THE GREEN HORSE

DALE PORTMAN

THE GREEN HORSE

My Early Years in the Canadian Rockies

—A PARK WARDEN'S STORY—

RMB

RMB | Rocky Mountain Books Ltd.
rmbooks.com
@rmbooks
facebook.com/rmbooks

Cataloguing data available from Library and Archives Canada
ISBN 9781771602266 (paperback)
ISBN 9781771602273 (electronic)

Cover photo: "The author next to Fifi at Hoodoo, Blue Creek District, Jasper, in Fall 1973."
Dale Portman Collection.

Printed and bound in Canada by Friesens

Distributed in Canada by Heritage Group Distribution and in the US by Publishers Group West

For information on purchasing bulk quantities of this book, or to obtain media excerpts or invite
the author to speak at an event, please visit rmbooks.com and select the "Contact Us" tab.

RMB | Rocky Mountain Books is dedicated to the environment and committed
to reducing the destruction of old-growth forests. Our books are produced
with respect for the future and consideration for the past.

We acknowledge the financial support of the Government of Canada through the Canada
Book Fund and the Canada Council for the Arts, and of the province of British Columbia
through the British Columbia Arts Council and the Book Publishing Tax Credit.

WILMORE
WILDERNESS
PARK

Blue Creek
Warden Cabin ×

Willow Creek
× Warden Cabin

JASPER
NATIONAL
PARK

Mt Robson ▲

16

16

16

Jasper ○

MT ROBSON
PROVINCIAL
PARK

Mt Edith
Cavell ▲

5

▲ Mt
Fryatt

93

Isaac Creek
Warden Cabin
×

Brazeau
Warden Cabin
×

Mt
Clemenceau
▲

× Athabasca
Pass

▲ Mt
Alberta

Kootenay
Plains
×

SIFFLEUR
WILDERNESS
AREA

Tsar ▲
Mtn

Mt ▲
Columbia

Lyells
▲

▲ Mt
Forbes

11

Recondite
Peak ▲

Ya Ha Tinda
Ranch
×

93

▲ Mt
Willingdon

Skoki
Lodge
×

BANFF
NATIONAL
PARK

40

5

YOHO
NATIONAL
PARK

Mt
Victoria ▲

Field ○

Lake Louise ○

1

Golden ○

1A

Banff ○

1A

Mt
Fidelity ▲

× Rogers
Pass

Deltaform
Mtn
▲ Mt
Goodsir

1

Canmore ○

1

Revelstoke ○

GLACIER
NATIONAL
PARK

KOOTENAY
NATIONAL
PARK

Mt ▲
Assiniboine

Mt ▲
Sir Douglas

40

KANANASKIS
COUNTRY

▲
Mt
King George

BUGABOO GLACIER
PROVINCIAL PARK

93
95

CONTENTS

✦ ✦ ✦

FOREWORD
THERE IS AN EDDY THERE, AND I'LL MEET HER THERE

THE LIFE OF DALE PORTMAN

Though a long shaggy dog of a story to be sure – and one that as the author points out would likely not pass the muster of social correctness today – we all loved hearing the Green Horse joke and laughed every time at the same places if only because its masterful telling symbolized Dale Portman at his exuberant best. But now, forty years later, we find that there was more to the story than we may have thought.

One of the great lines that Dale Portman repeated often in the telling of his legendary Green Horse joke concerns an eddy in the river where he intends to meet the woman of his dreams. It could be said that that is exactly what happened. Dale met his future wife in an eddy in time, and they carried on down that river for the rest of their lives. This book is a reflection on that eddy and that later journey.

There were many of us in and around that eddy at the time, and like all good memoirists, Dale remembers many of those of us he knew well early in his career with honesty first and fondness only when earned. But also like all good memoirs *The Green Horse* is not just about the eddy but about the character of the river itself; it is as much about the time in which Dale lived as it is about the people and events he remembers and celebrates.

You don't have to read deeply between the lines to realize the era that Portman describes was, like now, a time of intergenerational change: when the demographic cohort that grew up during the Second World War was in the midst of retiring; when new ideas about the management of national parks were emerging; and when Canada's national park system was growing and redefining its purpose and direction within the context of changing societal values. Whether we liked it or not, or even realized it, we were all drawn into that eddy.

You don't have to read deeply into *The Green Horse* to realize also that for our generation it was an era of extraordinary exuberance. We were all young and wild, in love with where we lived and overwhelmed always by the amazing landscapes and ecological relationships we found ourselves charged with protecting and interpreting. Though only a few of us, like Sid Marty, were at the time able to find words for the natural glory we discovered everywhere around us, it was an era during which we were all exposed to what the Romantics would have called the sublime. Though we could not articulate in words our feelings at the time, there was not one of us who did not push ourselves to the very limits of fear and danger climbing the peaks, crossing glaciers or rafting down swollen mountain rivers. What we could not explain then was that in breaking through those limits we often found ourselves face to face with something we never expected to discover: the transcendent glory of a wilderness world that at its heart was at once beautiful and terrifying beyond imagination. Even now, decades later, we still have difficulty finding words to describe the experiences each of us had on days when we were able to overcome the almost uncontrollable terror to which we sometimes unwittingly exposed ourselves by pushing ourselves to our physical and emotional limits in an indifferent and often dangerous landscape.

Even more difficult to put in words was how in overcoming fear and giving in to exhaustion we suddenly found ourselves open to the ineffable: the experience of overwhelming awe and reverence for the grandeur and vastness of the natural world that in a deeply personal way transformed our view of ourselves and redefined for each of us what had meaning in our young lives. We were, however, too young to know how to articulate this or respond appropriately to the sublimity we experienced; all we knew how to do was to occasionally go wild and let it all out howling at the moon.

Even though we could only seldom find the exact words for what mattered most to us, that did not stop us from being compelled to fight against those within the national park system who did not understand the depth of our commitment to protecting the landscapes that made such transformation not just possible but likely for any who were committed to experience them – not on terms defined by local chambers of commerce, according to the strict terms defined by the wilderness itself. You don't need to read far between the lines of this memoir to find this tension revealed. But it is also important to note, as Dale makes clear, that we were all equally exposed at that time to the dark side of the sublime; we were as haunted, as it were, by mountain gloom as we were by mountain glory. It was a dangerous time in our lives.

You didn't have to be a park warden to know that death was everywhere around us. None of us were adequately trained to deal with the terrible tragedies to which we were exposed on a regular basis. While wardens like Dale Portman took care of the mess, no one escaped the horror. Among the people Dale introduces to the reader of this memoir I am probably among the luckiest in that only four people I know died as a result of unfortunate encounters with grizzly bears. I count only a couple of dozen of my friends who were kicked to death by horses, died in avalanches or fell to their deaths in mountaineering accidents. When I look back I don't know how we didn't all go mad from the glory or conversely end up, especially the wardens, with Post-Traumatic Stress Disorder. Fortunately, however, the joy we found in one another and the simply irrepressible enthusiasm we had for where we lived and what we did kept us going in the face of what we were too young to know would become cumulative grief.

Despite all the risks and dangers, although our youthful exuberance was sometimes held needlessly back by the bureaucracy in which we worked, you don't have to read far into this memoir to see that this was a magical time and a place of huge opportunity for personal growth and adventure for all of us. It really was an eddy in time, an era in which to be qualified as a park warden in the National Park Service in Canada you had to be a competent horseman; be able to take care of yourself for three weeks at a time in the backcountry; be a capable enough mountaineer to be able to rescue other climbers when they were in trouble, while at the same time discharge duties related to upholding and enforcing the regulations of the National Parks Act. It was a hard job, and it took a special kind of man or woman to do it.

There were benefits, however, beyond deep immersion in place and time. These benefits largely took the form of relationships with remarkable others that came with the physical territory. Many of these were older park wardens, many of whom are named in this memoir. They were the people who kept us in check because we knew that they knew so very much more than we did and yet they cared enough about us to allow us not just to be colleagues but become friends. In their quiet observations and by example they taught us, whether we wanted to learn it or not, what we needed to know to be good at what we did and stay alive in service of the places we cared so much about. It must also be pointed that not all park administrators were disliked. Far from it. There were superintendents like Rory Flanagan in Jasper whom we all regarded with an almost holy reverence for his strength, consistency and courage in defending what we felt were the highest of national park ideals. We wanted to be like him. Then there were the mountaineers and mountain guides.

When Dale met his wife Kathy in the eddy in time that was Jasper, he married into an extended mountaineering family that included Kathy's father Don Forest and the famous circle in which he climbed, known as the Grizzly Group. As Dale notes in Chapter 13, this was no ordinary group of climbers, but a group of friends like Glen Boles and Mike Simpson who over time became legends in North American mountaineering in their own right. What was remarkable about them, however, was their humbleness. Through them, we learned that over time, sense of place can become a form of grace.

They are all here, everyone who was in the eddy in the river of time in the mountain national parks that Dale Portman so accurately portrays in this thoughtful, amusing and loving memoir. As Sid Marty wrote in one of his early poems on Jasper, "there are many stories of that place." *The Green Horse* tells some of the good ones. You are invited to read it with pleasure.

Robert William Sandford
Canmore, Alberta
June 2017

PROLOGUE

AS I REFLECT ON MY life, I realize it was the recreational opportunities I pursued in the mountains that gave me the necessary foundation to spend nearly thirty years working in a career I cherished. My earliest employments were at ski areas and summer resorts, where I was introduced to climbing and skiing. This was followed by an apprenticeship in the saddle, working as a packer, guide and wrangler for a couple of park outfitters: Bud Brewster and Bert Mickle. These skills allowed me to pursue a job as a park warden in 1969.

Once hired, getting a full-time job was not an easy task. Having a post-secondary education was becoming more important to becoming a warden than any practical skills a warden hopeful might possess. Though outdoor aptitudes were important, I needed to have my resume reinforced with a degree of some sort, particularly in the natural sciences. And so, I gained a college degree in resource technology from NAIT (Northern Alberta Institute of Technology).

A cherished highlight of my career was all the time spent in the saddle, leading one or two packhorses, going from cabin to cabin, and the many backcountry districts I had the opportunity to work in. In going about my duties, trails were cleared, game counts conducted, telephone lines repaired, environmental assessments written, assistance rendered to the park visitor, primitive campgrounds maintained and boundary patrols carried out. What added to the enjoyment was the chance to ski, hike and climb, to gain the skills required for mountain rescue and avalanche control, which led to my future as a dog handler. Living in the wonder of a mountain wilderness, solitude was often my companion, self-reliance my partner and wildlife my audience.

During subsequent years, I found myself writing down the many interesting stories I was either a part of or shared with the people I met and worked with. I wrote a couple of minor books on these subjects and helped my wife Kathy, also a retired park warden, write a book about mountain rescue in Canada. Mountain history has always been the cement that binds our books together. When not writing, we both get out as much as possible – riding, skiing, hiking, backpacking and, in these senior years, scrambling up the odd peak.

The path that is laid out for us in our brief mortal struggle on Earth is often veiled and enigmatic, but if we pay attention and observe closely, we can sometimes see the hazy signposts that help us understand our life and the path to follow. The mountains opened a doorway to a greater understanding of why I took a path that seemed at times obscure and dangerous to others.

Some of the training and work required risk that, in hindsight, gave me a greater appreciation of what life had to offer. I put great value in these experiences as they expanded my opportunities by giving me the confidence to undertake adventures I might otherwise have avoided. They also helped me understand myself better. To do so, I needed to build the confidence to deal with whatever circumstance was thrown my way. The warden service was the perfect vehicle for that.

Many of these stories represent my personal connection to the greater tapestry of western Canadian mountain history. This history includes the traditions and cultures of the many mountain communities I've had the good fortune to reside in, including my hometown of Cochrane, located at the foot of these beautiful, demanding mountains.

ONE

MY YOUTH

WHEN I WAS WORKING AND living in Jasper, people used to call me the Green Horse. What kind of horse were they referring to? You might think it was because I was inexperienced, untrained, immature, naive or unsophisticated. Although that might be true or partly true it had nothing to do with the name. You might think it meant I was fertile, verdant, new, fresh or unripe, but they do not apply either, nor does it mean I was ill, sick or environmentally friendly. No, it's because I was known for an off-colour, politically incorrect joke that resulted in the suggestion that if I painted my mighty white steed green I could win the heart of a beautiful maiden. Make sense? Of course not, but it's true.

* * *

ON A WARM day in June 2015, my wife Kathy and I left Cochrane, Alberta, on a 102-day venture across Canada and back. We were towing a 17-foot fibreglass trailer with a moderately large dog along as a companion, friend and arbitrator of the peace. The trip had to be designed almost completely around her, for if she soured on the adventure, the trip would be doomed. Of the many wet and windy days that Atlantic Canada conjured up that summer, some were a challenge, taxing us fully to keep her (and ourselves) interested and committed to the adventure.

On Day 86, on our way home, it was raining again, but Lily was still engaged and enjoying the numerous opportunities for a fresh walk and a new campsite. Although oblivious to its historic significance, she especially liked where Wolfe and Montcalm did battle as it gave her numerous opportunities to leave her mark and chase the odd squirrel.

After a lengthy hike across the Plains of Abraham, led by her, we eventually found ourselves wandering amongst the mist-enshrouded streets of the old city of Quebec. The quaint shops couldn't help but present themselves as cozy and inviting. We strolled along the pleasant Rue de Buade under the shadow of the Chateau Frontenac and came upon the D'Orsay, a restaurant/pub with an interesting menu and an alluring interior. We decided to dine there later.

We settled next to the window in our little alcove, taking in its warm interior and the rich rosewood bar nearby. Several people were sitting there discussing politics. When that conversation died, some-one piped up, "Let's talk religion." They were boisterous, probably visiting the city as part of a tour group, and they continued to order more drinks. A fellow from Florida, sitting alongside his rather drunk and apologetic wife, felt the city was too small to really enjoy. He much preferred larger metropolises like New York, Chicago and LA - he eventually included in his list Boston and Philadelphia. Interestingly, they failed to mention any worthy destinations in Europe or Asia. The guy from Florida did say he was looking forward to visiting Montreal.

Our food came and their conversation slipped into the back-ground. I was moved by the city, finding it a worthy destination, and it reminded me of a visit to Cadiz, Spain, with its old Moorish architecture and ancient walls surrounding the old town. It was from there that Columbus set sail in 1492 to rediscover the "new" world. Here the old walls are still standing, corralling a wealth of old stone buildings and churches. Forty-three years after Columbus's epic

My father and mother (Howard and Rose) with me.
SUSAN MITTON COLLECTION

voyage, Jacques Cartier set foot on what became known as Stadacona, eventually Quebec City. I fell in love with Cadiz decades ago, and I fell in love again that day with this jewel of North America.

My thoughts drifted off from our dining, the ambience of the place had muted somewhat and the bar conversation was now subdued. I started to think about travel and how I had embraced it in my early life. When I was five, we moved from Alberta to North Bay, Ontario. It was our family's first trip across the country.

While living in the east, I felt like I was only a visitor and that one day we would return to the West. I was born there, after all, and lived there for five years, but I had no memory of mountains. Even though I had no recollection, geography in school taught me they were a big part of where I had come from.

A CAMPING TRIP ACROSS CANADA

My first memory of the mountains came in 1954 as a young boy on a car trip across Canada, made more notable because we camped along the way. It was three years since our original move east, and this trip left me with significant and lasting memories. We owned a big canvas tent with an awning that stuck out front, supported by two aluminum poles. It seemed to consume the trunk space and weighed a ton, even when it wasn't wet from a recent rain. We left Ontario in mid-July, following the proposed, but still not completed, Trans-Canada Highway. We were heading west to visit my father's relatives in the interior of British Columbia, near Kamloops where I was born.

My father was in the Royal Canadian Air Force and now stationed on the outskirts of Toronto at CFB Downsview, a few thousand kilometres from our trip destination in British Columbia. Both my brother Rick and I felt that this was going to be an adventure. We couldn't wait to be on our way, to drive our parents nuts with our squirming and high jinks in the back seat. Of course, we had a midway stop that alleviated the road-trip pressure. My mother's parents and some of her family were settled around the small town of Winnipeg Beach, Manitoba, and we planned to stop and visit for several days.

Seeing our many cousins and visiting the beach attractions was – as expected – fun for two young boys. However, it was my first sight of the mountains that was an epiphany in every sense of the word. From the top of a big hill west of Calgary I got my first really good view of the Rockies. It was like coming home. The feeling was only there for a few fleeting moments, but it registered with me like a stamp in a passport. Off in the distance were rolling grasslands that extended into the timber-crowned foothills that marched aggressively up to the mountains beyond. Nestled below us was the small town of Cochrane.

In 1954 Cochrane was a cow town with no more than seven hundred people. The main street ran east-west. Most of the businesses were on the north side, facing south, allowing the afternoon sun to warm their windows and door fronts. We parked in front of a hotel with a tavern. Not far away were some hitching rails right out of a movie set. This boded well for us to see a cowboy, maybe on horseback, riding through town and verify our image of the Canadian West.

Our parents bought us ice cream from a nearby store and left us sitting in the back seat while they went in for a beer. We were there for an hour or so, long enough for the ice cream to fade as a bribe. The monotony was broken by the odd stringy cowboy strolling by in his faded blue jeans and dusty boots, often with a cigarette dangling from his lips. Some stopped and stepped into the bar. We peered at the doorway as they entered. We were disappointed not to see the expected gun belt and holsters being worn or checked at the door.

Mom and Dad finally came out and we headed for Banff. Dad mentioned that a fight was about to break out over an argument in the men's section and "that it was a pretty rough place and it was time to hit the road." This was music to my ears.

When I think about the Cochrane I saw as a boy, I am reminded of another town I would see many decades later. After a couple of long days driving a pickup truck down an endless dusty road in South America, our journey finally came to an end in a small frontier town. Scattered along the main street were a few vehicles, the odd vaquero on horseback and some necessary structures – hitching rails and a livery stable. The town was in a wide valley next to a deep-azure stream. Distant mountains could be seen in all directions. It brought back memories of my first trip west, and the town's name had a familiar ring to it, Cochrane – Cochrane, Chile.

We headed west out of town and soon found ourselves being edged in on the right by verdant green hills while extensive river flats spread out to our left. Swathes of hay swayed in the breeze. The odd stock corral lay abandoned next to the railway tracks that cut across the open fields. Dad knew the country and said it was similar to the cattle country around Kamloops and that spring must have been a wet one in these parts as the hills were still green and not scorched brown like they normally would be.

We finally approached the portal of the mountains, through which the Bow River carved its course. We were carried along in a sloped-back, 1949 Nash Rambler with the licence plate IOU – 82. On our right was the half-moon presence of Mount Yamnuska, like an exposed scale of a long-buried dinosaur. On the left was the less dramatic but still significant Barrier Mountain. High winds buffeted the car as we slipped through the gap. Soon Banff's park gates appeared, looking sturdy with their dark rock masonry. Here we bought our park pass, an attractive metal buffalo shield, which we attached to our front licence plate.

In Banff my parents bought me a snakeskin belt that I treated like a talisman on returning home. Decorated with coloured beads, the design was meant to mimic the pattern of a rattlesnake. It was made by the local Native people whose reservation was just east of the mountains in the foothills, within the hilly grasslands we had just come through. Back home I pointed out its significance to my friends who never did understand its Native origin and spiritual connection to where we had been.

We continued westward through a dynamic landscape, every turn presenting another vista, adding to our growing adventure and sense of wonder. After passing by the sentinel of Mount Temple, we arrived at the hamlet of Lake Louise and took the short drive up to see the famous lake. Yellow and red canoes were flashing their reflections on the glassy surface of the turquoise lake, trying to compete with the white, glaciated peaks in the background. The stately Chateau Lake Louise was surrounded by a myriad of flower gardens and tulip beds. If it wasn't for the spectacular setting, the hotel could have overpowered everything.

As my gaze lingered on the snowy ledges leading to the soft slope running to the summit of Mount Victoria, I wondered what it would take to climb the mountain. It was only later that we learned of the tragedy that occurred on those very slopes only a few days earlier. It would be a decade later before I learned the details. Three Mexican women and their guide had plunged to their deaths down the very face I had been staring at.

We continued to the famous Yoho Valley, 20 kilometres west of Lake Louise. It's a beautiful valley nestled under the towering shadow of Mount Stephen, which harbours the small railroad community of Field, BC a place I would later call home. It was so deeply tucked within the forested folds of the mountain's apron, that some houses at the back never saw the sun for three long months in the winter. We camped that night in Golden, BC.

We headed north the next day on the Big Bend Highway, following the Columbia River. It was 290 kilometres of dust and gravel. Towering above us to the west, and extending as an endless barrier, were the Selkirk Mountains. To the east, the majestic summits of the Rockies were being broken up by numerous, deep side valleys, concealing the spine of the continent: the Great Divide.

The road hung above the valley floor like a ribbon, clinging to the western slopes of the mountains. Many of the peaks to the west had glaciers nestled in their high cirques. Some were restless, sending ice, brawling and tumbling, down steep cliff faces, while others seemed more organized, like giant staircases placidly extending an invitation to explore further. It made the country look even more rugged and formidable.

There were numerous bridges that crossed the many torrential streams, and at the top of the bend was the small community of Boat Encampment. Here we crossed the broad sweep of the Columbia River on a bridge that seemed to float on the slow-moving surface. This was the wildest and most remote part of the trip.

Eight years after our adventure, a much shorter highway was built, which now climbs through Rogers Pass following the route the railroad took in 1885 and located halfway between the towns of Golden and Revelstoke. This section, which cuts the travelling distance in half, is even more spectacular, dominated by peaks that rival the Matterhorn for elegance and singularity. This relegated the Big Bend Highway (named after the famous bend in the Columbia River), to little more than a logging road. Today a lot of it is under water, covered by two huge dams, built to accommodate North America's appetite for hydroelectric power.

We arrived that night in Revelstoke after a long, dusty drive and stayed with relatives for a few days. Later, we entered a deep, forested valley, damp with cedar, past a small bottomless blue lake. We

Rick and I, camped somewhere on our cross-Canada road trip in 1954.

eventually came upon the site of the Enchanted Forest, a great stop in the middle of nowhere. I'm not sure on which occasion we discovered it, probably on our next trip in the early 1960s. In fact, this nature trail, complete with fairy houses, figures and a candy-cane house, first opened to the public on July 1, 1960.

Deep valleys dictated a twisting road that was narrower and rougher than what we had experienced in the Rockies. Finally, we spilled out onto more habitable land along the shores of Shuswap Lake. Sprinkled about were acreages and homes covered in tarpaper; this was mining country, after all. We eventually stopped in the town of Chase to visit more family and then reached our final destination, Kamloops, a few days later.

The route back through the northern States was just as eventful. I remember my dad having to use an axe to remove a large tree that lay across the highway, the result of a recent storm in Washington State. Farther along in North Dakota, a huge storm rained down on us, dropping frogs like hail and evoking biblical images of God punishing the Israelites. My mother, being a staunch Catholic, must have thought her days were over. I certainly thought so, listening to her occasional scream as the car skidded over the slick surface of bodies on the road. The last great wonder was the fresh, new bridge that spanned the Mackinac Straits between Lake Michigan and Lake Huron; it seemed to go on forever. The bridge was actually opened in 1957, three years later, and we crossed it for the first time in 1959 on our return trip to the West.

The journey left an indelible impression on me. In my formative years, we moved a lot because of military postings, and that left me restless with a desire to travel. Throughout life I found myself attracted to less-beaten paths in the pursuit of new adventures, exotic places and rich cultures. That first trip west, which both my brother and I cherished, set the table for me. Even today from time to time, I massage those memories as if they were smooth stones in my pocket.

We came west again in 1959, this time to stay. My father had been trying for a few years to get transferred back west, and he finally had the move approved. We settled into housing at the air-force base in Lincoln Park in southwest Calgary. Today, it's the site of ATCO Industries.

MY EARLY YEARS IN CATHOLIC SCHOOLS

When Kathy and I planned our trip east, large cities were not going to be on the itinerary. Contrary to the fellow from Florida who loved a "sprawling metropolis," we were the opposite. We had both lived in small towns throughout our adult lives, and the thought of visiting Montreal or Toronto was not appealing. I had heard too many stories from fellow travellers about navigating the Gardner Expressway and the 401 with their numerous lanes of hell. As well, from an educational standpoint, Toronto did not represent a great period in my life.

It's troubling now to reflect on my early school years in Toronto and realize how dysfunctional they really were. I spent Grades 1 to 6 there, and the first four years were wasted attending various Separate schools in the city. Being raised Catholic and being a minority amongst Protestants on the air-force base, Rick and I were bused from school to school. There were on average about fifteen of us each year that had to be bused, often long distances. We were like a collection of vagabonds going to one school for a few months followed quickly by relocation to another school, because there was no more room for us. We didn't belong to any particular school district. As schools filled up, we would get bumped. We felt like outcasts at recess, huddling about in the various playgrounds, avoiding contact with the rest of the students. I changed schools at least twice a year and in Grade 4 attended four different ones.

Catholic schools to me were nothing more than toxic cauldrons of ethnic animosity. No one seemed to get along and the lunchroom was full of strange food odours. The German kids had their smelly Limburger cheese, the Italians their sardine sandwiches, and the Eastern Europeans added to the aroma with cooked cabbage and sausage. There were few kids from our ethnic background in these schools outside of our little group, and we stayed to ourselves. After all, a few months later we would be bused to a new school requiring new adjustments.

The first few hours every day were spent studying the catechism of the Roman Catholic Church, before we got the opportunity to move on to math, science and the rest. Every night we had a couple of hours of religion homework, leaving me no time to study the remaining subjects that are so important to getting a proper education. We lined up for everything, and discipline was enforced by the sadistic nuns in their black habits. Our lines were kept straight with the use of yardsticks, which the nuns brandished like swords. I had a bit of a rebellious streak in me and I often felt the effects of their wrath. Crooked lines were bad habits not tolerated and quickly corrected by the swift discipline of the rod. Their other weapon of choice was their weighty rosary crosses hanging from their waists. They would swirl them like bolos, often bonking you on the head, much to their delight. It had to be hell for the Native kids in residential schools, back then, with teachers like these.

I pleaded with my mother every new school year to let me go to public school so I could be with my friends. It was hard to articulate what it was like, but she must have come to some realization of how disruptive it was to move from school to school. Eventually, an event transpired that led to change. My brother and I came down with ringworm. It was humiliating for us. We had to have our heads shaved and were forced to wear these ridiculous cotton toques over our scalps. We stood out like malignant tumours in crowded hallways and much ridicule was directed our way. In the spring, I told my mother I despised Catholicism and I was probably going to fail Grade 5 if it continued. My marks were so low by now I was barely passing on to the next grade.

Finally, she reneged, and I started Grade 5 in a public school, near the air-force base. It was like going from a heavy metal band to a Strauss waltz. Grade 5 started out as a great year, but just as my marks started to pick up, my parents separated. Once again, we found ourselves moving, now to Winnipeg Beach, and living with my mother's grandparents. I was now going to a one-room school that taught Grades 5 to 8.

Some of the farm kids were as old as seventeen before they advanced to Grade 9. One of the reasons for their failure was that they were absent a lot. Many were forced to help out on the family farms.

Obviously, it was not healthy for me to be exposed to these older kids, and I picked up some bad habits. I was hanging out with the wrong crowd, a crowd that was older and more experienced than I was. They were often getting in trouble with the police, usually because of vandalism. I tagged along, on occasion, and was exposed to a different sort of education.

Most of my mother's relatives lived in Winnipeg, 75 kilometres away, and we visited them on most weekends. This side of my family was predominantly Polish, and most of my male cousins were altar boys or studying to be one. Many spoke Polish and some were learning Latin. Trying to keep up with the rest of her family, my mother wanted me to start learning Polish and train to become an altar boy. This was the last thing I wanted, but to please her, I said I would try. I no sooner became an altar boy than we moved back to Toronto. My parents had come together again just in time for Grade 6.

I consider myself a mongrel. My father's side was half Irish and half English. My mother's side was a melting pot of Eastern European nationalities, Polish being the most significant. A lot of my characteristics, traits and temperament I identified with my Irish rather than my English roots. I fantasized that my creativity came from Yeats and Keats, my rebellious nature from the Irish while my stubborn bone-headedness a gift from the English. My adventurous and trail-blazing Polish side, I enthused, must have come from the likes of Copernicus and, of course, Joseph Conrad. One of my favourite books growing up was *Lord Jim*.

Grade 6 was my most stable and effective year, and I did well in school, especially in science, social studies and physical education. Math and English literature were a bit more challenging. The biggest thing about Grade 6 was that all the Catholic mumbo-jumbo was behind me. I quickly forgot most of what I learned about being an altar boy and the rudimentary Polish and Latin I had picked up.

REFLECTIONS ON A SOFTER AND POSSIBLY A GENTLER CHURCH

We camped overnight at St. Agathe des Monts near Mount Tremblay, and on the morning of Day 9, we found ourselves headed south, hoping to take the bypass just north of Montreal towards Trois-Rivières. In this way, we would escape the tangle of freeways that can trap you like a spider web within the city itself. We had the GPS on but she (her name was Hilda) didn't respond to the exit for Highway 640, and I took it on instinct. It was the right choice. After crossing the St. Lawrence River at Trois-Rivières, we headed northeast towards the Gaspésie (Gaspé) on the Trans-Canada Highway. On our right were several small towns and villages, one to two kilometres off in the distance, set in bucolic surroundings. At the centre of each community was the local Catholic church with its high steeple, rising above the surrounding deciduous trees. These quiet settings gave an air of tranquility and peace to the beautiful churches I had previously associated with oppression. The more forgiving views of a new and refreshing pope helped lessen my jaded view of the Church.

I never properly processed my educational upheaval in my formative years. When we moved to Calgary, my mother often sent Rick and me to Sunday mass on our own. She was going through a period of abstinence, her faith wavering. After a few weeks, we started walking past the church and spending the hour sitting in a small set of stands at a nearby baseball field. This went on for a few months until winter arrived. Not wanting to sit outside in the winter weather, we told our mother what we had been doing. She shook her head and because she was losing interest in attending mass, she relented on our own attendance. We, of course, were delighted. She kept her faith throughout life, but towards her later years, she became more evangelical. She followed Billy Graham and Oral Roberts daily on television. By the time I was eighteen, I had completely broken ties with any religion.

TORONTO WAS IN OUR REAR-VIEW MIRROR

The one thing that stood out when we moved to Calgary was how culturally different it was from Toronto. Instead of going to the closest

Stedman's store in Toronto, to steal something on a dare from my friends, I became active outdoors. I found the school kids in Calgary much more grounded than the duck-tailed hoods I was starting to hang out with in Toronto. In Calgary they talked about hunting and fishing or maybe going skiing on the weekend. It was a different world, and I embraced it wholeheartedly.

I began school in the seventh grade at Currie Junior High. I was twelve and had a whole new world of adventure spreading out before me that I could not wait to plunge into. My parents were behind me in these new endeavours and encouraged me to become a Boy Scout, as there was a troop nearby. This was a wise decision, as I would get further training in outdoor activity and camping under the guidance of experienced Scout leaders.

By Grade 8 my scholastic record was deeply rooted in C mediocrity, but my athletic prowess was well-established. That spring I was chosen the school's best physical education student for my endeavours in track and field.

Before joining the air force, my father had owned a taxi business in Kamloops, which left him with a love of driving and sightseeing, and we often took trips to the mountains. Winter did not slow us down, no matter how cold it got, which led to one memorable occasion when we drove up to Mount Norquay to watch the skiers. There, at the bottom of the hill stood the first park warden I ever saw.

He stood by an old green Dodge Power Wagon, wearing a faded green parka, a fur-lined cap and white army mukluks. His neck was open (though I believe it was -30) and his parka was zippered, maybe halfway up. He was older than my parents. He was in his late forties or early fifties, and even from that snapshot moment, he seemed to be overdressed, while the rest of us were bundled up tightly. He fit easily into his surroundings, much like an elk or bighorn sheep. I decided then and there, I wanted to be just like him.

THE SEARCH FOR PEGGY TELFER

A couple of years before I graduated from high school I spent the summer working for my grandfather in Winnipeg Beach. He owned a small grocery store located on the main road that passed through town. His store was at one end of the block while at the other end was Joe Boroditsky's store. Joe was Jewish. Most of the people who shopped at my grandfather's place were either Icelandic or Eastern European, and some were anti-Semitic. This was nothing new, for it permeated the halls and classrooms of the Catholic schools I was brought up in.

I liked Joe and I often went over to his store seeking friendship and someone to talk to. It was a lonely summer. He was a progressive sort who I remember sold coloured popcorn, much more upscale than what my grandfather sold. He liked me and often kidded around, accusing me of spying for my grandfather by checking Joe's prices against his. My grandfather chided me for not spending more time with my own people, whoever they were. I certainly had no friends in Winnipeg Beach.

I returned home that fall and spent a couple of restless winters in Calgary. I was decoupling from any desire to be involved in organized religion. My Polish upbringing and its prevalent anti-Semitism was something I disliked, and I was searching for some direction in my life. I certainly had a desire to leave my upbringing behind, along with many of the relatives and family I had grown up with.

In the spring of 1965, the search for Peggy Telfer spread across the pages of the *Calgary Herald*, and I was riveted by the news. It played out like a mystery drama for me, and still does, even after all these years. And I'm not the only one. The older climbing community in Calgary and Banff still remembers Peggy Telfer today, and if you bring up her name, many old-timers will say, "Of course I remember Peggy. She was such a fine gal."

The search stands out for me not just because of the images but also because of the huge press it received at the time. It occurred immediately before I left for the mountains, and it directed my focus to where it needed to be. The gripping portrayal of the search for this woman in the newspapers had me glued to the story, hoping for her survival and for the safety of the searchers themselves. Back then I knew nothing about the people involved, neither Peggy herself nor the men conducting the search. I've come to know many of them since, and they've helped me tell her story.

For several days in mid-May, reports of Peggy spread across the front page of the *Calgary Herald*. She was lost on the Illecillewaet Glacier in Glacier National Park near Rogers Pass, and a lot of skilled people were desperately trying to find her. The weather conditions couldn't have been more inimical. It was like looking for the proverbial needle in a haystack under the trying conditions, and it was extremely challenging for the searchers.

Peggy Telfer was a talented young ski instructor from Banff who was well-liked and well-known in the mountain community. She was a good friends with some of the big-name guides at the time, like Hans Gmoser, Bruno Engler, Mike Wiegele and Bob Geber. Through them, Peggy was introduced to ski mountaineering and what she lacked in experience she made up for in enthusiasm. During the Victoria Day weekend that year, she and a group of fellow ski instructors and friends from Banff headed to Rogers Pass in Glacier National Park for a weekend ski ascent of the Illecillewaet Glacier. They had arrived the night before at the Alpine Club of Canada's Wheeler Hut, located close to the highway and at the base of the route up.

The Illecillewaet is an impressive glacier with a number of minor peaks that can be reached on skis from high up on its névé. Today, from the summit of Rogers Pass on the Trans-Canada Highway, you can see the glacier, spreading out before you to the south. The setting is so spectacular you'd be hard pressed to forget it.

They left the warmth of the hut on May 15, in a long procession, working their way through the timber, using the friction of their climbing skins to help them gain purchase on the snow. Soon they broke out of the trees and onto the lower slopes of the terminal moraine. Then it was up onto the snow-covered ice, snaking their way, one after the other, ever gaining elevation. Somewhere high up on the glacier she got separated from the party. Maybe she was

Looking at the Deville Glacier from the backside of the Illecillewaet.
DALE PORTMAN COLLECTION

having problems with her climbing skins or there was an issue with her ski bindings, or maybe she was just getting tired, but for some reason the rest of the party was unaware of her plight and kept moving on. When the party reached the top of the glacier they realized she wasn't there. At this point a storm started blowing in, which greatly reduced their visibility and started covering up their ascending tracks. This forced the party to head back down in deteriorating conditions. They assumed that Peggy would also ski back to the hut. They assumed wrong.

Charlie Locke and Don Gardner were climbing on Mount Peechee, just east of Banff townsite, and remember the original storm that rapidly came down the Bow Valley that day, the day that Peggy went missing. "It moved in rather quickly," Don said, "with high winds and lots of snow filling the air." They also retreated down the mountain. Both of them remember her today and the tragedy that unfolded. Don also remembers Peggy as a very likeable person who was active outdoors and at one time had been a girlfriend of Hans Gmoser.

In a gathering whiteout, the group made its way back to the hut without incident but became concerned when Peggy wasn't there to welcome them. There was no sign of her skis as well. It was 1:30 PM when the warden service was contacted about the missing woman. Fred Schleiss, who had just taken over as the head avalanche forecaster at Rogers Pass from Noel Gardner, was the rescue leader. After interviewing the group thoroughly, he left at 3:00 PM with three wardens. Once up on the glacier, one of the rescuers was left behind to build a snow shelter for the group while the other two and Fred started checking out some of the crevasses in the area. When that turned up nothing they carried on up onto the névé and searched, but the light snow coming down obscured visibility. By 8:30 that evening they still had found no evidence of Peggy, and they turned around, heading back to their camp. They spent the night huddled in their improvised snow shelter, trying to keep warm.

They set out at 4:30 AM in lightly falling snow, searching again in poor light for most of the morning. As they proceeded up onto the upper part of the glacier, the weather started to deteriorate even further. The wind was now gusting up to 62 miles per hour, making it extremely difficult to confront without some kind of face protection. Ice was forming on their faces as their route headed into the wind. It became apparent that they could not continue into the teeth of the gale. They tried to sit out the storm high up on the névé, huddled together with tarps wrapped around them in an effort to hold off the wind. Finally, they were forced to retreat in visibility that had been reduced to 15 to 20 feet. They reached the highway at about noon, fortunate to have made it off the glacier as the storm intensified.

It was with heavy hearts that the rescuers had to give up the search until conditions improved. Warden Bob Lehmann wrote in his diary: "The survival of the rescue party was rapidly becoming questionable. If we encountered difficulties, the search for the missing skier would become greatly complicated. To continue the search was considered foolhardy. To remain in the face of the storm was impossible."

While the first party led by Fred Schleiss was still up on the glacier fighting the elements, Walter Perren arrived from Banff with four wardens. In further discussions with the ski group, it was confirmed that there was very little chance of her having survived if she was up on the glacier, as she only had a small daypack and possibly only a light jacket for added protection. Walter later said he felt Peggy's only chance for survival was if she had made it down into the trees somewhere, somehow. He sent a second party, led by Noel Gardner, up the glacier, and they met the first rescue party coming down. After reviewing what the first party had experienced and the deteriorating weather conditions, the second party turned around, as well.

That day during the height of the storm, two rescuers were sent out to check the forested areas below the glacier and in some of the smaller side valleys, in the hope she had made it to the safety of the timber. They found nothing. May 18 broke cold and clear, which allowed for the use of a badly needed helicopter. An aerial survey was conducted of the ridge leading up to what is known as the Steps of Paradise. The survey also included a search of the névé. Meanwhile, a ground party searched the area, and it was here that they found Peggy Telfer.

They came upon a pair of skis sticking vertically out of the snow. Just past the skis, jutting out of the surface was the end of a ski pole with the loop handle exposed. In the loop was a hand. She had laid down to wait for her returning chums, her skis crossed as a marker. The rest of her was completely buried in snow. Her death marked a big change in how ski parties behaved on trips in the mountains.

A pamphlet was produced on avalanche safety. The contents of the brochure included what should be carried in a daypack while travelling in avalanche terrain. The drawing on the cover was of a small hand with a loop around its wrist that was just sticking out of the snow. Peggy's legacy lives on in the measures that are now in place today to ensure safe travel in the mountains.

Willi Pfisterer, who was on the rescue and later was hired as one of two alpine specialists to replace Walter Perren, said, "It changed forever how ski parties conducted themselves in the mountains. The fatal mistake was to lose contact with one of their party members and leave her behind.... A responsible person needs to be assigned to take up the rear and make sure no one is left behind." The other point Pfisterer made was people should "not travel with such light rucksacks with nothing in them but air." This very experienced group learned a hard lesson that weekend. But it wasn't just a hard lesson for them; it was a lesson for all of the mountain communities and at the expense of Peggy's life.

The year she died was the same year I moved to the mountains to remain, but it would be four more years before the challenges of mountain rescue would become my challenge, as well. Before that I had a lot of country to ride, trails to explore and much to learn.

MY HALCYON SUMMER IN THE MOUNTAINS AT DEER LODGE

When I started high school at Viscount Bennett in Calgary, I met Rick Crosby who would play a pivotal role in my life not too many years later. He lived in Lincoln Park not far from us, but we only became friends when we were in high school. We had a common air force background, and we both loved going to the mountains. His father's family owned a lodge near Lake Louise, and he would go up there every summer to work as a bellhop. He mentioned that if I ever needed summer employment I could come and work there.

This would happen sooner than either of us expected. Outside of working for my grandfather a couple of summers earlier, my employment was typical of most high school kids in the area, caddying at the local (Earl Grey) golf course or cutting lawns. None of this was very inspirational. Neither was living at home. As Sue, Rick and I grew older, our parents grew apart, and we could sense the tension. Though they kept things to themselves, it was not a surprise when they separated again. That was soon followed by a divorce.

My sister has accused me on occasion of abandoning them after my parents' split. It was a difficult period, and home life was changing as I grew older. It was hard to say what the deciding factor was

My sister Sue, my brother Rick and I a few years after I made my home in the mountains.
SUSAN MITTON COLLECTION

(there were many). I certainly had enough of living in Calgary and after graduating from high school, there was nothing to keep me there. I had taken a second year of Grade 12, trying to matriculate by retaking my French and Math 30. I had a vague idea of wanting to eventually go to university, but I had no idea how that was going to come about. My parents certainly couldn't afford to send me. It was mid-June 1965, and all I had with me was a small duffel of clothing and a little money. The mountains had finally taken over and were drawing me to them.

I remember getting on a Greyhound bus in Calgary and arriving in Lake Louise late at night. The bus pulled up across from the roofed promenade that led to the Post Hotel, which was the designated Greyhound bus terminal at the time and my point of departure. I crossed the road and walked the promenade's loud, planked length to the hotel. Its entrance displayed a faint welcoming light over the reception desk.

Just inside, between the two doors were 60 or 70 square feet of floor space and a couple of chairs. This was adjacent to the locked main entrance, with the front desk visible on the other side. It provided a small sitting room with some diffused light coming from the reception area. It was midnight and this little space was where passengers sat and waited for their buses. It afforded me some inside comfort.

The bus made a sweeping turn out front – its headlights training on me for a second – before it swung back in the direction it had come. Its light beams probed ahead then locked onto some distant object, drawing it back to the highway. I momentarily felt alone and abandoned.

There wasn't a soul about and the likelihood of finding a taxi at that hour was nonexistent. In the clear, moonless night, I started walking up the road to the lake, located a couple of miles above the village. The hair on my neck stood up like antennae; I was on alert for any possible noise or movement. Dark and menacing objects seemed to lurk in every nook and shadow that the stars failed to illuminate.

After an hour, the prominent parapet of Deer Lodge appeared around the corner, and my lonely, nervous walk was about to end as I approached the door lit by a cheery light. Once inside, I looked around, appreciating the high arched windows with their maroon curtains and the Persian rugs scattered in front of the large stone fireplace, not to mention the room itself. Strewn about were deep, comfortable couches and straight-backed, wooden chairs competing for my eyes, like they had recently been abandoned and were now seeking attention.

The desk clerk gave me a quick hello as I approached. "I'm looking for Rick Crosby. I'm a friend of his," I said.

"Man, it's past one in the morning, he won't be up. I better get Marge," replied the clerk and he left.

Soon a short, severe woman followed him into the room and eyed me up and down. "Rick's in bed and can't be awoke. You'll have to come back in the morning."

Not wanting to walk back down the road again and not having put much thought into the evening, I mumbled that I was looking for a job. "Well, we can't do anything about that tonight. We'll look into that in the morning. And do you have a place to stay?" she asked.

"No, I was hoping to stay with Rick."

"That's out of the question. He can't be disturbed at this hour. You can stay in one of our guest rooms." I was quickly starting to warm up to this matriarch of the family.

I tracked Rick down at lunch the next day and moved into Cabin 10 with him that afternoon. I had been given a job that morning working in the laundry with two Polish sisters, making 75 cents an hour. They were both very proud of their Polish heritage and always referred to themselves as Polish first and Canadian second. They were from Vegreville and possessed that distinct accent I recognized from my youth. Of course, I considered myself Canadian first.

A week or two later, a mutual friend, Wayne South, showed up and started slinging hamburgers in the Inglenook Cafeteria. And so, those days went on to become the halcyon summer you fondly look back on for the rest of your life.

THE INTERESTING PEOPLE I MET THAT SUMMER

That summer Rick Crosby introduced me to climbing. He had been initiated into the sport by his fellow bellhops and a school chum back in Calgary, Chic Scott. At the time Chic was working for Brewster as a bus driver in Lake Louise and lived in the Brewster Block behind Deer Lodge. He had attended the same high school Rick and I did but was a year or two ahead of us.

Parties and get-togethers ruled many of the evening hours, and I met some interesting people. There was Ted, another bus driver with Brewster, who introduced his visiting mother to all of us as, "My mother, the breeder of champions." When I introduced my mother later that summer and used Ted's line, I got that withering look that a parent often gives a son when he's behaving like an idiot.

Chic, when he wasn't driving bus, was putting up new routes on a wealth of peaks in the area with his dependable climbing partners Don Gardner, Hudson Vipond, Gerry Walsh and Charlie Locke. Don was already quite a force in the mountain community. He had apprenticed with Hans Gmoser (who started the first helicopter skiing business in Canada) at his backcountry lodges, but

Don Gardner, Chic Scott, Charlie Locke and Neil Liske before their big ski traverse from Jasper to Banff.
DON GARDNER COLLECTION

he was better known for his cross-country skiing. He was one of the first Canadians to race competitively in the sport, which at the time was relatively unknown in Canada. He later went on to design hiking and Nordic ski trails in the mountains and eventually for the winter Olympics in Calgary. He later helped in the initial design of Vancouver's Olympic course.

Hudson had been climbing for several years, employed as a bellhop at the Chateau Lake Louise. He was raised in the East but was drawn to the mountains and spent several summers doing what he loved most, climbing. He was very capable at it, and he and Chic got up several peaks that summer. Their climbing exploits together went back several years. I met him again years later at a mountain film festival that Chic organized in Calgary.

Charlie was a stockbroker who went on to own and manage a number of ski areas and resorts in Alberta and British Columbia, one of them being his flagship, the Lake Louise Ski Area. Charlie was one of the first homegrown locals to get a mountain-guiding certificate, which kept him in elite company for several years, with only a few others joining the ranks for a period of time.

When I think about Chic and his climbing buddies, Andy, the poet who was also a climber and worked with Rick as a bellhop, also comes to mind. There were Fred and Marge who ran the place for the rest of the Crosby family. Victor Horvath, the bohemian artist from Budapest via San Francisco, who said he painted portraits for the Kennedy family, was also hard to forget. He did an oil painting on canvas for me of the trail leading up to Lake Agnes after a late summer snowfall that now brightens a wall in my study.

Who could forget Bill Hope who ran Brewster Transport in Lake Louise, a great guy who was unfortunately killed during that winter of 1965 on the Banff–Jasper Highway in a head-on collision with a government maintenance foreman. Slim Fleming was another legendary bus driver. And two of the most rugged characters I met were Bret Mitzel and Bert Mickle, who ran the two competing pony barns. Bret was younger and good looking; Bert was older and weather beaten.

Wally McPhee was the district warden. He was old and wise in the way of horses while his assistant, "The Kid" Jay Morton, was young and keen. Jay was one of the first wardens with a university degree to be hired in the mountain national parks. Two others wardens with university degrees come to mind: Sid Marty and Tim Auger. Their education helped, but more important, they were keen on the work and soon acquired the skills the job required. In time, they fitted in with the older fellows who brought experience and common sense to the job.

One of the persons working in the Inglenook Cafeteria was a waitress who could read palms. A few of the staff were lined up getting their hands read when I strolled by and looked on. I decided I would join the lineup. When she got to my hand, she gazed at it for a second and then threw it aside, abruptly saying, "I can't read that." That was an ominous moment, and I had no idea what she meant by it.

Later I consulted a book on reading palms and studied my life line, and it appeared to be broken or disconnected halfway along. I should have blown it off, but instead I let it linger. Knowledge of this broken life line settled back into the fissures of my subconscious, dormant, lying there only to surface when my self-confidence was challenged or in doubt. A premonition of early death would then coalesce in my mind, like a spider crawling out of some dark corner. I learned to push it aside, but it always lingered, and I was pretty sure I would be either dead or dealing with some serious health issue at the midpoint in my life. What it did do was make me more introspective than I had been. This idea that I would die young led me to trust my instincts but also to live life rather recklessly, especially in my early years.

THE CLIMBING ACCIDENT ON THE CLIFFS AT THE END OF LAKE LOUISE

One thing that happened that summer had a predominant effect on me and forced me to reassess objectives in my life. It almost bore credence to the fortune teller's reaction to my palm.

On August 10, immediately after work, Rick and I set out to do a route on the cliffs at the end of Lake Louise. Halfway up, Rick led out across a small ledge, traversing to the left. After getting to a good location, he set up an anchor belay and signalled for me to start the traverse. The handholds were extremely small, and the footholds were along a thin ledge of friable rock, which made it dicey. Not far into the traverse, I stopped as my handholds were getting fewer and thinner. I was standing on a small section of the ledge with both handholds at eye level when the thin rock under my right foot gave way. It shifted my weight to my arms, putting pressure on my delicate grasp on the rock. I immediately lost my first grip, followed by my second. I was clawing frantically at the rock, trying to gain some purchase, to no avail. Then my left foothold gave way. I was moving down, clear of the rock, penduluming across the face, feet first. At that point, I instinctively wrapped my hands around the rope leading up from my chest. I was not wearing a climbing harness, which was common at the time. The rope was only tied around my chest with a bowline. I hit the rock face with the right side of my body, and then I felt the elasticity in the rope as Rick began holding my fall. I absorbed most of the shock with my arms as opposed to my chest, which probably saved my back.

I had fallen approximately 82 feet when the rope finally held. Rick called down, wondering how I was. I said I'd done something to my hip but everything else seemed fine. I asked him how he was doing, and he said his hands were badly burnt by the friction of trying to hold the fall. I told him I was going to try to get to a small ledge just above me that I could probably just fit on. It was about 5 or 6 feet above my head. In those days, I could do twenty pull-ups with no trouble, so hand over hand, up I went. Once I reached the ledge I asked him to take up the slack. He asked if I could climb back up to where he was. He couldn't climb because of his hands.

Shock set in as the pain in my hip increased, and I realized how close I had come to killing myself. The last thing I wanted to do was climb back up and attempt to renegotiate the ledge again with my damaged hip. I figured it would be too dangerous, and I felt the only option we had was to remain where we were and wait for a rescue. Rick was in just as bad a shape as I was because of the burns on both his hands. Once they started to set, his hands hardened like plastic and he wasn't able to grip anything.

Once our situation had been assessed, I started to shake uncontrollably. This wasn't good because my perch was small, sloped slightly downward, and tenuous. Fortunately, at that moment I was distracted from my predicament by someone passing by on the trail below. I yelled our situation to him, and he immediately turned around and headed back to the Chateau Lake Louise, a distance of about a mile and a half, to let the wardens know. The distraction allowed me to stop shaking.

Rick and I periodically talked back and forth through the night, trying to keep our spirits up. I managed to rip my shirt loose from under my sweater and fasten it around my hip to staunch any bleeding. I spent the remainder of the time trying to maintain my perch on the small ledge.

At 3:00 AM, Walter Perren climbed up to where I was, wearing a headlamp, belayed by Ollie Hermanrude. Ollie was the district warden at Healy Creek at the time and frequently called upon to be a member of Walter's rescue teams. Walter was the alpine specialist hired to train the wardens in climbing and search and rescue. He set up a sturdy anchor and asked me if I was capable of looking after myself on the way down, as there was just the two of them. I felt I could. My hip had stiffened up, but I leaned back in repel fashion and managed to stay in that form for part of the way down. It was awkward, but I kept facing the rock for a stretch. At some point, I collapsed into the wall and turned the uninjured side of my body to the rock for the rest of the journey down. Finally, I was at the top of the slope next to Hermanrude. Getting Rick down was another matter.

It was going to be difficult to reach him from below in the dark with only a headlamp, but once Walter realized he was in a secure position, he decided to wait out the night. At first light, they set up a winch system in a secure location above Rick and brought him up. Ian Mackie, the assistant manager at the Chateau Lake Louise, drove me to the Mineral Springs Hospital in Banff in the back of his station wagon.

My doctor in Banff was Dr. Titamore. My hospital roommate was a young Peter Monod, who had broken his leg skiing. Dr. Titamore knew the Monod family of Banff well and was Peter's doctor, too. He would stop in on occasion when it wasn't busy and visit. Because I had been in a climbing accident, Dr. Titamore felt it was necessary to tell me the details of a rescue he had helped with eleven years previously, that of some Mexican climbers. No doubt he was trying to give me some realistic understanding of the dangers of mountaineering.

I spent a week in hospital. It turned out I only had a cracked hip, so my convalescence was much shorter than expected and I was back at work in just over a week. I hobbled around for the rest of the summer, and in early September I managed to gain the summit of Mount Niblock.

Putting the accident aside, it was a superb summer in all facets, even weather-wise, but in the early fall, after the Labour Day long weekend had passed, the tourists started to drop off dramatically. So, I moved to Banff in mid-September and found a place to stay.

ABOVE ROCKBOUND LAKE WITH JOHN GOW

Later that fall, once I had relocated to Banff, I met John Gow, a local climber who had heard of my accident through his climbing partner, Ken Moore, who had been a bellhop at Deer Lodge that summer. In mid-October, John asked me to join him and Ken in doing some bouldering above Rockbound Lake behind Castle Mountain. He felt it would be good for me to get back in the saddle (figuratively speaking) sooner rather than later, and so I joined them. It was a crisp morning when we took off from the trailhead. The sun came out soon after, and we had blue sky for a good part of the day. The boulders were made of prickly limestone, and once the sun went behind Castle Mountain the temperature dropped. Our fingers became numb, and we didn't feel the lacerations to our fingertips until later when we warmed them up and felt the sharp pain. That hindered my climbing opportunities for the rest of the fall.

It was good to get out and do some climbing with John and Ken. A few years later, John went on to get his mountain guide licence. Meanwhile, horses became my focus, and I put the mountain climbing aside for several years, probably ensuring a longer life. The old mountain adage, "If you survive the first five years of climbing you might live to an old age," was appropriate for me.

TWO

BANFF AND LAKE LOUISE

BANFF: THE EARLY YEARS

After my eventful summer at Deer Lodge, I spent the fall of 1965 working for a local building contractor, Bill Wilson, who was constructing Harmony Mall in Banff, which would house Harmony Drugs and Monod's Sports. The job was part time and only lasted a few months, so I had some free time on my hands.

Andy and Joan Knight ran a boarding house in Banff that a lot of us came and went from, during our early months and years there. The house was located on Lynx Street, and Rob Crosby (Rick's dad) owned it. It had several individual rooms upstairs, which Andy and Joan rented or sublet to staff working around Banff. It was like one big family and we all had access to the living room and the use of the kitchen. The living room was always a centre for conversation and relaxation. Most of us men, because of our lack of culinary skills early in life, preferred to run a tab at the old Modern Cafe, where Magpie and Stump is today. The local watering holes were either the King Edward or Cascade Hotels, which shut down early in those days. The Modern was just down the street on the same block as the King Eddy and became the magnet that drew everyone for the final meal of the day. Here you could carry on the social scene (minus alcohol) in a place where food was served, and it was always full after the bar closed.

Banff was a source of colourful characters back then, and one of the most unforgettable was "Timberline Jim" Deegan. Jim had a flair for making his presence known in rather dramatic fashion. On one occasion, after spending his usual lengthy time out in the wilds of Banff's backcountry, he was just a tad parched for that amber liquid that was drawn from the taps of the Cascade Hotel. So, after a shit, shave, shower and shampoo, he went down to see the boys at the Cascade and entered with much fanfare and bravado. As he sauntered up to the bar, he saw his buddies sitting about. Seeing this congenial company inspired him to instruct the waiter to "anoint the mahogany" and off they went with their trays full, passing out Deegan's round to all who were present. Then once everyone had been provided for and the din of the crowd had settled down, he stood at attention at the front of the bar and announced with great flair, "When Deegan drinks, everyone drinks." With that, he tossed his beer back in one thirsty gesture. A great roar came forth from the patrons and, in unison, all saluted Deegan's presence and drank from their glass. After taking another glass of beer off the counter, he downed it slower, savouring it and everyone followed. He then reached into his pocket and pulled out a dime. With one quick flip, he tossed the coin onto the counter and then announced to one and all, "When Deegan pays, everyone pays." That wouldn't be the first or the last time he was thrown out of the place.

In conjunction with that incident is the tale of his entrance to the Modern Cafe one night in an inebriated state, after the bar had closed. Feeling quite full of himself as he swaggered into the joint, he announced to one and all that he was "A Tiger in Tight Clothing, an Avalanche in Motion," and everybody laughed. However, a rather diminutive individual took exception to his claim, stepped up and decked him with one punch.

Another time, Jim came hobbling into town and complained to

anyone who would listen that his horse had bucked him off. One guy remarked that the horse was normally docile and it was unusual for him to do something like that – he must have been spooked. Jim said, "You know horses!" Then he started to explain the circumstances surrounding the event. "Well," he said, "I was out cutting trail with my axe and I came across this snag hung up on a limb high over the trail. I couldn't reach it from the ground so I positioned my horse in the right place then I climbed on. I had to stand up in the stirrups, and I got greater height by shortening them, which might have bothered another horse, but as you have observed, he is quite docile. Well, I took this large swing with my axe but missed the branch and hit him in his right shoulder. Could you believe it? He bucked me off."

A WINTER SPENT AT SUNSHINE VILLAGE

After my construction job ended, I began looking for winter work at one of the ski areas, hoping to learn how to ski and make some money. In the meantime, I filled my days by hiking some of the local trails and getting to know my fellow residents at the Knights' house.

There was an intriguing couple staying there, off and on that fall, a sister and brother in their early twenties. Faye was a striking woman with her dark beauty and a shy, mischievous nature. They were the son and daughter of Bert Mickle, and they seemed to enter the room like a fresh breeze through an open window. Don seemed to have a wild nature about him, emphasized by his unruly blond hair and hard to ignore, buckskin jacket. I felt they had an aura about them that radiated all that was wild and woolly about the surrounding country. We saw little of them that fall as they were out on the trail a lot, conducting hunting trips for their father.

One of the fellows staying at Andy and Joan's had just gotten a job at the Sunshine ski resort, working on the new Standish Chairlift that was under construction, so the next day I went up with him and got a job. I moved up and lived with the guys building the lift. They were a tough bunch. There was Gordon Brockway, who in the summer guided horse trips, Bobby Hall, who managed the construction of the chairlift, Bob Powell, Sunshine's area manager, and Lorne Tiffin, a friend of Gordon's.

Once the ski area opened for the season, I got a job as a lift operator. My base of operations was the Strawberry T-Bar where I loaded skiers most days. The lift serviced the gentlest runs on the mountain, which were commonly referred to as the "dope slopes." The odd time, my glove or mitt would be carried up the lift, caught between the tee and someone's backside. I made many a trip to the lost and found, replenishing lost gloves and mitts.

I had to constantly remind the skiers not to sit down on the T-bar. This was the novice slope, so there were a lot of beginners. Everyone instinctively wanted to sit down on the bar, but it is designed to pull you up the hill, not to be sat on. This last-minute instruction never seemed to penetrate their distracted brains, so quite often people would sit down and fall off the lift. Weekends were the worst, and some weekends were worse than others. On reflection, there seemed to be days when only the uninitiated were allowed on the hill.

Sometimes, I would be sidetracked doing something else at the lift station and skiers would try to load on their own. Occasionally, I would watch, fascinated, as they would bend over awkwardly, like a giraffe trying to drink water, while reaching for the tee. Then they would try to fit it between their legs from the back, appearing to me like they were trying to insert it up their ass. It wouldn't fit, so they would have to let go, but being spring loaded, the bar would fly wildly upward towards the cable, often caroming off the back of their heads on its way up. Stunned, they would look towards me, blinking, gasping like fish out of water, and then try it all over again.

One particularly bad weekend started with a couple of people falling off the lift while I screamed at them to "stand up, stand up!" Usually when they fell off they would try to drag themselves out of the way like wounded animals, concerned about escaping the onslaught of skiers coming up behind them. It was an act of self-preservation. This was never easy. After all, they had a 6- or 7-foot piece of wood strapped to each foot and a 4-foot ski pole wrapped around each wrist.

On rare occasions, you would get a couple of people who would fall off; usually one would fall knocking the other one down, and they would just lie there blinking, doing the gulping fish thing, in the middle of the track, saying nothing.

The topography of the Strawberry lift line leaving the station was such that the track climbed gradually up then levelled off for a ways. The skiers being pulled through this level stretch were hidden from my view for a while, until they started climbing up a steeper rise where they would reappear. One day, just after they had entered the hidden no-man's land, two people fell off in a tangle.

Because I couldn't see them, I continued to load skiers, not realizing I was sending them into a mess. Consequently, the people coming up behind crashed into the ones lying on the track, creating a snarl like rush-hour traffic. Still unaware of this growing catastrophe, I let an empty T-bar go by that had a faulty spring, causing it to drag on the ground. When it reached the pile of skiers, it got tangled in the writhing mass of bodies, skis and poles. The tee then stretched out to its fullest extent and started dragging the quivering and squeaking mass of arms and legs up the lift line, and finally into my view. As soon as I saw them, I stopped the lift and walked up the lift line to untangle the lump of human appendages and used ski equipment. This wasn't an easy task, and some of them had to remove their skis to disengage. Once I realized no one was hurt, I immediately saw the humour in it all, and it provided me with a "Tale with Ales," I could take to my fellow workers at the end of the day.

SUNSHINE CHARACTERS

There was a young man who often came up from Banff to ski at Sunshine. He was decked out in old ski-mountaineering equipment, wore an old orange anorak and looked like he didn't have two nickels to rub together. He was quite congenial with a cheerful disposition, and he got along well with the staff. I often had a chance to speak with him at the lift station. On some occasions, he could be seen skiing off in the afternoon with a big pack on his back. He would spend the night out in an igloo or snow cave and return the following morning with frost on his beard. When we had an occasion to chat, I found out he was a New Zealander. He talked about spending his youth hiking back home around Milford Sound and told me about a job he had once, hunting pesky deer that were as common as rabbits back there. His name was Lloyd Gallagher and everyone called him "Kiwi." He became a mountain guide for Hans Gmoser in the early days of helicopter skiing. Later in life, when he was married and had kids and needed a more secure work environment and a steadier income, he went to work for the Alberta government. He pioneered the development of an alpine rescue program at the province's first mountain park, Peter Lougheed, in Kananaskis Country.

Jerry Johnson was the ski school director at Sunshine Village. He went against the grain and employed mainly Canadian-born ski instructors. A significant proportion of instructors at Norquay and Lake Louise were European, mainly Austrian or Swiss, the odd Yugoslavian thrown in to liven up the atmosphere. By contrast, Jerry's crew was a virtual Who's Who of future movers and shakers in the Canadian ski industry. Roy Andersen, Norm Crerar, John Gow, Brian James and Peter M. Smith – all got their start with Jerry at Sunshine. There probably wasn't a better ski school director in the country. He had lots of competition though from Hans Vivian at Norquay and Mike Wiegele in Lake Louise.

In 1963, as a young ski instructor, Jerry started the first program for disabled skiers in Canada at Sunshine. He was inspired by Karl Hilzinger, a Calgary Stampeder football player who lost both of his legs in a car accident, and John Gow, who survived a plane crash near Golden, BC, but lost both of his feet to frostbite. Neither of them ever let anything get in the way of their return to the sports they loved.

Both Jerry and his wife Annie had a profound influence on the growth and development of the sport of skiing for disabled persons. They founded the Canadian Association for Disabled Skiing in 1976, and Jerry stayed on as its executive director for nearly thirty years. Both were inducted into the Canadian Disability Hall of Fame in the spring of 2014.

Lloyd "Kiwi" Gallagher guiding a group into Assiniboine in 1995.
DON FOREST ARCHIVE

After his years at Sunshine, Roy Andersen became the ski school director at Mount Norquay. He also followed in Bruno Engler's footsteps and became a well-established photographer in Banff. He helped develop the ski-jumping facilities in Calgary for the 1988 Olympics.

Peter M. Smith and Brian James both remained in the ski industry after working at Sunshine. Brian owned and operated a ski shop at Big White near Kelowna. Norm Crerar, who was also a competitive canoeist, co-owned and operated Silver Star Ski Resort near Vernon for several years with John Gow.

John Gow became an Association of Canadian Mountain Guides (ACMG) mountain guide in 1967, one of the first locals to come out of the new program that Walter Perren had envisioned. The airplane crash, which occurred in the spring of 1968, started out as an exploration of the mountains near Golden and ended as an epic journey to find help. He and pilot Bernie Royal were in a small aircraft, looking for suitable ski terrain in the countryside around Golden. They found themselves too low in a side valley, with an underpowered aircraft that could not climb out over the looming mountains at the end of the valley. They tried to make a tight turn inside the confined space, but, in attempting it, they lost elevation. Without the necessary power to complete the turn, they sliced into the trees. Bernie was killed outright and John was knocked out. When he regained consciousness, he found that he was injured but not incapacitated. He set out on an old logging road that had not seen a plough all winter, and the snow was bottomless. He spent three days struggling to reach help, but it was an exhausting task. When he was eventually found, it was immediately apparent that he had badly frozen legs and feet. Amputation was inevitable, leaving an 8-inch stump below one knee, and he lost a good portion of his other foot. That didn't stop him. With prostheses, he regained his ability to ski and ventured into climbing again. Just eighteen months after the accident, he completed the Gooseberry route on the back of Tunnel Mountain – no small feat – and he has been an inspiration for both the disabled and challenged ever since.

Two other individuals come to mind who ran the professional ski patrol at Sunshine: George Capel, the ski patrol leader, and Guenther Boehnisch, who worked for him. Back then the ski patrol at the four ski areas in the national parks – Sunshine, Norquay, Lake Louise and Marmot Basin (in Jasper) – were run by the Canadian National Park Warden Service. Along with the patrolling and first aid part of the operation, George and Guenther were also involved in the fledgling avalanche-control program, under the direction of Walter Perren. George, along with a couple of others from Sunshine, later started up the successful Abominable Ski Shop franchise that we still see today. Guenther went into business and built up a successful landscaping company.

SUNSHINE'S UNIQUE POSITION IN OUR MOUNTAIN NATIONAL PARKS

Back in the 1960s, Sunshine did not have the varied and extensive terrain that Lake Louise had, or the steeper slopes that Norquay possessed, but it was overly compensated with an abundance of snow. With its gentler ski terrain, it received a disproportionally greater share of young women (back in the day, we referred to them as "ski bunnies") who wanted to learn how to ski. This kept the ski instructors busy, both on and off the slopes. Sunshine was also the only ski area in the Canadian Rockies with on-site hotel accommodation, so if you were a ski instructor, fraternizing with the guests was part of the job description. The hotel was completed at the start of the 1965 ski season along with a new chairlift. The on-site hotel was the first and last of its kind in the mountain national parks.

In 1968 Imperial Oil tried to get on-site accommodation approval for Lake Louise but was turned down because of environmental concerns and a huge environmental lobby. Previously, Banff had been turned down as a possible site for the 1964 and 1968 Winter Olympics, showing the growing concern about excessive development in our national parks.

THE SUNSHINE SWIM TRUCK AND BANFF'S FAMOUS HANGOVER CURE

Every Wednesday night, we'd clean out the back of the old Dodge Power Wagon, throw a couple of mattresses into its covered back and head to Banff for the weekly swim night. After a lengthy session in the hot springs, soaking in +100°F temperatures, we would head for the Mountain Holm and a Swiss-style restaurant called the Tom-Tom Room, and enjoy their hot rums, Gluehwein and fondue. Unfortunately, I was under the legal drinking age of twenty-one, and without some fast talking or false documentation I was never sure if I would get served. On the times I was successful, I was part of the group, and it was great. But because it was a small town, the waiters soon got to know everyone, and as time went by, getting served became more of a challenge for me. I rarely had enough money to bribe my way in. If I failed, I spent the rest of the evening, walking lonely Banff Avenue, breaking the tedium with a coffee at one establishment and a bite to eat at another.

Before Banff became a big-time resort destination, the Sulphur Mountain Hot Springs was the great Banff hangover cure. After partying until the wee hours, morning always seemed to arrive abruptly. But you could always rely on the cure. When you took it depended on your work schedule the next day. If it was a day off, the morning swim was the priority of the day. Otherwise, this delight might have to be delayed until evening.

The treatment started with a hot plunge, followed by a hot steam, then a cold shower, repeated as many times as you could stand it. The final plunge and steam were prolonged a bit longer but were not followed by the cold shower. From the pool, you went directly to the massage room, where an attendant wrapped you in flannel blankets then placed you on your back on one of the tables. The next twenty minutes were devoted to sweating the poison out of your system. The treatment was often followed by a visit to a cocktail lounge on Banff Avenue, where you were required to consume a hot toddy. You had to drink it quickly, to get your heart racing to induce another cleansing sweat. The secret was to have the discipline to leave after the one toddy. I always preferred the cure at night as the hot rum was an important part of the program but not recommended for a mid-morning or an afternoon session. The toddy probably defeated the purpose of the pool plunge and sweat, but at our age, no one paid much attention to logic.

THE UIC SKI TEAM

A lot of the guys and gals living in Banff at that time were on the "UIC ski team," a term that referred to people who worked in the summer and took the winter off, using unemployment insurance to support their skiing. This was long before MP Joe Clark made reference to it. You might think it a less than admirable way to go about things, but the system in Canada cried out to be abused. There were even Brits and Australians who were on the team. They qualified because they were considered British subjects. The Aussies picked up skiing quickly, as a lot of them had a surfing background. The majority of us, though, went to work every day and only managed to sneak in a few ski runs. Up at Sunshine, if it was on your day off, you had to make a decision: a trip to town to do your laundry or a day on the hill. I had to do a lot of juggling to get my skiing in.

RESTLESS FOR A SPRING BREAK

Cliff and Beverly White bought the Sunshine Village ski area in early 1960 and by 1964 were looking to develop it further. They sold part interest in the ski hill to Power Corporation, a large and well-known company from the East. The money financed the new on-site accommodation and Standish Chairlift. In the middle of the 1965–66 ski season, the popular husband and wife team managing the hotel were let go, and the Whites took over management. In late April, a decision was made to extend the ski season one more week.

By this point, most of the staff were getting restless. A lot of them had summer jobs with other hotels and resorts, and they wanted a break between the two busy seasons. Many of the staff were talking about heading to San Blas, Mexico, for a break and wanted to get on their way. As the season wore on, many of the staff quit. That left a skeleton crew to try and get through the final weekend. It was now well into May, and even I wanted to be down in the valley where there were rumours that spring was gobbling up the lingering drifts of rotting snow. But I was trying to build a life in the mountains, so I stayed on, amazed at the endurance of the snow at 7,200 feet. There was still great skiing, in increasingly lovely, warm weather, and the management intended to wring the last bit out of the season.

On the final day of the final weekend, some of the lift operators rebelled and started drinking early, which resulted in mayhem at one of the lift stations. A fellow by the name of Harry, who went by the nickname "Needles," was loading people on the Wawa T-Bar in a cavalier manner, then deliberately stopping the lift. The first part of the lift line is up a steep incline and when the lift stopped there was always a bit of a roll back, a few feet, before it actually came to a complete stop. Suddenly the skier's momentum was going in reverse for a few seconds. Because of the steepness, it was a rather abrupt stop, and one or two people would fall over backwards when this occurred. That would be the exact moment Needles would start the lift again, dragging them up the hill, their legs and skis wrapped around the tee. It wasn't a pretty sight or safe by any means, but Harry thought it was hilarious. They sent me down to relieve him of his duties.

We called him Needles because he liked to knit. He was no shrinking violet, though, in a physical sense. He stood a little over 6 feet and weighed a good 210 pounds. As I tried to bring some sort of normalcy to the situation, two local Banff boys (George and Murray), who were also working as lift operators, soon joined Needles, drinking in the lift shack.

When Gordon Brockway, who was by now considered management, came down to survey the situation, he found Needles, George and Murray, hanging from the T-bars by their arms as they returned to the lift station. At one point, they had to be 50 feet above the ground. This is a hair-raising thing to do when you're sober, considering the distance and time you're exposed, but a piece of cake if you're intoxicated. The trio had performed the stunt a couple of times without incident, while I continued to load people, shaking my head. I had a difficult time explaining to the skiers why these people were hanging from the tees, and I gave up after a while. Gordon put a stop to their fun before they injured themselves.

By this time, some of the other lift operators were now getting into the party mood, so Gordon and Bob Powell, the area manager, sent the incapacitated staff home, while management and a few of us who were sober ran the lifts for the rest of the afternoon. Gordon never got upset; he took it in stride and just made sure that when the day was done, it would end without incident or harm to anyone. It was a small miracle that no one was hurt. The ski area closed the next day, and we spent the time packing up our belongings and saying our goodbyes. Many were suffering from massive hangovers.

ON THE ROAD TO SAN BLAS

Orville Byrd (one of the cooks) and I decided to hitchhike down to Mexico and join those who had left earlier for San Blas. It was one of those quiet Mexican fishing ports that became a haunt for California surfers in the 60s. It had black sandy beaches, good surfing, mainly on the beaches south of town, and ankle-biting sand flies that came out as soon as the sun went down. Even if you weren't a surfer there was still a lot to see and do. In particular, there was a boat excursion up a quiet river through mangroves to a deep pool and waterfall. There was a small restaurant there that served simple food and beer. Because the town was a fishing village, it had good, inexpensive seafood in the many little restaurants, cluttered around the central plaza. If you wanted some beer or wine with dinner, you just brought it with you, and there was no corkage fee.

Orville was a huge man with a bushy beard, so it was difficult hitching. He wasn't a wise choice as a hitchhiking partner. It took us a week to get to San Francisco, and we were both pretty discouraged by then. We decided to split up: he took a bus south to LA, and I took one north, back to Vancouver. He made it as far as Tijuana, while I was back in Banff within a week, after a stop in Calgary to visit my folks. I would get to San Blas, but it would be eighteen years later.

On returning to Banff, I wanted to work at something that could

San Blas, Mexico, with old church tower.
DALE PORTMAN COLLECTION

help me later, possibly in a career with the warden service, but I settled for a job at Deer Lodge again. If a job opportunity arose that involved working with horses, though, I knew I would seriously look at the offer. I wasn't a novice around horses, but I had no practical working experience with them. As air force brats living at Lincoln Park, some of us would go down to the local pony stand and rent a horse for an hour or two. At the time, the air base was on the outskirts of Calgary. The stables stood where Mount Royal University is today, and we only had to stroll across a large open field to get there. It was open grassland all the way to the Sarcee Indian Reserve (Tsuu T'ina Nation). I started going there with a small group of friends but once I got to know the people running the place, I would often go there on my own. On a couple of occasions, my father came along just to check things out, see the horses and talk to the people. My father had an interest in race horses that he passed on to me.

MY PREVIOUS EXPOSURE TO HORSES

At the time, my dad's youngest brother, Kenny, was involved with thoroughbred horses as a trainer. The two of them were very close, and after Dad retired from the military, he bought some thoroughbreds as claimers and started training and racing them.

Kenny started out as a stable hand in his youth, and then he became a jockey because of his slight stature. When that career ended (when he grew older and gained weight), he established himself as a horse trainer. He was very good at it and was soon hired by renowned Calgary newspaper publisher Max Bell, who had a racing stable.

The Bell Ranch, which he owned and operated with his business partner, Frank McMahon, was located near Okotoks, Alberta, on the Sheep River. His racing and breeding facility was called Golden West Farms. Located on the land is the prominent, glacial deposit, an erratic rock that Okotoks is named and known for (o'kotok means "rock" in the Blackfoot language). The rock is revered by the Blackfoot people. By the late 1960s, it had also become a local landmark in the climbing community.

The ranch was a large spread that held magnificent facilities for raising, breeding and training thoroughbreds. My father would often take us there on weekends where we would roam about and explore the countryside, as well as watch the horse operation. Once in a while, I got to ride one of the quieter working horses that were kept there. I always rode bareback, and on one occasion, I fell off while loping across the field in front of my dad and uncle. When I got up, I heard my father say to my uncle, "I guess it doesn't run in the family." That kind of hurt, and I wondered if he'd ever ridden bareback.

There was a guest house on the ranch where Bell's friends would stay and visit. Bing Crosby was one of them. That made everything more exciting for us as we never knew when he might show up and we would get a glimpse of him. It was foolish optimism on our part but you could always hope. We spent hours going over my uncle's stacks of racing magazines. By now we had a sister, Susan, who was still in diapers and loved to wade in, knocking over the various piles. Through these magazines I came to know the blood line of most of the thoroughbred champions. Man of War, Omaha, Citation, Seabiscuit, War Admiral, all come to mind as greats of the past. Our visits were a few years before Northern Dancer's successes at the Kentucky Derby and the Preakness, and his third-place finish at the Belmont Stakes.

Next to E.P. Taylor, who owned Northern Dancer, Max Bell was the leading breeder in the country and the most prominent in western Canada. He was introduced to horse racing by the American Hall of Fame jockey Johnny Longden, who said of Bell, "I owe everything I have to that man. He was the finest man I have ever met in racing."

The racing partnership Bell had with Frank McMahon also involved Bing Crosby. Frank knew Crosby from his university days in Spokane, Washington, and the three of them were involved in several stake race victories with co-owned horses. The three of them owned Meadow Court, who won the Irish Derby in 1965. In the winner's circle, Crosby sang "When Irish Eyes are Smiling" for the crowd. He and McMahon won the 1968 Queen's Plate on Merger. One of their biggest successes was Four-and-Twenty, who won the 1961 Santa Anita Derby and

WHO'S LAUGHING

Medicine Hat, Alberta, July 26, 1975. 5 1/2 Furlongs,1:09:3
Owner-Trainer: H.Portman,Calgary.   Howard Boggs up
Dewey Boy (2nd)   NEW TRACK RECORD   Tatayet (3rd)

Dad's Who's Laughing in the winner's circle at Medicine Hat, Alberta, in 1975.
DALE PORTMAN COLLECTION

the Hollywood Derby in the same year. Crosby and McMahon also co-owned the great Majestic Prince, who won the 1969 Kentucky Derby and the Preakness

Bell was a great philanthropist whose name is on many facilities in Calgary. Shortly before his death, he founded the Max Bell Foundation, which awarded millions of dollars in grants for medical, veterinary, sporting and educational causes. He also helped finance the Vancouver Canucks' entry into the NHL. His FP Publications was Canada's largest newspaper syndicate in the 1960s.

Frank McMahon was the founder of Westcoast Transmission, a natural gas pipeline company that opened western and northern Canada to oil and gas markets in the United States. In 1960 Frank and his brother George helped finance the construction of the football stadium named after them, McMahon Stadium. *Time* magazine said he was the man who did the most to open Canada's northwestern wilderness to resource development.

By the time I found myself working in the mountains, Ken and Dad had a small racing stable based out of the track in Calgary. They had a few winners, mostly claim horses. One that comes to mind is Sickles Prince. My sister kept all the old photographs from that period, which I enjoyed going through while writing this book.

WORKING FOR BUD BREWSTER AND BRET MITZEL

I had no practical experience that would help me get a job as a guide or wrangler at one of the riding stables in the Banff/Lake Louise area, but then I met Skip Brochu. I had arrived back in Lake Louise after the trip south with Orville and was settled into my work at Deer Lodge. It was about this time that I met Skip, who worked for the Brewster Riding Stables. We started chumming around together, and he eventually lined me up for a job with Bret Mitzel, by inflating my horse-handling skills.

Two books that I really enjoyed growing up were *Grass beyond the Mountains* by Rich Hobson, the first of a trilogy of books about the Chilcotin Country, and R.M. Patterson's *Buffalo Head*, about ranching life in southwestern Alberta. Another of Patterson's books, which fascinated many, was *Dangerous River*.

I had to quit my job with Deer Lodge, which I struggled with, as they had been so good to me, but it was early in the season and they had adequate time to find a replacement. I found myself guiding one-hour rides from the lakeshore near the Chateau Lake Louise. The pony stand location consisted of a large teepee and a small kiosk. The main stables were well away from the lake front, next to the Brewster Transport facilities, under a kilometre away. Being situated near the lake made all kinds of business sense, as this was where the largest concentration of tourists was.

The operation was nurtured along by an old codger who was as cranky as a she cougar giving birth to a roll of barb wire. Old Ralph, as he was known, was ninety-four and still able to get around with a lot of spunk. He wore a buckskin coat that made him stand out from the rest of us and he was famous for this regalia. All kinds of tourists got their picture taken with him, and just the sight of this old mountain man would draw the crowds over – and he played the role, with great relish. With his drawing attraction, many would get in the spirit and go for a ride.

Ralph looked after everything at the site, and our hourly rides would come and go from there. He walked around, inspecting every-thing we did, cussing at this and that and making sure we didn't step out of line. At times, he was a pain in the ass, but we never complained as he had a sharp tongue and even sharper wit.

Skip's life revolved around being a cowboy, and he spent his winters down in Arizona training polo ponies. He looked like he had just walked out of a Zane Grey novel, and he played the cowboy role naturally and to the hilt. I always enjoyed his stories, even if some of them, I suspected, were a tad embellished. He was also a few years older than me, and he became a bit of a mentor, both at work and play.

I started to do well with the cash tips, as I watched some of the more experienced guys perform their craft. One of them, Bill Soderman, had a real gift of the gab. He actually liked to take people out for a ride and entertain them. Most cowboys back then would grunt a few words at the beginning of the ride and fall silent for the remainder of the trip. If they were asked a question and they didn't know the answer, which was often, they would make something up. All flowers were alpine buttercups or mountain daisies, and birds could be broken up into four categories: dickey birds, raptors, ducks and LBJs (little brown jobs).

Bill's nickname was "Saucer Eyes," and the birds he didn't know, which were many, were often referred to as "rosy-breasted pushovers" or "rosy-breasted bed-thrashers." He reserved these expressions until he really got into it, especially if there was a young attractive female on the ride. He had big round eyes that bulged out when he got excited or laughed. His thin lips, wide mouth and pale complexion, didn't add to his appearance. He wore a black hat, black boots and jeans, and had a knack for attracting the ladies that played counter to his poor looks. He was also a treat to be around.

The hour-long rides got to be repetitive and tedious as the summer rolled on, but once in a while you were given a table scrap and got to go along on a half-day or, even better, a full-day ride. This only happened when it was busy and the other guides were tied up. These longer rides were the domain of the more experienced cowboys.

I use the term "cowboys" loosely, as there was little similarity between them and working cowboys outside of wearing the cowboy boots and the hat, while on a horse. That said many of the more experienced guides did have a ranching background. The one-hour rides were at the lowest rung, but guiding them gave you the opportunity to play the role to the maximum. Guys who only two weeks before had a stammer and a stutter on Yonge Street, now had a Montana drawl that some of us thought authentic.

The adage "bullshit baffles brains" seemed to apply to everything around us, including very gullible tourists with a high tolerance for bullshit. Back then the entertainment became how good you were at being cheeky to a guest, without going overboard and offending them. If you pissed them off, though, it didn't matter – you'd never see them again and the Gorbies (a local name for a tourist) seemed to accept being treated this way. This was a few decades before Banff's business people got serious about hospitality training and providing the visitor with a first-class experience and some decent service delivery.

This poor attitude towards tourists was endemic throughout the industry in western Canada in the 1960s and 1970s. The product provided to tourists was often unsophisticated, and there was no desire to pass on any level of quality to enhance their experience. A lot of the businesses realized their staff had much to learn. The managers began to take notice of the rising level of service provided in other parts of the world. The attitude finally changed when some of the Banff businesses started to address the problem seriously, and they only had to look as far as the Canadian Pacific hotel chain for an example of how to do things right.

It was disappointing to see how little food you got on your plate when dining in Banff back then, especially compared to restaurants south of the border. If you went stateside, your plate was heaped full and you always got a friendly "How are you all doing?" and "You all come back now" response from the waiter or waitress. In Banff breakfast often consisted of two puny eggs, two or three stingy pieces of bacon and a plastic garnish that you would eat because you were still hungry. Being served on a large white plate further accentuated this meagre offering. Some even had the audacity to serve the toast on a separate plate. Needless to say, no hash browns were to be found anywhere. American tourists were usually very polite about hiding their astonishment when they realized that was all they were getting for their money. If the exchange rate had not been so favourable, it might have been a different story.

The old "Skier's Special" at the Paris Restaurant was the exception. They served this huge steak on a large wooden plate or platter. The steak was cut thin, maybe ⅜- to ½-inch thick, but it covered a big area and the French fries lay on top in substantial quantity. There was no other place on the platter to put them. On top of all of this was often a fried egg. I don't remember anything else that came with the serving, outside of some garlic toast, but it didn't matter, you had lots to eat and it was very popular with the staff around Banff. It reminded me of what I got years later when travelling in Argentina and Chile. The Argentine people were proud of their beef, and so was Ossie Treutler, the proprietor of the Paris Restaurant.

The cheeseburger deluxe you got at the Brewster Cafe above their garage was one of the best you could find in the country. The burger was topped with a fried egg that took it to another level. That broken yoke dripping down the sides was awesome to bite into.

Bob Sandford, back in the day.
DALE PORTMAN COLLECTION

Hospitality training appeared in the early 1980s when Bob Sandford was hired by Brewster Transport. It was taken up by some of the other major employers in the area later, mainly influenced by Bob's training. Eventually even Parks Canada hired him to provide the training to its staff. Bob had worked for several years as a naturalist in Jasper and Banff. He was a very creative and dynamic individual who brought a lot of energy to this new position, and it was important that this phase of the training be successful and that the business people and their staff bought into the program. Management accepted the training well before the workers did, and Bob found it a struggle to sometimes get the staff on side. This was a hugely important stage in the development of sophisticated tourist delivery in our mountain national parks during the 1980s.

But all of this came after my summer at the horse stand by the lake. As the summer moved along, I tired of the endless days of one-hour rides. I started to volunteer for barn chores and stayed back to clean up the horse stalls at the stables, adjacent to the old Brewster block.

Here you could have some solitude, listen to some Frankie Lane tunes and work at your own pace in an unhampered environment without Old Ralph's charmless presence.

JOSÉ THE DONKEY

After our visit to Quebec City, on Day 89, we headed southwest into the Eastern Township region of Quebec, south of Montreal. Just south of Sherbrook and not far from the town of Coaticook near the Vermont border, we found a lovely campground and claimed a wonderful campsite next to a field of horses. Lily was in heaven. She loved domestic animals, being brought up around horses, and she couldn't wait to make friends. She sniffed the horses through the wire fence and they quickly accepted her. A hinny – a male horse crossed with a female donkey – came over to investigate and showed great interest in the dog. The hinny dropped its head allowing its ear to be exposed to the dog's nose. It was a gesture of friendship and trust and Lily took the opportunity to get a good sniff of its ear. It was a wonderful sight, and it took me back to when I was starting out as a guide and a particularly feisty and infamous donkey.

One day I was witness to a breakout that happened often over the years. José, the donkey over at Timberline Tours, the Mickle stables, got loose and came over to see how things were faring with the Brewster string and all their dude horses. The Brewster horses at the lakeshore were only tied by their bridle reins to a long rope stretched between two trees. Horses never did like surprises, and José was deemed an alien. At this point, many of the Brewster horses had never seen a donkey before. José seemed oblivious to the terror his presence created as he amiably wandered about in the pursuit of poppies – that donkey loved poppies.

As the grey midget appeared on the horizon, the horses snorted. As José advanced, the horses' eyes rolled back in their heads and they flew back in varying degrees of panic. Some broke their reins and landed on their haunches, while the rest hopefully settled down somewhat and looked on nervously.

What really unnerved them, though, was José's foghorn bray. When that little donkey brayed, all hell broke loose. The more skittish horses by now had commanded the whole string to bolt, which left us madly running about trying to settle them down. Amongst the flying feet and falling bodies was Old Ralph, who waddled bowlegged into the fray, expressing himself like a dog's anal glands, foul and profane, trying to bring some control to the situation. Of course, the donkey couldn't figure out why there was so much commotion going on as he passed by on his way to the abundant poppy beds surrounding the Chateau Lake Louise.

José never did take a liking to the Brewster cowboys, they were always cursing him and trying to shoo him away. Many of the cowboys thought the donkey's wanderings were a deliberate act on Bert Mickle's part to stir up the competition. José's only focus, though, were those poppies near the Chateau, and near Deer Lodge. He would always leave the white ones, because he preferred red. José's breakouts usually ended with Bert getting a phone call from the Crosbies or Ian Mackie, the manager at the Chateau Lake Louise, or Bret Mitzel, asking him to come and get his damn donkey off their property.

There is one enduring story of José that comes to mind. As has been noted, he often was allowed to roam freely around the yard of the pony stand, and he became a focus for the tourists who came to check out the horse operation. He was always chasing other animals away, but one day a small black bear cub showed up without a mother. The poor thing had probably lost its mother to a collision with a vehicle or a train. José stepped in as the new mother and comforted the newly orphaned little tyke. The cub was seen curled up at night with José and would stick near him throughout the day. June Mickle, who was running the pony stand at that time, was the owner of José and had a fondness for all animals. She was quite pleased that José would care for the little cub and hoped for the best. However, it was still early spring and without its mother, the cub had little chance of survival. She phoned Wally McPhee, the warden, and he came and picked it up and had it transferred to the Calgary Zoo.

Towards the end of the summer, the boys were having a party in the large communal bunkhouse area where we all stayed. Gordon Brockway and a couple of other cowboys had driven up from Turner Valley to visit Bret, and a party quickly broke out after the chores were done. A one point in the evening I accidentally knocked over a partly full whisky bottle. Bret was pissed off and collared me as I made some feeble attempt at apologizing to him and the inebriated crowd. We ended up in the hallway where he drifted me a good one on the side of the head. I hit the wall while disjointedly, trying to maintain my balance. Bret was a big man.

I managed to regain my balance and being a peaceful sort, and outgunned, I decided to get the hell out before he tagged me with another one. As I went down the hall, he informed me I was fired. At that point, Gordon stepped out into the hall and told Bret to pick on someone his own size. Bret turned around and said, "You're my size," and hammered Gordon, breaking his jaw.

I retired to the friendlier confines of the stables where I saddled a horse and went for a ride to clear my head. The next morning Bret rehired me and Gordon spent the rest of the fall with his jaw wired shut, sipping things through a straw. I was the lucky one; I only had a sore jaw and a bruised ego. Oh, how I miss that cowboy culture back in the good old 1960s.

BUD BREWSTER AND THE BREWSTER CLAN

Bret managed the stables but it was owned by Bud Brewster, and Bud would show up on occasion to check on the operation, often accompanied by his wife Annette. Usually, after they had checked on how things were going and had talked to the staff, they would saddle up and go for a ride up to Lake Agnes or the Plain of Six Glaciers.

The Brewster clan had been around Banff since its inception. John Brewster was Bud's great-great grandfather. He had come out west in 1886 from Kingston, Ontario, following the completion of the Canadian Pacific Railroad across Canada and the creation of Canada's first national park in 1885, eventually called Banff. His wife and four sons – Bill, John, Fred and Jack – came out and joined him in 1888. They started a dairy operation near Banff, next to Vermilion Lakes, and a horse ranch in the shadow of Mount Yamnuska, at the entrance to the mountains. One of John's sons, Jim, started a horse-drawn carriage business in Banff that eventually evolved into Brewster Transport. Another son, Bud's grandfather, Bill went into the outfitting business and built the Kananaskis Guest Ranch near Seebe.

Bud's father, Claude, was Bill's son, and once Claude was old enough, he took over managing the business while maintaining a significant presence in the Banff area. He was a quiet, unassuming person who was a humanitarian at heart. He had a close, supportive and friendly relationship with the local Stoney Indians near Seebe. He was also very active in both local and federal politics and a personal friend of Louis St. Laurent, the prime minister at the time.

Bud eventually took over the operation from Claude and continued to expand the business, both in Banff and Lake Louise with Brewster Mountain Pack Trains out of Banff and Lake Louise Stables at the lake. He built a backcountry lodge at Shadow Lake, a hotel – Brewster Mountain Lodge – in the town of Banff, and a golf course at the Kananaskis Ranch near Seebe. He signed a lucrative contract with the Trail Riders of the Canadian Rockies and the Skyline Hikers that kept him busy setting up base camps throughout Banff's backcountry. Bud had many talents, among them being a cowboy, a carpenter, a businessman and an entrepreneur. But beyond that, he was a great employer who looked after his staff.

THREE

FAYE AND DONNY

MY RELATIONSHIP WITH THE MICKLE FAMILY

It was June 22, 2015, and we finally set off on our journey east with Newfoundland as our ultimate goal. But it wasn't an easy departure. Kathy had recently finished a book on June Mickle, *One Woman's Life in the Foothills and Mountains of Western Canada*. She had sent it off to the publisher in early February and was waiting for an editor to be assigned. The edited version didn't show up until a couple of days before we left. On top of that, a friend, Donna was going to move in to look after the place. She had recently sold her house in Calgary and had nowhere to live. Kathy now had to review the book and send it back, but we were leaving in a couple of days. She did as much as possible and had the manuscript copied out, then madly tried to help me pack up and get our trailer shipshape.

Our departure was about as stressful as it gets, and we decided that we would not stop moving east until we got to Prince Edward Island and then finish the editing there. It was hanging over us as we travelled east. When we got to Kenora, Ontario, we checked into a campground that had good Internet delivery, and we camped near their tower to get the best reception. Kathy couldn't bear having the book looming over her for the next couple of weeks. It had the potential of putting a damper on the trip. For two solid days, we sat down in front of our computers and completed the editing and sent it off to the publisher. Now we only had to wait for the proofread, which caught up to us in PEI.

The idea of writing June Mickle's story partially grew out of my involvement with the Mickle family back in the mid-1960s and Kathy's personal relationship with June and the family. June moved to Cochrane in her later years, and Kathy had a wonderful relationship with her as the book took shape. As I drove east towards Thunder Bay, I couldn't help but reflect on those early years and unforgettable experiences they rendered. My relationship with the Mickles was one of the most important ones of my life.

THE FALL RIDE INTO SKOKI LODGE

In the fall of 1966, Skip got hired on with Timberline Tours for the fall hunting season with the Mickles, and I got offered a job, as well. I was quite thrilled with this new opportunity to see some of Banff's more remote backcountry.

It didn't take long to move. I had little in the way of possessions and it was only a 100-yard walk through the spruce trees from Brewster to the Mickle operation. The pony stand was a collection of older, rust-coloured buildings with a corral, covered stalls and attached tack room. It all hung together in confusion; all the parts' sole association being a dirt parking lot and the weathered vehicles it sheltered. It wasn't falling apart, but it had the feeling of age steeped in some sort of equine history.

One of the first things Skip and I did was trail eight or nine head of horses up to their trailhead operation located at Temple Lodge. This 7-mile trip took us down the old tramline used in the early days by the CPR to haul luggage and freight up from the passenger train. This route led us past the Post Hotel, the Esso gas station and Boyle's store. We crossed the Trans-Canada Highway near the entrance to the sedan

Bert in camp at the 1967 Spring Roundup.
DON MICKLE COLLECTION

lift, followed Temple Road as far as Fish Creek and then picked up a trail that paralleled the ski-out run and past the small and somewhat shabby Eagle Warden Cabin.

Temple Lodge was at the end of the road: a lovely old two-storey log building built by Banff's Peter and Catherine Whyte back in the 1930s to facilitate travel to Skoki Lodge. The couple had seen how successful Assiniboine Lodge was and thought a similar lodge would work in the Lake Louise area. They contracted Ken Jones to construct Skoki Lodge, and the legendary skier and guide did a superb job. Sir Norman Watson came into possession of the two lodges, under dubious circumstances, and was now leasing both lodges to the Mickles. It was from Temple Lodge that the trail took off for Skoki and the Red Deer Lakes country. The lodge acted as a base of operations for the backcountry part of the Mickle business.

Skip and I arrived late in the afternoon and were met by Bert Mickle, his wife June and two Millarville cowboys, Bob Haney and Keith Foster. Skip and I corralled the horses and then came up to the lodge where Keith and Bob were throwing things into a couple sets of pack boxes. Bert was sitting on the steps supervising.

He stood up and came over and introduced himself to me. He already knew Skip. I was a punk kid shaking hands with the fiercest Black Bart of all outfitters. He was the toughest looking man I had ever laid eyes on. He wore a stained black Stetson with the curl on each side flattened against the peak part of the brim. His long face was worn and weather beaten, wrinkled like the hide of an elephant. His narrow eyes were hooded by big, bushy eyebrows, and his sideburns came down to the level of his mouth, which wasn't overly big or wide. A rolled cigarette hung precariously from his thin lips, over a nest of black hair protruding like steel wool from the V of his shirt. In the middle of it all was a flattened nose, pasted to his face like the brim of his hat. I gulped and said hello.

It was a big group that headed for Skoki that early evening with twenty loose horses and the addition of Charlie Weatherly, an old hand from Sundre. The first mile or so was through groves of downy larch, along with stands of balsam fir and Engelmann spruce, until we reached an open, subalpine meadow.

The meadow surrounding Halfway Hut was cluttered with small clumps of balsam fir, while along the edges of the meadow were larger stands of fir and spruce. The hut was a small, one-room cabin used by skiers in the winter on their way to Skoki. In front of the cabin and to the side was a small community of balsam firs that acted as a barrier to the wind and provided something secure to tie a horse to.

We came over a boulder-strewn crown of land and there before me was Ptarmigan Lake, the first alpine one we were to ride by. Bert called me kid as we gained the low pass, pointing out the surrounding peaks, Redoubt, Ptarmigan, and Pika. Looking back, you could see the sweeping lines of the ski runs and the distant sentinels surrounding Lake Louise: Mounts Temple, Aberdeen, Lefroy, and Whyte. In the other direction, off in the distance, you could see the trail skirting the shore to the left and then steadily angling up to a major pass.

Ptarmigan Lake and Boulder Pass from Deception Pass on a moody day.
DALE PORTMAN COLLECTION

Bert was enjoying himself, and I was exhilarated by the view of horses and cowboys spreading out before us as we crossed the stretch of alpine. Now there was only a hint of krummholz here and there before we left them behind, heading up towards Deception Pass. Finally, we gained the pass and stopped for a moment to take in the spectacular views that were falling away in both directions. Bob Haney finally led off down into the Skoki valley leading the packhorses. It seemed like just a short time later when I could see a column of smoke, then the main lodge, surrounded by three or four cabins. Everyone came out to meet us as we rode by to the corrals, which are located below the lodge.

Rita Smith, Bert's sister, put together a big supper and later everyone sat around playing crib and talking about the next day. I woke up in the dead of night in a strange bed and for a while I had no idea where I was. I had to piss like a racehorse but was disoriented by the total darkness that obscured the room. I desperately needed to find a way out – my bladder was ready to burst. I groped around for the door and soon realized I was in a small room, and then I remembered were I was: Skoki! I examined every crack and corner until I finally brushed the door latch. I stopped. My eyes were slowly adjusting to the scant moonlight, and I could see a pitcher silhouetted next to a slowly materializing window. With relief, I peed into it, then found the bed and went back to sleep.

Next morning, I heard a knock and was up in a flash. I called out that I'd be right down, grabbed the pitcher and dumped the contents out the window. I had the pitcher in my hand as I went downstairs, intending to rinse it in the creek before going to breakfast, but Bert surprised me at the bottom of the stairs as I snuck towards the door. I stashed the pitcher next to a small bookshelf. I didn't want him to know that I had used his lovely enamel pitcher with its unique floral design as a urinal.

Bert asked me to go down to the corral and let Keith and Donny know breakfast was ready. Off I went and when I got back, I searched madly for the pitcher, but it was nowhere to be found. Quickly I slipped into the kitchen and sat down for breakfast with everyone else. I reached for a slice of toast and then watched in frozen horror as Bert poured himself some juice from a very familiar pitcher. He brought the glass to his thin lips and drank. An expression passed over his face, a delicate hesitation or reflection, more quizzical than anything else – as though he was trying to identify something, an aftertaste, subtle but distinct. Then, as suddenly as the expression was there, it was gone, and he poured himself another glass. If I admitted to my secret it would have been the shortest job I ever had.

OVER PIPESTONE PASS AND DOWN THE SIFFLEUR

Skip headed back to Temple while a small group of us trailed the horses out to the Siffleur for the start of hunting season. Bob Haney and Keith Foster took up the lead while Don Mickle and I followed, driving the horses down the trail to the Little Pipestone River. Shortly after leaving Skoki, we skirted Merlin Meadows on our descent. Donny pointed out Merlin Castle, a significant rock formation that could be seen in the distance as it stood jaggedly against the talus slope. In an hour or so we arrived at the Little Pipestone Warden Cabin, where we forded the Pipestone River. We had a ways to go to get to the hunting camp, located approximately 26 miles away.

It was a pleasant ride up the valley, as we passed through old stands of jack pine, broken up here and there by small meadows. On occasion, the trail dipped down to the river. At the end of a long, timber-covered bench, we stopped to gaze over the land ahead. Spreading out before us was Singing Meadows. A slow, meandering stream ran through the open grassland, and off to the right, Singing Falls slipped down a smooth face, like a giant water feature.

On our approach to Pipestone Pass and still in the trees, we came upon an old warden cabin and stopped for lunch. The window shutters and door were covered in nail spikes, sprouting from them like a porcupine's quills. It was a determined deterrent for any grizzly that wanted to get inside without the necessary key. We continued up the valley, staying near the creek, and soon broke out into the alpine. The notch of the pass could be seen off in the distance.

From the pass, the undulating alpine terrain of the upper Siffleur River spread before us. The high hidden pockets and hollows were ideal for concealing the caribou that lived there. In fact, it was so perfect that for the longest time, it was only rumoured there were caribou there, as sightings were so scarce. But if you took the time to look, you might catch the sight of an old track or two in the fine shale. If you stopped to glass, you might even catch them, cooling off, away from the tormenting flies on the east-facing snowfields, where they were easier to spot.

Clumps of krummholz started to appear around us as we headed down the valley, and soon we came to a trail junction. To our right was Clearwater Pass, its summit 500 feet above us. We eventually entered

Isabella Lake and the Dolomite Valley.
DALE PORTMAN COLLECTION

a mixed forest of spruce and pine that revealed the old remnant of an abandoned warden cabin. We continued down the valley and eventually we broke out into an old burn that was next to a grassy meadow. Scattered about were young pine trees growing up around the burnt deadfall. This was to be our campsite for the night, and it offered us a grand view down the valley towards Dolomite Creek.

The campsite was referred to as Wildman Camp, but I don't think it had an official name as there wasn't much there, just some running water, a bit of firewood, level ground and a view. The two packhorses were soon unpacked and the horses turned out to graze. The possibility of a supper now took on some significance.

After supper, which didn't take much to prepare outside of building a fire and heating a couple cans of beans, we settled in for the evening. With much glee and fanfare, Donny reached into one of the pack boxes and pulled out a bottle of whisky, which he swiftly uncorked, much too easily in retrospect. He tossed the bottle back and took a swig, then spat it out. Without hesitation, he cursed his sister, Faye. She had replaced its contents with tea and what Keith called her was even less flattering. There was no match to Keith, or better-equipped mouth, in a situation like this. He made Old Ralph sound like a choir boy.

We were off early the next morning with hollow stomachs as our eggs were only shells thanks to Faye. Her name came up frequently over the next hour or two, and her ears must have been burning back in Lake Louise. Keith expressed it best in the end when he said, "I'm so fucking hungry, if someone shit on a piece of bread, I'd eat around and under it." Faye and Keith were always rubbing each other the wrong way, and while she felt sorry for Donny, it was too much to resist getting back at Keith.

About that time, we arrived at the Dolomite stream crossing, uncharacteristically wide at that point, running over a floor of boulders, and it took some time to push the horses across. Soon we were back into a deep mossy forest that offered little in the way of scenery outside of possibly seeing a leprechaun or two, or maybe a spruce hen. Then we came across the boundary of Banff National Park. It was identified by a narrow slash (cutline) up through the trees perpendicular to the trail. The path then meandered farther into the shadowed timber for another 2 miles before breaking out into a small clearing of swamp grass. From here you could see the start of a seismic road. It was near here that Bert had his hunting camp.

As the four of us sat around the fire that night, little did we know that all of us would follow the same path and join the warden service. Bob and Keith would eventually become chief park wardens (CPW) in various national parks, Donny would become the cultural resource expert for Banff National Park, and I would remain in the field, turning down the odd opportunity for advancement to concentrate on training and handling search and rescue dogs.

For the next couple of days, we were kept busy setting up the hunting camp; a cook tent was erected, some wall tents put up for sleeping and a food storage area. We brought loads of firewood in, bucked it up and split it into suitable lengths for the wood stove. We cut a separate pile of kindling and once everything was in place we sat back and waited for Bert and the hunters.

THE MILLARVILLE MAFIA

The Millarville Mafia was a term created by one of the assistant chief park wardens in Banff in the early 1980s, Keith Everts. He was referring to four individuals who were from Millarville, three park wardens and a fourth who was Banff's barn boss. They were old friends who now worked for the warden service but at one time they also worked for Bert Mickle. They were Don Mickle, Bob Haney, Perry Jacobson and John Nylund. There were two others in the "mafia": Keith Foster and Dave Wildman. Also from Millarville, they both worked for Bert. Keith also became a park warden and eventually the CPW of Grasslands National Park. Dave was a rancher from the area who later moved to a spread near Sangudo, Alberta, on the Pembina River. Later, membership in this clan was extended to Lee Edwards and myself. Lee worked for the warden service as a packer in the early 70s after working for Bert and at this writing lives in Bragg Creek west of Calgary. The three criteria for acceptance into this unusual club were: one, you had to have worked for the Mickles; two, you grew up near Millarville; and three, you worked for the warden service. You had to meet two of the three to be considered.

We lost Keith to a heart attack several years ago, but the rest of the group still keeps in touch. Perry and Dave visit regularly and Perry, Bob, Don, Johnny and I are part of the Park Warden Service Alumni Society and get together at meetings and other events. We see a lot of each other, and I saw Lee at a book signing in Bragg Creek for Kathy's book on June Mickle. Donny and I have remained close friends and provide a good source of yarns at various functions. We also don't let facts get in the way of a good story.

Forty years later, when we were both in our sixties, Donny Mickle wrote a story about his early upbringing in the foothills, southwest of Calgary near Millarville. It was titled, "My Friend Ben," who was his first personal horse and his favourite mount on the many horse chases he participated in. I used the story as the basis for a narrative I did on his life and some of our shared adventures in the mountains. His story poignantly reveals what it was like to be brought up in the foothills of southwestern Alberta and puts a lens on how the Mickles came to the mountains.

DON AND FAYE GROWING UP WEST OF MILLARVILLE

Don begins his story by stating that everyone should have at least one horse in his or her life. Some are fortunate to have many but there is always one that stands out. This, I assume, can extend to all pets that the reader might identify with. For Mickle, it was Ben.

His earliest memories are of their original family homestead near the Elbow River, west of Calgary. It was called Mission Valley Ranch and was located just north of the Elbow River and just west of Highway 22. On the south side of the river was the Vince and Jackie Robinson place, and to the east of the highway was Clem Gardner's spread, and to the west was the Copithornes' and Batemans'. From here the family moved to their new Square Butte Ranch west of Millarville in the pastoral rolling hills of southwestern Alberta.

There were always horses around. June Mickle believed that a gentle horse was the best babysitter she could have for her two children, Don and Faye. They acquired many interesting equine friends in those early days. It was always interesting for the two of them to try and mount these tall horses at such a young age. They would catch a horse and lead it over to the corral, climb the rails and crawl on his or her back. They soon found out that if the horse could shuffle away from the fence, they wouldn't be able to mount, so they took turns pushing the horses against the rails while the other mounted. In this fashion, they rode bareback around their land, one being led by the other.

Faye's first horse was May, a hairy little bay mare that kept her company for most of the day. Donny's first horse was Midget; then he graduated to Glassy, who had one white eye that looked like it was made of glass. Once mounted on their two favourite horses, they would race across the fields or wander onto the forestry reserve that bordered their land, up into the hills that were heavily timbered, providing cover for a band of wild horses.

When Donny was about ten, his school buddy Glenny stayed over for the weekend. Both boys wanted to go riding so they pestered Faye to allow Glenny to ride her horse, May. She initially resisted, hinting at her future propensity for being difficult and uncooperative whenever she was confronted by some of Donny's wilder friends. After much pleading, though, she reluctantly gave in. Faye was never mean in her abjections but did get retribution with some very inventive pranks. The empty egg shells and tea rather than whisky was a good example of her edgy sense of humour.

The boys immediately began galloping around with their cap guns in hand, playing cowboys and Indians. As Donny related, "I looked at 'Black Bart' coming out of the trees and fired my cap gun. Suddenly I found myself sitting on the ground in front of Glassy. He stood glaring at me with his glassy eye and blowing from his flared nostrils."

Later, over dinner, he told his dad about what had happened. Bert laughed and told him that he had the same problem when Glassy was a young horse. He had been out hunting and on spotting a deer had taken a shot from the saddle – never a wise thing to do. Glassy immediately blew up, burying his head between his front feet. Bert was bucked off with his rifle still in hand. Bert said, "He never had any use for gunfire from that point on." That ended his tenure as Wyatt Earp, and the gunplay off of Glassy around the OK Corral.

Many of the older horses were harnessed to pull. The scene could have been taken from a Van Gogh painting, the family raking up freshly cut hay under a hot afternoon sun, the hay dumped into the horse-drawn sweeper. The occasional wasp nest would be stirred up with the possibility of turning a tranquil day into chaos, as a friendly old horse became a wild runaway.

Each summer, after the hay was cut, baled and stacked, following a timeless tradition, the family would ride west into the mountains of the frontal range to relax before winter arrived. Bert had a trapline in the forest reserve near what was the north Sheep River (now

Early photo of Don and Faye in front of their horse.
DON MICKLE COLLECTION

Threepoint Creek). He had built a log cabin along its bank and the family spent holidays there. Using the cabin as a base, they would venture farther into the recesses of the frontal range and camp in the many remote meadows hidden up some small side valleys. There was always lots of wildlife to observe and bull trout to catch in the creeks. Bert liked to hike the ridges and glass for game, so it was natural for Donny to be equally at home riding or walking.

On one occasion, when Bert and June had to head home early to finish the haying, Faye, Donny and a friend, Elaine Bateman, were left by themselves for a few days at the cabin. It must have been a hurried departure as the youngsters were not left with much food. To enhance their meagre larder, they spent the time catching fish and picking berries. One day the three of them rode about 5 miles to their favourite berry patch. A black bear was already there, helping himself to the juicy berries, so they left him alone, not wanting to interrupt his glutinous foraging. He would need the berries more than them in the winter months to come. There were all kinds of things to keep them busy for those few days, and it was an opportunity to gain some self-reliance.

They were down to their last box of Kraft Dinner when their parents showed up with fresh supplies. The next day the family packed up the necessary supplies, gear and whatnot and rode to the big muskeg that lay in the shadow of Forgetmenot Mountain. It had a canyon on its south end that they eagerly wanted to explore. They were fortunate to observe a cougar and a black bear together near the campsite. This was a rare sighting, for cougar are nocturnal animals and not often seen at any time let alone in daylight. Seeing the two predators together was indeed a rare sight.

They rode by old horse traps along the way, which signified the presence of wild horses in the area. As they passed by the traps, Donny could tell his dad was deep in thought, reflecting on the thrill of chasing wild horses. Little did he know that a decade later, both of them would be pursuing these feisty critters, often trying to recover the mares from the stud who had stolen them from their own stock. The studs would intentionally knock down their fence, which bordered on the reserve, to get the mares. They would have to repair the damage and then the chase was on, rounding up the mares again. June often thought Bert did not mind as it gave him an excuse to get on another horse chase.

One of their day rides took them up to the fire lookout on Forgetmenot Mountain, where they visited Curly Sands, the first fire-lookout ranger and an old family friend. In his substantial arsenal of stories, Curly had some fascinating tales that captivating a ten-year-old girl and a twelve-year-old boy for hours. They probably even believed some of them were true.

More horses came into their lives as the years passed. The family eventually moved farther into the mountains, to Banff National Park, where they became guides and outfitters. By then, their herd had expanded to about a hundred head, and Donny can still remember the names of some of the special ones: Chico, Annabelle, Fancy, Pick-Pocket, Babe, White Lady and Jitterbug were just a few that came to mind.

FINDING A SUITABLE SADDLE HORSE

In 1964 Donny met Ben, a four-year-old, running quarter-horse colt from Tip Johnson's stock. Tip was a well-known horseman who had a string of quarter horses, including his stallion Tip Top McKue. Tip was Donny's step-grandfather, who had passed away earlier that year.

Donny's grandmother was kept busy selling off Tip's many horses, but she kindly said that Donny could choose one the colts. The horses were pastured at Don Thompson's ranch east of Black Diamond, so Donny went there to look at the four colts in his corral. Three of them were registered quarter horses, and Ben was a grade horse with some thoroughbred in him, commonly referred to as a "running quarter horse." He was a rangy-looking bay with wide-set eyes that looked at Donny cautiously through a shaggy forelock.

Don Thompson, a good friend of Tip's and a noted rancher and horse-man, could see that Ben had caught Donny's eye. He told Donny that Ben had been ridden a few times and that he was Tip's favourite, even though he didn't have papers. He was just what Donny wanted, and they soon had him loaded up for the trip home. After leading him into the corral, Donny gently placed his saddle on Ben's back, put a light snaffle bit in his mouth and stepped into the stirrup. He seemed well-broke, and as Donny settled into his seat, he realized the horse was also broke to rein.

He was riding Ben around the corral one day when Faye, who had been riding in the forest reserve, arrived on her horse, Gypsy. She was now nineteen years old and had been riding in the reserve looking for her old saddle horse, May. She had been out looking for a band of wild horses that she thought May had been running with. May was now approximately thirty-five years old and had a knack for opening gates, slipping out and joining the wandering band. She was easy to catch, but she often took some of the Mickle horses along for the adventure. The year before, Faye had retired her by turning her loose to join her friends in the hills, which was a kind gesture. It was a salute to May for being such a loyal companion.

Gypsy, her new saddle horse, was a high-headed, dark-brown mare who Faye was very proud of. She was fast and could easily outrun anything that Donny had been on lately. Faye looked at Ben, his head hung low, looking sleepy. "We should have a race, wake your new horse up," she said. He accepted the challenge on one condition. Ben was young and just getting his legs under him so they wouldn't run them very far.

He left Gypsy like she was standing still. Ben obviously loved to run, but it took some time before he finally found the brakes, which was convenient under the circumstances, as the fence was fast approaching. In the many years they were together, this was a problem they never totally rectified.

It would be a few weeks before the family started to round up the horses for their new guide and outfitting business, and Faye would finally have some steady money coming in. Donny had just returned from spending the winter in Rogers Pass, working for Noel Gardner on avalanche control and taking weather data.

The family's new business venture came about from a chance encounter. Bert and June had gone to visit Bert's brother, Jack, and his family in the Columbia Valley of southeastern British Columbia. They stopped at Lake Louise to visit an old family friend, Ray Legace. Ray had run the Lake Louise guide and outfitting business for many years and got to know Bert years earlier when he wintered some horses on the Mickle spread at the old Mission Valley Ranch. Bert and Jack were often enlisted to break the new colts over the winter.

On this occasion, in the early 1960s, when he saw Bert again after many years, Ray was convinced that he had found the right family to take over his business. He even offered to stick around and travel the trails with them to get them started. The Mickles were excited about this new adventure and raised the money to buy the outfit by selling some land in the foothills.

In the fall, at the end of the season, Ray would turn his horses out on a forestry lease near the Ya Ha Tinda Ranch. They wintered there on the abundant montane grasslands outside the eastern boundary of Banff National Park. This open country allowed the ponies to roam the hills with unlimited freedom so that by spring they differed little from the "wildies" that inhabited the same land. The family now had the challenge of rounding the horses up themselves. Donny had acquired Ben a few weeks before they were due to head for the Red Deer River to gather

Don Mickle riding Ben in his parents' corral at Spruce View, Alberta.
DALE PORTMAN COLLECTION

the horses. To get him hardened up, he started riding him every day.

He was beginning to take the seemingly gentle horse for granted, thinking that he had him completely under control. But Donny soon realized that Ben was only under control when he wanted to be. This became very clear one morning when he threw the saddle on but failed to notice the tightness of the horse's sides as he adjusted the cinches. When he was reaching for the breast collar, there was a huge and hairy explosion in front of him. Suddenly, there was nothing but air where the horse had stood a split second before. Ben bucked so hard that the loose stirrups were clapping together over his back like they were applauding him on. The horse bucked, roared and farted across the pasture and back again, then suddenly stopped in front of Donny. He seemed to be grinning at me, Donny recalled, and then he mounted and they trotted away as if nothing had happened. It was a while before he took his horse for granted again.

One day, Faye and Donny rode out to the nearby hills. Their west gate opened out onto an endless expanse of wilderness before touching the slopes of the mountains. It was only a few miles from their gate to the top of Square Butte, a prominent ridge that stretches for miles north and south. From their vantage point on top of the butte, mounted on Ben and Gypsy, they could look over the tree-covered hills that led to the frontal range. It was a spectacular panorama, from Allsmoke in the south to Banded Peak in the north. All of a sudden, Faye looked down in the valley and spotted two riders. They were leading a familiar horse and winding their way through the aspen forest situated below their vantage point.

Faye, of course, wanted to ride down to meet them. It was Ivor Lyster and Ernie Sylvester, two local cowboys, who had been out chasing wild horses. Following along with a rope around her neck was Old May. Ivor said that he had been chasing a band of wildies, and he managed to rope the last one as the rest galloped into the trees. He was a little surprised when he discovered the old mare was halter broke and obediently followed them home. Faye stepped off Gypsy and parted some hair on the rear of the old mare to show the boys the Mickle brand. They seemed a little embarrassed when Faye turned the old mare out again. May totted happily back towards where she had last seen her mustang friends. Ivor and Ernie were well-known in the area as wild and daring riders with a reputation for their horse-chasing skills, but Faye was not above teasing the boys about their catch that day. As a matter of fact, she was renowned for her teasing and the many tricks she played – especially on vulnerable young men who were lured into trying to impress her, which usually accomplished nothing.

FOUR

A MOUNTAIN WINTER AND A SPRING ROUNDUP

A WINTER WORKING OUT OF TEMPLE AND SKOKI LODGES

We had finally reached the Gaspé region of Quebec by Day 9, and the Chic-Choc Mountains were rising to the south of us. At the town of Sainte-Anne-des-Monts, located on the coast, a road leads up into an area that has been set aside as a park. It has become a destination for summer tourists seeking wilderness experiences. In the late 1990s, during the winter, the area had become popular as backcountry skiing gained popularity in eastern Canada. My mind flashed back to the early days in Banff and reminded me of my first introduction to ski touring in the backcountry near Lake Louise.

During the winter of 1966–67, I was living in Banff, drifting from job to job and staying at Andy and Joan's place, when I bumped into Don Mickle. It was late January and they were looking for someone to help out in their coffee shop in the basement of Temple Lodge, which acted as a day lodge for the downhill skiers. There would also be an opportunity to help out at Skoki. I jumped at the offer.

I arrived in Lake Louise in early February and got a ride up to Temple Lodge on the morning ski bus with Slim Fleming. I had first met Slim while working at Deer Lodge, and I was always captivated by him and his many mountain tales. Once there, I was put to work in the coffee shop in the basement, slinging hamburgers and serving chili to the day skiers.

After a busy weekend, Bert started organizing a trip into Skoki and wanted me to come along to help. I found myself skiing in with Faye and June while Bert drove the snowmobile, pulling a sled full of provisions. I had inherited an old pair of hickory skis with bear-trap bindings and managed to scrounge up a floppy pair of leather ski boots. I owned downhill equipment but this touring gear was new to me. I was about to learn the challenges of ski touring and the use of climbing skins.

From Boulder Pass, we followed poles across Ptarmigan Lake, spaced out every 50 to 100 yards. They had been installed by the warden service to mark the way during poor weather and limited visibility. It was clear and bright for our trip over Deception Pass that day.

Bert dropped the sled at the top of the pass then returned to pull Faye and June up. I fumbled putting the sealskins on my skis but finally succeeded. They worked well and when I got to the top I wasn't too far behind. The three of us all took spills on the way down but outside of some snow on our toques and down our necks, it was pretty uneventful. Certainly more uneventful then the many challenges I would face during the rest of the spring.

I was looking forward to seeing the lodge, now buried deep in snow. We were kept busy for the next couple of days getting the place in shape to receive guests for the coming weekend. I shovelled out both entrances to the lodge and all the cabins, and I built some steps down to the creek to fetch water. I shovelled the snow away from in front of the wood shed and cleared an area for splitting firewood. But most important, a path and entrance to the outhouse was established. I was kept busy splitting wood while Bert went out to Temple for another load of supplies.

Using an old fiberglass sled, I hauled firewood to each of the cabins and topped them up with kindling. I was continually hauling water as June and Faye seemed to have a voracious appetite for the stuff. I would deliver pail upon heavy pail that would quickly disappear into the kitchen. All I ever saw was two pairs of hands holding out empty buckets. It wasn't until Saturday morning that I got around to shovelling off the lodge roof. The guests arrived Saturday afternoon for a four-day stay. I was kept hopping throughout; hauling water, washing dishes and keeping the wood supply up for the stoves.

On Sunday it was decided I would I would join the guests, showing them the way up to the Natural Arch. Bert wanted me to act as a guide; there was one big problem with that – I'd never been there before. That didn't matter. He said, "It won't be a problem," as he described the route to me that night. I was now a ski guide who had one day of ski touring under my belt and no clue as to what difficulties I would encounter along the route. If I was going to have any credibility with the guests I would have to demonstrate a confidence I didn't have.

Bert sometimes ran his business with a casualness that would give most outfitters and guides today a nervous breakdown. By today's standards, no one would be allowed to sneeze let alone guide without being fully trained and certified. Even the most minor accident can lead to a costly legal suit. But Bert was no different than many others back then.

I struck off in the lead over Skoki Pass and down to the Red Deer Lakes. Once we broke out of the trees near the lakes, one of the guests seemed to know where he was going, and it all seemed to match Bert's description so I let him take over. He liked being out front and that suited me fine. He probably also sensed I was new at this. We stopped to view the Natural Arch, and then we carried on across the meadow above us, heading towards the Bonnet Glacier. We stopped at the edge of the clearing and had lunch then turned around and headed back, following our ski tracks.

It was getting close to dusk when we got back. It was an ambitious day for both the clients and me, and Bert had to have some concerns about sending someone as green as myself to lead. It showed in his greeting and delight at seeing use safely return. I was pretty tired and was amazed at how tough and fit this lot was. Many of them were in their sixties and early seventies and didn't seem to turn a hair.

Bert sent me out Tuesday morning to break a trail over Deception Pass for the guests, as there had been fresh snow overnight. When I got to Temple, I leaned the skis up against the building and went inside. A couple of hours later, the guests arrived and one of them was none too pleased when he got there. Someone had taken his skis, and he had fumed about it all the way out. He had no choice but to use mine. There was only one person who could have done that and that was me. When I left in the morning I had accidently grabbed the wrong set – they looked so much alike to me. I only wished the bindings hadn't fit my boots so well, otherwise I would have realized my mistake. No number of apologies melted his icy stare, so I beat a retreat to the coffee shop and started flipping hamburgers.

AN EPIC TRIP INTO SKOKI WITH TWO CLIENTS

This occasional winter guiding was something I hadn't counted on, and it was intimidating. I dug around in the lodge library, looking for something, anything, on winter travel. When that didn't pan out, I scammed a ride to Banff on a rare day off, and at Monod's Sports, I found a book that had recently come out, called *The Avalanche Enigma*, by Colin Fraser. It was gripping, and I sat up late at night devouring its pages. It certainly helped me understand the basics of avalanche safety, the art of travelling through avalanche terrain, and simple avalanche search and rescue. It also talked about the mechanics of snow and why it fails at times.

Shortly after that, Bert asked me to escort (guide) a couple into Skoki. We left on an overcast day with no significant amounts of snow forecast. When we reached Boulder Pass, we stopped to take in the view. Looming in the distance off slightly to the left was Deception Pass. As we started across Ptarmigan Lake, the weather closed in on us, and soon we were engulfed in wind and snow. It deteriorated even further, and somehow, we lost track of the poles. I thought about sitting it out but the couple were eager to carry on and get to Skoki, so we set out again. We were in semi-whiteout conditions, and I found myself troublingly disoriented at times. Immediately the terrain started to climb. We worked our way up towards the pass as the terrain became steeper and steeper. I had them spread out, as the book had recommended, so there was some distance between us in case an avalanche did release, and we kept going. The feel of the land seemed different than what I had experienced in the past, but I put it down to taking a different line to the summit of the pass.

Partway up, the weather lifted momentarily, revealing what I thought was the pass. When we gained it nothing felt right. Everything was different than what it should have looked like in the dimming light. I had been over Deception Pass once in the fall and twice recently and this didn't seem right. I hadn't come across any poles since leaving the lake, and I had the feeling we were in a different pass. I couldn't be sure, though, as Deception Pass is wide, and we could have gained it at a different point. Then the doubt crept in and my logic started to crumble. Like divine intervention, the clouds started to lift and for a brief period I could see down towards Skoki. What I saw was Skoki Lakes, which you can't see from Deception Pass, and the reality of our situation became crystal clear. We were on Packer's Pass. I had made a huge mistake, for this pass lies west of Deception Pass on the west side of Packer Peak.

I had been breaking trail all the way up but still had to wait on several occasions for the two guests to catch up. They were from Toronto and had little skiing experience, but they had heard about Skoki and were determined to get there. I couldn't believe the circumstances I was in, not knowing whether to go back or carry on. We could drop down to Ptarmigan Lake and try to find the poles leading to the right pass, but that would add too much to the day.

I briefly considered travelling across the expansive slope under Packer Peak to avoid losing elevation and gain access to the proper pass. But this choice would require crossing some dangerous avalanche slopes. Even going back to the lake would put us in dubious

Skoki Lakes before freeze up in the late fall.
DALE PORTMAN COLLECTION

terrain again. I knew people had travelled over Packer's Pass in the summer, so I reasoned we could do it on skis, as well.

The option to return to Temple was something I was not going to consider. It would be like retreating from battle and I wasn't at that stage yet. I decided to carry on as if it was just a normal outing and we had just reached Deception Pass. I was going to need everything I had learned in the book and exercise a lot of caution on the descent. I kept our predicament to myself as we headed down, and I had confidence in that decision. The terrain between the lakes and us looked doable, but the crux would be getting down through the cliffs that lie between and below the two lakes. With that in mind, I started to side step down the slope towards Skoki Lakes. I would reassess our descent, trying to keep my bearings when the lakes occasionally came into view through the swirling clouds.

The weather hadn't been able to make up its mind all day and it was no different now. One minute you could see the features below, the next they were gone. I led them down very carefully, not wanting to slip over a hidden cliff or get caught in some steep terrain trap and kick a slide loose. Once in a while the weather lifted, just enough for me to get my bearings and select a promising course. We got down far enough that some of the features remained in view, especially the line of trees below.

Finally, we were standing above Upper Skoki Lake. The guests were getting concerned about why it was taking so long to reach the lodge. I was concerned about spending the night out, for it couldn't be far off in the diminishing light. When we reached the upper lake, I knew we had to find a way down, past or through the cliff band to the first lake. I could see the meadow beyond the lower lake off in the distance – it was our Shangri-La. We managed to breach the cliff band and reach the lower lake.

It was night now as I followed the upper lip of the cliff, desperately looking for a break in its length. I was pretty tired and started to feel fear rise within, as I couldn't find a break in the rock. The scrub fir that inhabited the top edge of the cliff made it even more difficult to find a route. On occasion, some light filtered through from a partial moon, allowing some visibility, and then I found a way. It was a steep, wind-scoured slope, and it was the only way down.

I went first, sliding on my edges all the way. When I reached the bottom, I stepped aside and had the woman come down next, followed by her husband. From here it was relatively easy to reach the main meadow and the ski trail coming down from the elusive and well-named Deception Pass. When the lights of the lodge finally came into view, it was 8:00 at night and instead of being elated at the sight, a wave of exhaustion settled over me, as I struggled to take my skis off. Bert and June were happy seeing us finally arrive safely.

I slept well that night and awoke just in time to catch breakfast. I was surprised they had let me sleep in. I was quick to get back to work, hauling water and chopping wood. Bert knew what I had gone through when I told him I'd mistakenly come over Packer's Pass. Thankfully, the remainder of the winter was tame and uneventful for me but not so for some others.

AN AVALANCHE ACCIDENT ABOVE PTARMIGAN LAKE

We closed down the lodge in mid-April, and Bert and I spent another delightful week putting up wood. The sun was strong during the day but it was cold at night, a solid crust formed on the surface of the snow. We snowshoed a trail to each of the dead standing trees we had marked to be cut, and once the track had set overnight, we could walk on it. We dropped, limbed and cut up all the trees, into manageable lengths. We then hauled them by snowmobile and a sled to a stacking area near the woodshed. Looking back, it was one of the most memorable weeks I ever spent in Skoki. Each night was a starlit feast of celestial bodies, burning holes in the dark velvet sky. Each day the heavens saw deep blue skies. This pattern of warm days and cold nights seemed to go on forever. After a week of putting up wood, I was back helping out in the coffee shop at Temple for the remainder of the ski season.

There was avalanche accident that winter that was significant for a few reasons. First, it happened below Packer's Pass in a terrain trap that I later learned has caught and killed several people over the years. Second, it was terrain that I had been exposed to in my misadventure over the pass, without harm. Third, it involved people I knew, friends of mine, and it was the first live avalanche recovery in these parts. After this successful rescue, the crew received a merit of honour award from the Canadian Ski Patrol Association.

As a park warden, Jay Morton was now involved with the ski patrol program at the Lake Louise ski area. He was in the patrol hut on the Temple side of the mountain, working on snow-reading data when a snowmobile raced up and Ron Hall burst through the door. He came in to report a man caught in an avalanche near Ptarmigan Lake on the way to Deception Pass. The small party, headed for Skoki Lodge, had apparently gotten off route (sound familiar?).

Skoki Lodge, winter of 1967–68.
DALE PORTMAN COLLECTION

It was the end of the day, and most of the staff had left the mountain, leaving Jay to close up shop. Gordon Brockway and Ron had been breaking a snowmobile trail up towards Deception Pass with the intent of getting to Skoki. Travelling up past Halfway Hut towards Boulder Pass, they met a young man skiing down at breakneck speed. He was on his way out to report his friend had been buried in an avalanche. Fortunately, he had seen the two men on snowmobiles and stopped, waved and had already got their attention.

After working for years in the mountains, Brockway was familiar with avalanche searching and knew what to do. He sent Ron off to report the accident to the warden service on his snowmobile, while he and the survivor headed to the site on his machine. Once there, he determined from the survivor where he thought the last-seen point was and marked it, then started looking for any evidence on the surface of the snow.

Once Ron arrived and told him what happened, Jay immediately sent him back with avalanche probes and a hasty search kit that was always stored in a locker, for just such an occasion. He then got hold of park headquarters in Banff by radio, telling them what he knew about the accident, what steps he had taken, and he asked for backup. A group from Lake Louise was organized quickly, and soon they were headed to the site on snowmobiles with more gear and equipment.

Once Ron reached the accident site with the equipment, both men started searching with probes. By now the victim had been buried for one and a half hours, and statistically there was little hope that he would be found alive. The survivor was in poor shape and unable to render much assistance outside of pointing to where his buddy might be located. Not long after, and taking some direction from the survivor on where to search, Gordon yelled, "I've got him!" Ron and Gordon started digging with shovels and quickly reached the victim. They were shocked – he was still alive. They made sure his airway was clear and had started tending to him when the rescue party arrived. He regained consciousness and was quickly transported back to the ski area and a waiting ambulance, which took him to Banff.

The guy had survived because of the quick action of Ron, Gordon and Jay. There was no confusion, everyone was versed in what to do, and they responded in a professional manner. That's not always the case in avalanche accidents, especially back then, when the people involved knew little and were poorly equipped to deal with such events.

THE MEN'S READING CLUB IN BANFF

It was January 26, 2016, and Chic Scott had invited Kathy to talk to his men's book club at the old Crosby house on the Whyte Museum property. She was there to talk about her most recent book on June Mickle. I was invited along. The group specialized in reading about

Recovering a body in an avalanche.
DALE PORTMAN COLLECTION

subjects that pertain to the Banff area. They became aware of her book on the history of mountain rescue entitled *Guardians of the Peaks*. I was a co-writer of the book, albeit in a minor way, and so I was included in the discussion of both books. One of the members attending the meeting was Roy Andersen from my Sunshine days, who I had kept in touch with over the years. He told an interesting story about an avalanche that he was involved in that same winter I worked there. I had long forgotten the incident, but that was probably because so little was made of it at the time.

He was on his way up the Strawberry T-bar, trying to catch up to a pupil who was waiting at the bottom for him. After getting off at the top and skiing down into the Dell, which is below the headwall of the Standish Chair, he saw two skiers enter the slope above. The area was fenced off and out of bounds to skiers. Suddenly the slope released, and he only saw one skier. A wall of snow was now heading his way. He had little time to react, and luckily the snow came to rest before reaching him. Because he originally saw two skiers, he proceeded up onto the deposit and started looking around. He found a ski tip sticking out of the snow and so started digging with his hands. He soon uncovered the skier who was still breathing and conscious. The fellow was wearing a volunteer ski patrol jacket. Roy went down to the ski patrol shack and reported the occurrence to Bill Vroom, the warden on duty. Roy explained what happened but Bill was only interested in who the culprits were so that he could charge them for skiing out of bounds.

After Roy had finished his story, I turned to Kathy and said, "How the hell did we miss that one?" We had gone through all the rescue reports in Banff and that one hadn't turned up, and to make matters worse, I had worked there that season of 1965–66. She said, "They never filled out a report on the accident!" This was amazing. We realized it was the first unrecorded live recovery in an avalanche in Banff (or elsewhere in western Canada). But it wasn't the only first. Ironically, the two skiers became the first in the country to be charged under the National Parks Act for skiing in a closed area.

MY INTRODUCTION TO CHASING HORSES IN THE SPRING OF 1967

My career as a trail hand started when I was a nineteen-year-old, guiding for Bud Brewster and Bret Mitzel at Lake Louise. I turned twenty that summer. It wasn't until I went to work for the Mickle family a year later, on a more permanent basis, in 1967 that I felt I was really becoming part of the mountain culture. My initiation took place that spring when I was invited along on their spring roundup. It was two weeks of hard riding over rough and varied terrain on the Red Deer River near the Ya Ha Tinda Ranch.

Earlier that spring I had my first opportunity to head out with the boys and chase some wild horses. A couple of days earlier they had come down from the slopes of Square Butte, knocked down a section of their barb-wire fence and ran off with a number of mares. We set out two days later to retrieve the mares.

My saddle horse was White Ranger, a leggy grey thoroughbred with a hard mouth and lots of speed, but as I soon found out, little else. Each of us rode off in a different direction to find some horses. Bert's theory was that once one of us located some, we would report back and then put a plan in place to round them up.

Ranger and I were working our way up a hillside of mixed spruce and aspen when he suddenly stopped. I looked between his cocked ears. Standing quietly in front of us in the trees was a herd of horses looking like they had been caught in a game of hide-and-seek. Many had the shaggy, thick appearance of a wild horse, but several had the slicker coat of a groomed, ranch-bred horse. They started to nervously move off to the right, and then, with gathering energy, took off. The strategy is to try to stay with them until they start to tire out and then attempt to herd them in the right direction or gain some control over them, but this required the help of a second rider. I knew I was supposed to report back with their location, but the plan started to lose its appeal as the excitement of a chase grew in my mind. Although the likelihood of being successful was remote, I couldn't help myself, and I decided to stick with them and see what happened.

Ranger and I burst into a meadow at the top of the hill only to see the tail end of the herd disappearing from sight. For some reason, I came up with a new plan and thought I could rope one of them. As I looked down at the lariat, fumbling with its tie-down, trying to untie it, I failed to see a large, overhanging branch. I landed on my backside as Ranger raced off ahead. I got up and ran after him as fast as I could, yelling for him to stop as if that was going to help, only to be hindered by my riding boots and stovepipe chaps. Fortunately, the bridle reins were dragging beside him on one side while the lariat had uncoiled somewhat on the other side, making it difficult for him. I continued to yell until I finally managed to get near him and grab the reins. Within seconds, I was back on, and we were streaking over the crest of the hill, trying to gain some distance on the horses and deal with the lariat at the same time.

I was riding pretty loose, just trying to stay with him as dips and hollows, rocks and clumps flashed by. We raced madly over the top of a flat, open summit, and then a gully suddenly appeared on the right.

Pat Haney in front of the Corners Forest Cabin during the 1969 spring roundup.
DALE PORTMAN COLLECTION

Ranger veered wildly to the left, almost pitching me out of the saddle and onto the ground again. Somehow, I managed to hook the toe of my riding boot on the cantle of the saddle and tried to claw myself back into the seat. I grabbed everything within reach – saddle strings, slicker, saddlebags – but what really saved me was the coiled lariat that held fast and took the strain. Then Ranger swerved back towards me and I gained the saddle again.

We hit the trees on the other side of the crest as I caught sight of two rumps disappearing from view. We rocketed downhill through a stand of poplar, bouncing off tree trunks like balls in a pinball machine. Soon rails started to appear on my right, then over on my left. I couldn't believe my luck. These were the long wings of a catch corral, set in place specifically to catch wild horses. I could see the horses bunching up ahead of me, as the corral reached out to contain them.

They were now all in the corral, and I thought, "Wow! Bert is going to be slapping me on the back when I show him all the horses I caught single-handed on my first big chase." But the show wasn't over yet. I needed to dismount quickly to slide the rails across the front of the corral to hold the herd, but my horse wouldn't stop. I pulled on the reins as hard as I could, but Ranger had the bit in his teeth, and we plunged forward until we hit the rails at the back of the corral. I looked over my shoulder only to see the horses dashing out of the corral and up the hill. We stood there, the two of us, Ranger's sides heaving, his nostrils flared, his tongue working the bit in his frothy mouth, while I gasped in hatless wonder. It was over. They had gotten away. I started to feel the pain in my knees from having ricocheted off some of the poplars on the way down. Later, when I rode up to the top of the hill and carried on across the open summit, I found the spot where I had been knocked off by the branch. It was marked by my missing cowboy hat.

I met up with the rest of the group later and told my tale of missed opportunity. After a few hours, we ran into the same bunch of horses and were off crashing through the timber again. For Ranger and me, however, the chase was over. He was spent from the morning run, and we soon lost contact with the group. I had managed to lose my hat again. I spent some time searching but never found it. I got a good ribbing from everyone later.

Eventually, they chased the horses down and herded them easily into our corral. (No doubt assisted by the energy they had expended in my original pursuit of them.) The wild ones were separated from Bert's mares and led down the road several miles and turned loose. We crossed our fingers that they would keep their distance and not complicate things by trying to retrieve the mares again. Bert gave me a blue polka-dot cap as a memento of my missed opportunity, and I often wore it over the next few years when chasing horses.

In late May we headed for the Red Deer River and our campsite near the Ya Ha Tinda Ranch. As in previous years, the first task was catching all the horses that had wintered on the open range south of the Red Deer River. Then we would trail them up to Scotch Camp, just inside Banff National Park, where we would ride down some of the colts a bit, to take the spring buck out of them. Then came the 38-mile ride up the Red Deer River to Red Deer Lakes and then over into the Pipestone Valley and down to Lake Louise.

The first morning, and almost every morning after that, we saddled up and crossed the Red Deer River. It was swollen from spring runoff, and the horses were often forced to swim. It was a cold wake-up call, and as we rode we got soaked at least to our crotches if not our waists. Once we gained the other side, we followed a straight seismic cut, perpendicular to the river, up a steep hill until we broke out at the head of a large meadow that stretched south for some distance. The four of us – Bert Mickle, Don Mickle, Ron Hall and I – rode into this expanse with our eyes peeled, looking for any sign of horses. I was riding a dark-bay mare, Annabelle, who I knew little about other than she was fast.

In the middle of the meadow and some distance off was a herd of horses. As we moved up on them, along the edge of the timber, they spotted us. They instantly broke for the timber, a third of a mile away and in the opposite direction from us. We kicked our horses in gear and headed after them. Annabelle was running hard, but in the wrong direction. We were off by 30 degrees as she stretched out, happy just to run, extending out and grabbing as much ground as her long stride would give her. I tried desperately to turn her head, to pull her around, using my right rein. I had her head pulled so much to one side I thought she might lose her footing and trip. That's when I came up with Plan B, using both reins. It took some effort, but with my thighs braced against the swells of my saddle, I managed to get enough purchase to bring her to a complete stop. I then pointed her in the right direction and let off on the reins. It was like going from zero to thirty in two seconds. The others were now well ahead, but at least we had something to pursue.

I saw the group of horses enter the timber followed several seconds later by Ron, Bert and Donny. Annabelle and I were on the right course, but we still had considerable distance to make up. We entered the trees at full speed and the instant transition from brightness to darkness was both terrifying and exhilarating. I narrowly avoided being knocked out of the saddle by deadfall. I leaned down and over to the right as far as possible as Annabelle just managed to pass under one massive branch. Timber was whipping by on all sides and, with the lack of control I was experiencing, disaster was inevitable. I also realized that Annabelle had no game plan and was just running for the love it. We had completely lost contact with the others. After another sustained effort, I brought her to a halt, with no confidence in her ability to safely follow the chase. At this stage in my education, I certainly hadn't acquired the skills of Dave Wildman, who had ridden Annabelle on many a chase.

We rode northwards, back across the meadow towards camp, at an antsy trot. She wanted to run and I had to work at keeping her pace reasonable. Eventually, we settled into a brisk walk back to the river's edge. I felt a dismal failure as we swam back across the river. I wondered how the guys were making out. Back at camp, June Mickle was no help. "Dale, after all that riding, where are all the horses?"

"Well, June," I answered wearily, "if I knew, I wouldn't be here now." I glumly cast my eyes towards the fire. Sensing she had scratched my fragile ego, she asked me if I wanted some coffee.

It seemed like a long time, but it was probably no more than an hour before I heard horses splashing in the river. Ten minutes later they were tying their horses up and loosening off their saddles. They said they had captured about fifteen head – a good start to the roundup. Everyone settled around the fire with a cup of coffee in hand and for the rest of the evening, they related the events of the day. They laughed as each of them took turns telling their part in the story of the chase. I stoked the fire, made sure there was lots of fresh coffee and listened with envy.

A few days later, a couple friends of the Mickles showed up – Dave Wildman and Ivor Lyster. They were two Millarville cowboys with lots of horse-chasing experience. Dave had worked for Bert a few years

Roundup camp dinner in front of tent. Left to right: June Mickle, unknown,
Dale Portman, Paul Peyto, Bert Mickle, Gord Brockway, Grace Mickle, Ron Hall.
DALE PORTMAN COLLECTION

earlier. Ivor was the brother of Gerry (Red) Lyster, a park warden in
Banff. Because of the added manpower, Bert decided we would ride
down to the forestry cabin at The Corners – where the Panther and
Dormer Rivers meet – the next day and try to round up as many horses as
possible. June decided to join us on the ride, adding colour to the group
with her red hat and buckskin jacket. I was still hoping to be of some
use on this roundup and had a gut feeling that today would be the day.

Again, we found ourselves riding south through the first big meadow
and then entered the timber at the southern end. Two rode off to the left
to check out a hidden meadow, while the rest of us continued to ride
south through the trees. Before long, we flushed a group of surprised
horses out of the bush. Not wanting to push them too hard, we fell back
at a gentle trot. Soon we were joined by other horses that just seemed to
appear. Almost by accident, we had a small band, trotting ahead of us.

We broke into another large meadow, the horses growing in
number. Seeing the open terrain ahead, their leader put his head down,
bucked a couple of times and took off. That was the signal for the rest
to follow as they quickly gathered speed. Now in a mad gallop south,
we were picking up horses everywhere. No one wanted to be left out.

Suddenly there was a crashing noise to our left and out of the timber came about ten head of horses and a few bewildered elk, followed by a couple of yelling cowboys. Eighty head now spread out before us in a wave of undulating colour and dust as we galloped at full speed. The elk wisely made their way to the edge of the flank and then peeled off to the right and came to a standstill, probably surprised by the spectacle.

Exhilarating shouts could be heard from all over the valley. A couple of riders on each side moved up along the flanks, trying to prevent horses from breaking off like the elk had. All the while, The Corners grew closer. The horses knew the route; the chase was all about control now. As we raced along, mud and gravel flew past our heads, and our faces were splattered with dirt. We couldn't be more thrilled. After several miles of hard riding, we saw The Corners. As if on signal, the horses slowed down enough for us to guide them easily into the big corral with its extended wings.

We had captured more than just Mickle horses. We spent time sorting out the herd and releasing some of the other horses. After a rare opportunity for a lunch break, seldom enjoyed in a leisurely fashion, we began the task of trailing the herd back to our camp on the Red Deer River. Ron and I went up front to lead the procession, while the rest followed behind, urging the horses along as needed. We had to set a good pace up front, one that would keep the horses moving, while the riders in the rear had to be careful not to push them too aggressively. Crowding them could set them running past Ron and me. It was all a matter of subtle judgement, and after a few miles, the horses started to string out in single file and settle into an easy pace. A pecking order was established that they would try to adhere to for the remainder of the day.

After ten days of hard, exhilarating pursuits, we successfully rounded up all the horses and shod a good many of them. We were now set to trail them through to Lake Louise. The next morning saw us leave the Big Horn campsite with a hundred head of horses, followed by June Mickle driving the truck with our camp and duffel in the back. Things stayed relatively tame as we negotiated the winding road that led across the Ya Ha Tinda Ranch. It lay between our former campsite near the Big Horn and the mountains we were headed for. As we entered open country, though, everything changed.

Once the horses hit the flat, they burst into a gallop. A few at the front threw their heads down and bucked. One let out a sharp fart that sounded like a cannon shot, and as if they'd heard a starting pistol, they started to charge past Bert who was in the lead. I could hear him yelling as he rode hard to keep ahead. The whole herd was now in pursuit, fanning out as we tried to keep them flanked. After a couple of miles, they finally settled into a nice easy lope along the fire road leading to Scotch Camp, our destination.

Scotch Camp is the staging area for two backcountry warden districts and has a large, well-fenced pasture with a good set of corrals. It's strategically located just off a fire road that led to the Banff townsite, 30 miles away via Snow Creek Summit. The cabin is an attractive log structure, stained dark brown, with sleeping quarters separate from the dining room and kitchen area. Jimmy Simpson – the son of Jimmy Simpson Sr., a legend in the Canadian Rockies – and his wrangler and cook, Jeff Wilson, greeted us when we arrived. Both were based out of Num-Ti-Jah Lodge in Banff National Park and were also there to round up their horses.

Simpson's horses wintered up near Tyrell Creek Flats, which sits just inside the park and straddles both sides of the road leading from the government ranch. An alluvial meadow marks the junction of Tyrell Creek and the Red Deer River. Jeff Wilson worked for Jimmy in a variety of ways, usually guiding out of their pony stand at Bow Lake. When hunting season came along, he wrangled, packed and cooked for Jimmy's clients.

That afternoon, Bert sorted out the colts and fillies and some older horses that needed to be "topped off" every spring. We all gathered down at the corrals to watch Ron Hall ride the buck out of one of the colts. This was a great way to end the day after an invigorating ride from the government ranch, and I enjoyed every minute of it. It was exciting to watch someone riding a green-broke colt from behind the safety of the fence.

Dave Wildman on Moonshine in the corral at Scotch Camp.

Donny was the next one up. Bert passed around a bottle of whisky and each of us took a pull from it. I was savouring a good swig when my perfect day fell apart. Donny was trotting a now-submissive three-year-old around the corral, waving at us like we were spectators at the Calgary Stampede. He took off his hat and bowed to the crowd. Bert leaned over the fence, looked at me and said, "All right, kid, you're next." A knot of fear formed in my stomach. I thought this show was for the more experienced hands and that I was just a spectator. I wasn't making much money after room and board and there wasn't much left for danger pay. I don't remember there being any of this in the contract I hadn't signed. There was no escaping Bert, though.

The first horse I climbed on bucked me off, leaving me dusting myself off and chasing him unceremoniously around the corral. Donny held him for me while I climbed back on and rode him until he quit bucking, which seemed to take forever. My shirt hung outside my blue jeans as I rode the second colt. As the horse kicked skyward, I felt a tug on my shirt, and most of the buttons popped off. I had hooked it over the saddle horn at some point. I was bouncing around all over the saddle as the colt worked out his pent-up fury. I felt I was going to come down well forward of the saddle on one or two occasions, which probably would have curtailed any riding for a while and probably any ability to sire kids in the future. Miraculously, I stayed on and even earned a round of cheers from my whisky-fuelled audience. I rode another horse, and by the end of the day I was sore from the pounding I had taken in the saddle, but it was tempered somewhat by another good pull of whisky.

The day's events were a blur of adrenaline, excitement, fear of failure and whisky. I suppose I passed some sort of initiation that day, but that was the furthest thing from my mind. More important, I had survived in good health and received pats on the back for making it an entertaining afternoon – it certainly had been for everyone, even me.

A lively night followed. Everyone sat around the table swapping stories as bottles of rum and whisky appeared from various duffels. Bert and Jimmy were old friends, and Jeff knew everyone there, except me. I sat back and took it all in, and after such an eventful day, I was the first to hit the sack. I woke up early, about five in the morning, and went out to feed and water the horses in the corral. Jimmy Simpson, Jeff Wilson and Bert's brother-in-law, Norm "Coyote" Smith, were still up, sitting around the table, playing poker, with a nearly empty bottle of Hudson's Bay overproof rum as the only visible excuse for keeping them there. It was parked in the middle of the table, attracting them like moths to a lantern. I felt as if I were living in a cowboy western movie.

Andy Anderson, the district warden, had told Bert and Jimmy where the cabin key was hidden as a friendly gesture. In those days, the relationship between outfitters and park wardens was closer than it is today. There was little backpacker activity in the remoter areas of the park, outside of the odd mountaineering party attempting to bag a faraway peak. The outfitters spent their summers in the park and were an extra set of eyes and ears for the district warden. This mutual association also provided a natural stepping-stone to anyone working in outfitting who wanted to start a career in the warden service. That window of opportunity closed, though, by the mid-1970s when hiring criteria emphasized a university degree in the natural sciences.

FIVE

DALE AND THE MICKLES

GAINING A UNIVERSITY DEGREE IN THE SADDLE

Following the horse drive, I worked out of Temple Lodge with Donny for the summer, running trips into Skoki and the surrounding area, which included the Red Deer Lakes. We were often packing supplies from Temple to Skoki or taking guests in on horseback. Some wanted to fish while others wanted to just ride and see the countryside. We had a lot of variety in our working day, but one thing you could be assured of was being up at five in the morning, jingling horses. The days were long and often extended well into the evening. On the odd occasion, when there were no clients at Skoki, you could steal off and do some fishing in the nearby lakes. There was usually an opportunity to get to town once a month.

I didn't own a vehicle so I had to bum lifts down the road to Lake Louise, and then catch a bus to Banff. I would catch another bus back to Lake Louise, which left me 5 miles from Temple, where I found myself walking up the road, occasionally at night. If I was lucky I got a lift with ski area staff. After a while I decided that I didn't really need to go to Banff. I could find everything I wanted in Lake Louise.

After numerous trips into Skoki that summer, I started to see a pattern developing. Around one or two in the afternoon, about when I was skirting Ptarmigan Lake, especially if it was hot, it became a real challenge for me to stay awake, even with clients along. One day I found myself riding in alone without packhorses. I nodded off and woke up suddenly when my saddle horse stopped in his tracks. Standing in front of me were two hikers with a puzzled look on their faces. "How can you do that and not fall off?" one asked. I was surprised myself.

DRUMMOND GLACIER AND THE GHOST OF HALFWAY HUT

One memorable trip that summer was packing glaciologists out of their camp at the base of the Drummond Glacier. Their site was in a spectacular setting in a meadow, not far from the blue ice of the glacier. I was looking forward to the trip and a chance to get away from the routine at Skoki. Donny and I left Temple late in the afternoon and got to Skoki just before supper.

The next morning we had trouble finding the horses as they had snuck around the drift fence at Merlin Meadows. That led to a late start heading out for the Drummond on the 8-mile ride. When we arrived, the glaciologists had already left. We had missed them as they had walked out via Baker Lake, but their gear was still there and it was a bigger pile than Donny expected. He wasn't happy. We didn't have enough packhorses to haul it all, which led to Donny venting about scientists being the cheapest bunch around, always trying to save a nickel on much-needed horse flesh.

The glaciologists had been coming to the Drummond Glacier for a several years now, and every time, they underestimated the number of horses needed, trying to keep the costs down. They seemed incapable of understanding how much a horse could carry, or perhaps they didn't care. After Donny's venting, we got down to packing it all up and loading it on the horses. The loads were awkward, heavy and needed to be carefully watched as we went down the trail. We didn't want to sore any of the horses.

It was 9:00 PM when we left the Drummond, and we still had a five-hour ride to Temple that was probably going to take six. Stopping at Skoki was out of the question. We had to get everything out to Temple because clients were scheduled to be guided into Skoki the next morning.

Because the loads were so large, we couldn't see if the pack saddles were balanced, and we had to stop several times to examine the packs, and look for chaffing or rubbing. A few times we repacked because of shifting loads. Donny's resilient sense of humour and good temperament was absent. Silence followed us down the trail. No playful banter between us, as we were focused on the loads as dusk dwindled into night.

Donny had some "bennies" that he had come across somewhere, so we swallowed a few. There was a full moon out and the sky was clear, a spectacular night for a ride, unappreciated by the two of us. As we rode past Baker Lake and started the climb up to Ptarmigan Lake, we finally broke into conversation. The two of us talked about Paley and the ghost that supposedly haunted Halfway Hut. Dr. Christopher Paley was a mathematician from Boston who was killed on Fossil Mountain in an avalanche in 1938 while staying at Skoki Lodge.

At the time of Paley's death, Peter and Catherine Whyte were running the lodge, and the accident haunted Peter for the rest of his life. On the day of Paley's death, Peter had told him the avalanche hazard was high and to stay away from steep slopes and not to travel on his own. Paley's stubborn independence and arrogance cost him his life. The rescuers managed to haul the body as far as the hut and spent the night there, before heading out to Lake Louise the next day. There had been many strange occurrences at the hut since then, and many people believed that Paley haunted the place.

I had heard a bit about the haunting from Janice Crosby, who I had worked with at Deer Lodge. She knew a friend who repeatedly tried to stay there but couldn't because of this annoying spirit. As we rode along under a canopy of stars that night, Donny filled me in on what he knew. He said from a distance people would see a light through the cabin window and smoke coming out of the chimney. When they approached and looked in, the table was always set and a candle burning near the window. There was no sign of any occupants. This sent a chill up my spine as we headed across the alpine, towards Ptarmigan Lake and Boulder Pass.

It was nearly one in the morning when we hit the pass and stopped to check the packs. The moon was still as bright as ever, the bennies were working and the cabin was easily visible from where we were. It had smoke coming out of its chimney and a light was coming from the window, and I think the two of us went at least one shade paler.

We never said a word as we rode down towards the hut. When we were at the nearest point the trail came to the hut, about 60 yards away, we stopped and I got off. I whispered to Donny, over my shoulder, I had to find out, so I crept towards the light. I got to the window and peered in and then as quickly as I looked, I ducked from view. I scuttled back to the horses and climbed on my mount and Donny said, "Well, what?"

"There's a couple in there, making out," I said. "And I don't know if they saw me but let's get the hell out of here. I feel like a peeping Tom." Donny laughed nearly all the way to Temple while I pondered how coincidental it was that Don told these tales on the very night someone was staying there. It was a million and one chance we would ride by them that night.

PACKING A SUSPICIOUS LOT UP THE PIPESTONE

Later that summer the two of us were sent to pack a group into the upper end of the Pipestone River. The group was starting to create some controversy with the warden service in Lake Louise. They were a religious bunch that had been packed into the head of the Clearwater River the previous year, hauling in some rather strange gear. Shovels and metal pans were noticed in their duffel, which Bert mentioned to the district warden, Andy Anderson, when he was discussing how things went over the summer. This year, the new Cyclone warden was Joe Halstensen, and he had been informed about the situation and was keen on having us keep a close eye on them and what they were doing.

When the group showed up, they had a lot of gear but they wouldn't let it out of their sight, even while we packed the horses. A couple of them had also stayed back, standing guard over their gear while the remainder of the group headed for the trailhead at Mosquito Creek. We couldn't help but notice. Joe showed up as we were still packing up. At one point, he managed to take us aside. There were no shovels or pans visible, but that didn't mean anything, and he said, "If you have a chance at the other end, see if you can get a peek at their equipment. They're probably up to no good." We said we would try to help out, and he left on that assurance.

Our route was up the Pipestone Valley from Lake Louise rather than via Temple and Skoki. The first 9 miles was a boring ride through an old spruce forest along a muddy trail with rotten corduroy. We finally got some relief when we broke out into a huge meadow near Point Camp. We had brought no food along outside of our lunch, which we consumed like vacuum cleaners at our planned stop at Point Camp. From there we headed farther up the Pipestone, passing the warden cabin at Little Pipestone and then finally coming upon Singing Meadows. A few miles past there, we arrived at the trail junction to Fish Lakes, then farther along we passed the old warden cabin with the grizzly claw marks. We arrived at the proposed campsite not far beyond. It had been a long day.

We unpacked the gear, duffel and food supplies and found some collapsible army surplus shovels tucked away in their duffel and some tin prospecting pans. The hikers arrived just as we were ready to leave, having come over North Molar Pass via Fish Lakes, a much shorter route. As we prepared to depart, one of them said to another, "It looks like it's going to rain tomorrow. That should help." That was a pretty strange comment, considering it rained far too much in this country and no one wishes for rain when they're camping. That sounded suspicious.

Thanks to Joe's hospitality and a key, we retreated to the old Pipestone cabin. It was stocked with some provisions, and our supper consisted of packaged soup and Kraft Dinner. After our simple supper, we crawled into bed, Donny taking the lower bunk while I took the top one. There wasn't much headroom for me as a log purlin was located just a foot above my head.

In the middle of the night, Donny blurted out, "There's something furry crawling up the wall."

I awoke, immediately thinking it a was grizzly bear. I bolted upright, whacking my head on the log above me, leaving me momentarily dazed. A grizzly bear was still foremost on my mind, motivating me to disregard the pain. How could you not think grizzly with all the telltale claw marks on the logs outside the cabin? "What's going on?" I yelled.

"Oh, it's all right," Donny said. "It was just a mouse that ran across my face. Good night."

"Thanks a lot," I said, rubbing my head. We both had a good laugh over it in the morning. That would be the last laughing I would be doing for a while.

In the morning, we found the horses not far away. We tied them to some trees above the cabin where they could be saddled. Omega, one of the packhorses, was watching me like a sniper on a rooftop as I approached from below, with a saddle blanket in my hand. I was nearly beside him when he swung his back end towards me and let fly with both his hind legs.

Suddenly I was in a heap at the bottom of the small rise, writhing in pain. I managed to get up on one leg and hopped around holding on to my right leg, almost nauseous with pain. He had kicked me in the thigh with both feet and sent me down like a discarded pack of cigarettes. I was sure he had broken my femur as the waves of pain coursed up my leg. Eventually they subsided into a deep throbbing ache. When Donny reached me I was as white as a ghost. I had quit dragging myself around like a wounded animal, finally stopping long enough for him to assess whether my leg was broken. It was hard for me to remain still; the pain was so intense. I felt little relief despite discovering it wasn't broken.

I pulled my denim pants down and there in the middle of my right thigh was the imprint of two hoof marks on the meaty part of my leg near the scar on my right hip. I needed about a half an hour to settle and collect myself. In the meantime, Donny saddled and bridled my horse, Annabelle. Omega had a reputation for kicking and I was not his first or last victim. I had forgotten about his quirkiness in that moment, but I would never forget it again.

We were 25 miles from the trailhead, and somehow I had to get back up into the saddle and ride out. I knew that the sooner I got up there, the better, before my leg really stiffened up.

Donny saddled the remaining horses and then helped me up onto Annabelle. Once I was on the horse, I was there for the duration of the trip. We couldn't trot so it was going to take about eight hours to reach the trailhead. I was laid up for a few days with a huge hematoma on my thigh. Though it was difficult to walk, riding was possible, once I managed to get up in the saddle. Fortunately, it was my right leg that was injured. The one I threw over the back of the saddle to mount and not the one I needed to stand up on to gain the seat. This allowed me to continue to be effective at work, hampered only when not in the saddle.

We returned ten days later to pick up the Pipestone group. In the meantime, Don had passed on to Joe what he had learned. He had a chat with the group leaders when they arrived at the trailhead, telling them of his suspicions. He had no substantive evidence to lay a charge but they never came back and we can only surmise that gold was what they were looking for. There is colour to be found in the North Saskatchewan River, and they were camped near Pipestone Pass, which divides it from the headwaters of the Siffleur River that flows into the Saskatchewan. It was probably a good place to look but it just happened to be illegal in a national park.

FISHING AND HUNTING IN THE FALL OF 1967
It had been a hot, dry summer. When the fall season approached, the Alberta Forest Service imposed a fire ban on the area Bert hunted.

The Baumanns, a couple from Switzerland, were coming early for their hunt so that they could get a fishing trip in before the season opened. Hans was in his early seventies and slightly overweight but still spry enough to hunt, while his wife was in her early sixties and much more active. They certainly enjoyed being in the Canadian Rockies, which they often compared to their beloved Swiss Alps.

I was along to help Bert with the packing and wrangling while June guided the two clients on horseback. The Baumanns had been on a trip with Bert a few years before and were eagerly anticipating this one. We stayed only one night at Skoki as they were both looking forward to sleeping under a canopy of stars. We made the trip down to the Pipestone River, and then carried on up to Singing Meadows. We camped at the north end of the meadow, a mile below the trail junction to Fish Lakes. From our tents, we could look back at the spectacular north side of the Drummond Glacier, while in the foreground, Singing Falls slipped melodiously over a smooth rock face to water the green pasture below. Today, because of the ongoing encroachment of tall willow and bog birch – the result of a century of fire management, a changing climate and a lack of grazing from both horses and elk – you would not be afforded that stupendous view.

The next day we travelled over Pipestone Pass into the Siffleur River drainage and then up and over Clearwater Pass to the east. We camped by an idling stream in a lovely meadow near Devon Lakes, 2.5 miles from the pass. We planned to spend four or five days there, before continuing our trip down the Siffleur to the hunting area just east of Banff National Park.

I took Hans up to the first Devon Lake to fish, but when he saw the lake he declared, "There's no fish in that lake!" He was wrong. He had his limit of ten pan-sized brook trout in about an hour, so we spent the rest of the time exploring all the nooks and crannies around the two lakes. We had a nice picnic lunch by the lower one. I guess one of the least flattering things I could say about him (that his wife would probably agree with) was that Hans could be obtuse at times. I thought he was thick-headed and imperceptive.

Indianhead District Warden headquarters.
DALE PORTMAN COLLECTION

When we got back to camp, he told Bert all about his exploits in catching the fish, including how good an eye he has for fish habitat and how he was going to prepare the fish for tonight's supper. I had caught a couple, so I added them to the larder and spent what was left of the afternoon cleaning them under his watchful eye. He seemed to relax watching me, and it was at times like this that he would drop his guard and reflect, bringing up his memories of hunting chamois in the Alps. I was too young, it seemed, to be taken seriously by him, but there were times when he seemed to warm to my presence. In those days, I looked younger than I really was. He possessed that old country, colonial attitude and didn't hesitate to remind me that I was not his guide. That was fine with me, although at times I struggled with his arrogance and had to bite my tongue.

Pack string heading up towards Clearwater Pass from Devon Lakes.
DON MICKLE COLLECTION

We were having "Blue Fish" for dinner, his specialty, and he was very fussy about how they needed to be cooked. The fish were dropped, head included, into a pot of boiling water and left to simmer for ten minutes – and he timed it. They were then taken out and eaten immediately, smothered in lemon and butter with salt and pepper. They were delicious, so much so that I was sent back the next day to catch more while the Baumanns had a camp day.

Two days later, I was sent on horseback to the backcountry warden station at Indianhead to find out if the fire ban had been lifted in the Siffleur area. It was a long ride, about 12 miles one way. To pass the time, and thinking I was the only one in the country, I started singing a Marty Robbins tune with much gusto and animation. "Bullet in my shoulder, blood running down my vest, twenty in the posse an' they're never going to let me rest…" It was a shock when a lone backpacker met me coming around a bend in the trail.

I was embarrassed as we exchanged greetings. I am one of the worst singers in the world. He showed no ill effects from my screeching, though, and I was surprised to see a cat perched on the top of his big pack. The traveller's name was Doug Lamond. He was from Montana but he had come north to seek opportunity in the Canadian Rockies. He was a certified mountain guide who also knew his way around horses, and I saw him several times over the years, usually on the trail somewhere. On this particular day he was hiking on his own, just with his cat, and he said he could relate to my solo laments to the puzzled creatures of the forest. It was a strange encounter, indeed. When I got to Indianhead, the place was boarded up and the windows shuttered. I had a quick lunch on the steps of the porch then headed back, arriving just in time for supper.

The next day, the Baumanns went for a day ride with June, down valley to Clearwater Lake, while Bert and I bucked up firewood and mended some tack. He was expecting Don and Eddie Hall, Ron's brother, to arrive with a couple of hunters later that afternoon. Accompanying the group was a friend of the family, Hank, a plumber from Calgary. He was a big, heavy-set guy who was not used to riding, and when he got to camp he was pretty saddle sore.

The two hunters arrived in better shape than Hank, but they certainly didn't have the sense of humour or outgoing personality that he brought to the campfire. Donny mentioned to Bert that they had seen Jay Morton in Lake Louise and he had told them that the fire ban in the Siffleur had been lifted. That explained why no one was at Indianhead, and it was welcome news to Bert.

Both outfits packed up the next day and headed for the hunting camp on the Siffleur River. Hank was so saddle sore he came up with a novel plan to protect his ass. He produced a foam sleeping pad and put it over his saddle then climbed on, hoping it would help. Fortunately, he had an understanding horse. I guess it helped, for that's how he rode for the rest of the trip, but it certainly looked weird. The only excitement that day was Old Blondie, the stove horse, getting poked by a tree branch. The mare took to bucking and managed to dump both the stove and the tent.

When we got to our destination, all of us were kept busy putting up the camp and getting firewood. Hans was hoping to bag a moose, with Bert as his guide, while Don and Eddie guided the two clients from Ontario. They were a couple of grocers who were decent guys and good about sharing their whisky. The two got drunk every night and hunted goats every day. I was the wrangler, so I got to go on some of the day hunts to look after the horses. They both were hunting mountain goats, so they would ride to where it got too steep for the horses, dismount and carry on by foot. I would stay with the animals. If they left camp on foot, I was left behind putting up firewood.

On one memorable occasion on that trip, all of us headed east on the seismic line for a few miles until we reached the turbulent Porcupine Creek. It's a nasty horse crossing if you are planning on continuing east. It was choked full of huge boulders on a side slope that offered few opportunities to cross. We avoided the crossing and headed up the creek valley, following old game trails, around some deadfall and lots of trees. After an hour or so, we broke into the open where we found Porcupine Lake, which rivals Lake Louise for its deep shade of luminous turquoise. It was so remote that few people had seen it. It remains isolated today, largely because the Siffluer Wilderness became a protected area that doesn't allow overnight camping or horse use. A few years after it was protected, a devastating fire ravaged most of the drainage, making it even harder to navigate. I doubt if more than a handful of people have seen it since those days.

Above the lake, we encountered extensive flats covered in mountain avens, which made for easy travel and an opportunity to glass the surrounding country for game. Here the groups split up. Bert and Hans went looking for moose, while Don and Ron continued to examine the

Dale Portman with Porcupine Lake off in the distance.
DALE PORTMAN COLLECTION

slopes. There was no sign of goat so we headed farther up the valley. No one had any luck that day, and we all met back at the lake. Dusk settled swiftly across the valley as we skirted the lake on our return to camp. Nightfall crept in quickly. It was a moonless night with an overcast sky that kept the stars hidden while cloaking the valley in darkness. Deep beneath the trees, we fumbled along in the dark, 8 miles from camp.

Bert was in the lead on Chico, a great jingle horse with a nose for finding the trail. He gave the horse his head and the rest of us followed in single file. I clasped the reins and hung on to the saddle horn with one hand clinging to my hat with the other, which I used to protect my eyes from clawing tree branches. Chico wove a course back through the trees exactly as we had come. He didn't hesitate once. According to Bert, he dropped his head on occasion to verify something with his nose, but the scent he followed often was what lingered above the ground in the undergrowth, residual from our trip up valley. I was impressed with this feat and in awe of his skill.

In hindsight, that was the day I became interested in scent and the mystery surrounding it. It was an important motivating factor for me to become a dog handler later in life.

Supper was late that night, and throughout the meal, I repeated how impressed I was with Chico's talent. There was little interest from the others in adding to the discussion as they wolfed their food down. I guess it was hard to eat and talk at the same time, and I didn't want to distract them, watching how intent they were to feed the old pie hole. Someone could easily poke an eye out with their fervent desire to finish off what remained on their plate, as they wheeled their forks dangerously about. I shut up, concerned about the safety of those in the cook tent. Only Bert understood my excitement, but he was a notoriously picky eater.

The next day, the two grocers got their goats high above camp, so everyone was in good spirits when we sat around the dinner table that night. While having a few drinks after dinner, a visitor rode in. It was Park Warden Jay Morton with some bad news. He had made a mistake telling Don and Eddie that the Siffleur was open, when in fact it was closed. As soon as he had arrived at his district cabin at Indianhead, he had unpacked his packhorses and turned them loose, then headed our way with the news.

That didn't stop our evening celebration, and as it was too late for him to return to Indianhead, Jay turned his saddle horse out. He was now happy to join us in putting a dint in the alcohol. We had to leave the next morning, which was unfortunate because Hans hadn't gotten his moose. The good thing was that the two grocers had all this booze that needed to be drunk. There was no way we were going to pack it out. The party picked up a considerable amount of tempo on that realization.

When Bert was a young man, a close friend of his, Lawrence Whitney from the Siksika (Sarcee) Reserve, taught him how to chicken dance. It's a traditional Blackfoot dance and Bert was now passing it on to us. We were trying to follow him around the fire in a manic rendition of it. By this point, a substantial amount of the alcohol had been consumed and, miraculously, no one fell into the fire.

Jay Morton with saddle over his shoulder.
DALE PORTMAN COLLECTION

Finally, we headed for bed. We needed to pack up the camp the next day and an early rise was necessary. Jay was protesting he had nothing to sleep in when Donny threw him a couple of saddle blankets. Our heads were heavy, and we only wanted to sleep and we had little sympathy for him. Throughout the night, he kept trying to crawl into various occupied sleeping bags, which resulted in an interrupted night of cursing and pleading as the temperature dropped.

When Don and I awoke at dawn to the sound of the alarm clock, we found Jay huddled in a ball with his slicker covering him. I woke him up and offered him my sleeping bag, but now that he was awake, he just wanted to get his horse and get back to the comforts of his district cabin.

Bert wandered in to the cook tent when we had finished lighting the stove. His mission was to get the coffee on while the three of us headed off to retrieve the horses. When we got to the river, it was evident they had crossed and one of us had to wade the river to bring them back. We drew straws and Donny lost. In fine form, he pulled out a bottle of Listerine, guzzled the contents and stepped into the river. To this day, Jay swears that Donny drained the mouthwash by the shore of the Siffleur River, without batting an eyelash. Don to this day maintains he only put it to his lips as a parting gesture and did not drink any of it. I've always backed Jay on this story, much to Donny's annoyance. When we got back to camp with the horses, we let everyone know about Donny's hangover cure. Bert enjoyed it while June gave him that look only a mother can give her son after he does something so stupid. It was something she was used to. All he wanted to know was if there was any beer left, to get rid of the awful taste in his mouth and further ease his hangover.

Jay got an early start and June headed out with the clients while the rest of us pulled the camp down and packed things up. Despite having not gotten his moose, Hans had had a good trip, and he and his wife were going to come back the next year. A few days after we left, it started raining, and it rained for a good stretch, enough to lift the fire ban on the Siffleur and just in time for the start of our next hunt.

NURSING BERT BACK TO HEALTH ON THE SIFFLEUR

On the next trip, Bert's saddle horse stumbled badly, and he was tossed off onto some pretty rough ground. He threw his back out and cracked a few ribs, so he was bedridden for a time. The hunters left shortly after that, happy with their hunt. I found myself alone with Bert in camp while he healed and I looked after things. I would go out and jingle the horses in the morning, bring them in for the day and turn them loose in the evening. We always kept one or two horses picketed nearby. He slowly healed as I bucked up firewood for the next hunt and prepared the meals.

Bert won every crib game I played with him on that trip. I caught him cheating twice. He would sneak extra points while pegging out or counting up his hand. When I confronted him, he just laughed and dealt another hand, paying little attention to my objections. I had to watch him like a hawk just to win one game, which never happened. I vowed never to play him for money after that.

The approach to Clearwater Pass looking west towards the Siffleur.
DALE PORTMAN COLLECTION

My favourite jingle horse was Chico, but he was kept in only when it was his turn to be picketed. The valley was wide and the meadow stretched for a few miles or so on both sides of the river. At that time of the year, the horses would often find some small clearing on the periphery of the trees, well-hidden from the naked eye. With Chico, all you had to do to find the other horses was ride along the trail towards Banff National Park, parallel to the meadow, and at some point, his head would inevitably pick up and his ears would perk forward, he would give a whinny and take off at a trot.

One morning I went for the horses and found some of them missing. I brought the others in and then returned to look for the rest. I searched all day without luck, and eventually I gave up and came back to camp. Bert was feeling better and the following morning we set out, heading into the park. A couple of miles along, Bert picked up their tracks. Chico was with the ones who were missing, so Bert's saddle horse was Cinnamon. We were now relying on Bert's skill as a tracker to find the sneaky breakaways. Soon we were crossing Dolomite Creek and heading up the Siffleur Valley. He could see where they had left the trail to feed and where they came back and continued to follow the trail. Just past the junction to Clearwater Pass, he got off Cinnamon and started inspecting the ground. He looked up, gazing east towards the pass, and then started heading off, following fresh tracks. At the summit of the pass stood Chico, Amigo, Annabelle and the rest. Bert took the lead and led them back down, with me pushing the rest from behind. They soon were strung out in line along the trail, heading back to camp at a comfortable pace to protect Bert's ribs.

It was about 9 miles to camp, and I certainly had time to reflect on how proficient Bert was with tracking. I learned a lot that day and eventually developed a keen eye for sign on the ground, which I used to my advantage in following behind a tracking dog later in life. There would be more than a few occasions as a dog handler when I wondered if the dog was off track. I was always looking for sign – a broken twig, a scuff, a footprint – and when I found something, my confidence in the dog was reinforced.

RIDING NAKED ACROSS THE KOOTENAY PLAINS AND ANOTHER BIZARRE EVENT

One trip to Banff later that autumn was both bizarre and memorable. After Bert recovered, I had been left at the hunting camp in the Siffleur. Bert told me that if they didn't return by a certain date, I was to secure the camp, put the food up the bear pole and ride out to the highway with the horses. When the date arrived and no one showed up, I got busy closing down the camp and securing it.

It would be an 18-mile ride to the highway, and when I got to the Saskatchewan River on the Kootenay Plains, I would need to cross it with the horses. Even in the fall, there was a stretch in the middle that the horses had to swim. I was going to have to hitchhike back to Lake Louise, so I put some thought into the river crossing. I didn't want to be wearing wet clothing while trying to thumb a ride. I stripped down to my white briefs, tied my clothes in a bundle around my neck and swam across the river sitting on my horse. I had little trouble pushing the others ahead of me across the river as they were looking forward to the green grass on the other side.

Once we were on the far shore, I pushed the horses across a huge meadow, part of the massive Kootenay Plains, in the direction of an aspen grove I could see off in the distance. I was loping along in wet riding boots, clothing streaming off my neck, when a vehicle passed by in the near distance followed by another a minute later, dust billowing from the gravel road. I must have been an apparition to those passing by. Such a peculiar scene to witness in the middle of nowhere while driving the future David Thompson Highway.

When I got to the stand of aspen, I stopped, tied up the horses, put on my clothes and unsaddled the horses. I piled all the tack together well inside the aspen stand and covered it all with a tarp. I hobbled and belled the horses and turned them loose. I got a ride right away and soon found myself in Lake Louise. My girlfriend at the time was living in Banff, so I got on the passenger train and took it there.

I headed right for the bar car at the back of the train, sat down and ordered a beer. I was still wearing trail clothes so I sat next to a guy I didn't think would object too much to the smell of sweat and horseshit. I was trying to avoid the women in the car and I attempted to be as inconspicuous as possible, but that didn't last. The guy I sat next to was a slightly built, older man. He looked over at me and began eyeing me up and down. His eyes locked on mine. A look of recognition spread across his face, as I quickly became troubled, and he said, "You're one of us. You came over in that spaceship with us, 24,000 years ago." I didn't know what to say. Everyone's head swivelled alarmingly in our direction. They were now focused on me, wondering what I would say. If Donny had been there he would have looked at me and said, "I don't know how you attract them Portman or how they're attracted to you but you have a way of picking real winners."

I looked over at the guy like he was radioactive and said, "No, that wasn't me. I slept in and missed the flight. I was on the one with Adam and Eve." With that I drained my beer and left. I couldn't get out of there fast enough. I found a seat at the front of the train and never looked back. I was the first one off when we got to the train station in Banff.

As I've already said, Annabelle loved to run. She was a dark-bay mare of medium build and had a narrow, slightly irregular white blaze on her handsome face that accentuated a finely featured head. She was unusually intelligent and would have made a fine dude horse if she could only give up her wild urge to run – but on looking back, who would want to remember her as a dude horse. She was a very spirited mare who would be a good mount for any seasoned rider with a light but firm hand, who wasn't chasing horses.

Annabelle was one of the greatest horses I've had the good fortune to ride in my various careers working with animals. My first encounter with her resulted in a runaway, but I continued to have confidence in her as a guide horse. The two attributes that come to mind in describing her are that she truly had a great heart as well as courage. She gave it all, and when she stretched out, to gain ground with her long stride, her nostrils widened. She was born to run and a treat to experience. I fondly remember how evident this was on one occasion with Donny, chasing some horses up the Pipestone near Point Camp. The ponies had crossed the river and as we approached at full gallop, we saw a deep hole looming in the river that was something we would normally ride around. Not her. She launched herself at full speed into the swirling back-eddy and disappeared with me up to my neck in water. Once we gained the mainstream of the river, which wasn't swimming water, she looked back at me like, "Why did you ask me to do that?" She was a fine saddle horse. Donny had an amazing story about her that he passed on to me a few years later.

Back in the summer of 1962, the Mickles were in the process of buying Timberline Tours from colourful Lake Louise outfitter Ray Lagace. They planned on working closely with Ray that summer, learning the operation, the horses and the country itself. Ray ran the business that summer and, though in essence the Mickles worked for him, the business profits went to the Mickles and Ray was paid wages. It was a setup that worked well for all involved. They also had the lease to Temple and Skoki Lodges. Temple was strategically located across from the backside of the Whitehorn ski area and at the base of the Larch ski run and Poma lift. It was also conveniently located at the trailhead for Skoki and the Red Deer Lakes country of the upper Red Deer River.

Donny was based out of Skoki that summer with old Ray who looked after the guests. He was learning a lot about the horses and the country. He did what I would take over doing years later: he jingled horses in the early morning, hauled water, split and hauled wood, guided clients and travelled the network of trails in the area. Bert and June spent their time at the pony stand with June concentrating on the business end of things. Faye spent her time filling in where she was needed, but she also travelled a lot between the homestead west of Millarville and the pony stand at Lake Louise.

There was nearly a hundred head of horses scattered amongst the three centres – Skoki, Temple and the pony stand – as well as at Point Camp, located 12 miles up the Pipestone. Point Camp was considered the holiday retreat for horses who were infirm or needed a break or were too young for long trips. There was a small tent camp with a set of corrals on a treed prominence of land that extended out into a large open meadow. Here the horses roamed freely in the open grassland.

One morning at first light, Donny, along with fellow wrangler, Richard Regnier, went down to the corral to get their saddle horses. Three horses had been kept in that night, one of which was Annabelle.

They silently saddled the horses with sleep in their eyes and quiet on their minds then quickly mounted and rode off down towards Merlin Meadows a mile away. There was no sign of the horses in the meadow, but there were fresh tracks heading down the trail towards the Pipestone. The horses had managed to break through the drift fence. A couple miles along the trail was another meadow, where Donny hoped the horses might have stopped to feed before pursuing their quest for freedom. The delinquent horses stood in the middle of the meadow as though waiting for them.

As if by signal, the horses stopped feeding and looked up at the relieved riders. Richard and Donny approached cautiously, trying to circle around to the left of them. They wanted to station themselves between the horses and the direction they were headed. It didn't work. The horses bolted and the chase was on. Richard and Donny madly tried to cut them off, but the horses had too much of a lead. They were quickly into the trees and running hard. As Donny followed into the woods, he saw a low branch directly in his path. He tried to pull Annabelle up, but there was slim hope of that. She had already picked out her route and it was directly under the branch. She drove Donny straight into the bony limb and it swept him out of the saddle and onto his backside. He remembers being momentarily knocked out and having a lump on his head. The last he saw of Annabelle was her rump undulating in pursuit of the rapidly vanishing horses. She never looked back. Donny got up, brushed himself off and made sure he was still intact. There was nothing to do but walk back to Skoki.

He hobbled into the lodge, and there was Ray with all the guests, sitting in the kitchen. Now, old Ray was famous for his lisp. When he saw Donny, he exclaimed, "Jethus Donny. What did you do? You've lotht your horthe and thaddle and you look like hell! Now, I think you're going to be riding thkin ath [skin ass or bareback] for a while." He added, "You better take old Midnight, the only horthe left in the corral. Yeah, you've done very well, Mishter Mickle."

Donny got little sympathy from Ray and a few hours later, Richard returned with most of the horses; but there was no Annabelle. He had last seen her running crazy through the bush, past the horses, headed in the direction of the Pipestone River. With that information, Donny climbed on old Midnight – bareback – and headed in the direction the horses were last seen with little in the way of food and no concrete game plan. He'd obviously had enough of Ray's blistering and sarcastic wit but more was his concern for Annabelle's well-being.

For two days, Donny rode with little rest and only a quick meal as he occasionally passed by Skoki. He covered all the surrounding countryside, all the meadows and favourite haunts with no luck. Then on the third day, he found himself down in the Pipestone Valley again. In a meadow just east of where the trail from Skoki and Red Deer Lakes reached the valley, he found a piece of rein from his bridle. Annabelle had been here for a while at least. He headed to Point Camp, 4 miles downstream, to see if the resting herd nearby had drawn her there.

By chance, Donny met his dad at Point Camp, who had heard of the missing horse by "moccasin telegraph." Bert had come to look for Annabelle, as well. Donny was relieved to see Bert – he was someone who had chased many a wild horse in his younger days, was quite the bushman and, as we well know, a good tracker.

They then separated and Bert headed up the Pipestone towards its source, while Donny concentrated on the upper Red Deer River. That was the last they would see of each other for quite a while.

Donny returned to Skoki that night, where he expected to meet Bert before heading off to Red Deer Lakes the next morning. When Bert didn't show up, Donny left early the next day on his own, bareback again on old Midnight. After checking out the meadows around the lakes, he headed downstream 8 miles, towards Horseshoe Lakes. The timber-covered valley opened for a brief period as the spectacular Drummond Glacier appeared off to the left before the timber closed in again. He checked the meadow below the face of the glacier; no signs of a horse. There was no relief from the deep timber until he reached Shingle Flats; again, no signs of a horse's presence. At the Sandhills Warden Cabin, he met District Warden Jerry (Red) Lyster. Jerry eyed Donny up and down with a critical eye.

"Why are you bareback on that old packhorse?" He asked with a frown on his face.

"I've ridden four days, looking for my horse and my gear," Donny answered, filling him in on the details.

"Well, there's no horse sign around here," Jerry said. He tied up the diamond on top of his packhorse and then swung up into the saddle and rode off with a grin on his face. Looking back, he said, "I guess riding bareback ain't all that bad. But if I spot your horse or saddle I'll send a message out to your dad. I'll be staying at Cyclone for the next little while so if you're at Skoki we can touch base in a few days." Cyclone Cabin is only 4 miles from Skoki.

Bob Haney (on Annabelle) and Dave Wildman, circa 1960s.
DON MICKLE COLLECTION

In the meantime, when Bert and Donny parted company, Bert headed up the Pipestone Valley to check out a long string of open meadows beside the river. A couple of miles past the junction with the Little Pipestone, he found a fresh horse track on the trail. Bert was riding Chico, the obvious choice when looking for a runaway.

When Bert found the track, old Chico lowered his head and sniffed the black earth. His nostrils flared fully and he snorted hard, like a bellow on a flame. He lifted his head and looked up the valley. Without further ado, he headed out in a slow easy trot. It was 11 miles to Pipestone Pass. Bert kept his eye on the ground. The fresh horse droppings were encouraging. It didn't look like the horse they were following had ever stopped to eat.

When they reached Singing Meadows, they stopped and looked around. There was no sign of Annabelle, so they kept riding. Chico never hesitated – he had a job to do and a track to follow. The horse travelled at a steady trot, and Bert was impressed with Chico's new-found energy for as much as Annabelle liked to run, Chico loved to track.

They reached the old Upper Pipestone Warden Cabin, marked by grizzly claws, but still no sign of Annabelle. Then finally, they broke out of the trees 2.5 miles from the pass. For a moment, Bert thought he saw the silhouette of a horse on the skyline of the pass, but he wasn't sure. Even as the terrain steepened as they approached the pass, Chico's pace didn't slacken, until they crested the summit. Chico stopped and there was Annabelle, looking wild and crazy. She stood there, trembling in terror as if the first misstep would send her off on another panicky run. There wasn't much left of the saddle on her back. It was perched precariously in place, held by the rear cinch that had slipped back, and was now flanking her. It was barely a saddle as the stirrups, front cinch, breast collar and bridle had been stripped off by her close encounters with the trees.

Bert approached slowly on Chico, ever aware that Annabelle could bolt at any moment. The horse was crazed with fear as they drew close, and Annabelle swung with lightning speed, kicking Chico in the chest. Chico didn't even flinch, and again they approached. Suddenly Annabelle bolted, forcing Chico and Bert to follow in pursuit. As she ran across the pass, Chico came up behind her. Annabelle cocked her leg and fired again, kicking Chico in the shoulder, narrowly missing Bert's leg. He swung Chico around and managed to cut Annabelle off. She came to an abrupt halt. Ever so carefully and with a soft soothing voice, he dismounted. He spoke to her for a long time in the same fashion and eventually managed to get within arms' reach.

He slowly touched her chest and trembling shoulder as he talked to her. Concealed behind his back in his other hand he held several loops of a rope. Annabelle was coiled like a spring, quivering, but she stayed where she was. She seemed to understand that all this was necessary, but the instinct was to bolt. Slowly, he worked his hand up her neck until he was standing next to her. In a comforting tone, he whispered placating noises as he carefully moved his hand over her nose. At this point, she relented and buried her head in his armpit, releasing all the tension from her body.

After he placed the rope around her neck and improvised a halter, he went about trying to take the saddle off. While all this was going on, Chico grazed quietly on some nearby forbs as if nothing had happened. The saddle readjusted and secured in place, Bert mounted old Chico and took off for Lake Louise, leading Annabelle. Chico was stepping out like a colt again, satisfied everything had turned out well.

The next day a pack string arrived from Temple, and Donny found out to his great relief that Annabelle had been found. Meanwhile, Ray's pack trip was nearly over, so Donny rushed off to meet up with the group. When he caught up to them later in the day, "moccasin telegraph" had already reached them.

"Yeth Donny, you're pretty good with people and you can shoe a horthe well, but your father's a much better horthe-turd detective than you are," Ray said to Donny as he rode into their camp.

SIX

LAKE LOUISE

THE MEXICAN WOMEN ON MOUNT VICTORIA

1967 ended on a tragic note when Walter Perren suddenly passed away from cancer. He had come to my rescue in Lake Louise, and over the two years since that event I had heard a lot about the man whose climbing skills and character bordered on legendary.

Like Conrad Kain and the Feuz brothers before him, Walter Perren's name is synonymous with guiding and mountaineering in Canada. He is considered the father of mountain rescue. He had the formidable task of trying to convince a bunch of broken-down cowboys, who happened to be park wardens, that they had the ability to climb and rescue people in distress. To most wardens, a rope was for lassoing a horse or tying a diamond hitch. They didn't have the confidence needed to hang from a rope on a mountainside or even comprehend why they should. But there are always a few in most organizations who are willing to try something new, something out of their comfort zone, and that was to be the case within the warden service. How mountain rescue in Canada was developed within the confines of the federal government is an interesting and enduring story.

It really started back in 1954 with the tragic accident of the Mexican women and their male guide on Mount Victoria. After the tragedy, great concern arose from the Canadian Pacific Railway about their guides becoming more and more involved in mountain rescue. The magnitude of the accident and the rescue that followed was unprecedented. I first learned about the disaster while visiting Lake Louise with my family back in 1954. A decade later, after my climbing accident and in the hospital, Dr. Titamore told me the rough circumstances surrounding the story.

The summer had been late coming that year, and by the end of July 1954 after a particularly harsh winter, the mountains were still covered in their snowy winter mantle. The seven young Mexican women stood in a knot on the shore of Lake Louise, conversing eagerly in hushed tones about the effect the beauty of the lake had on persons seeing it for the first time, like them. Eventually, their young eyes locked on the expansive face and the central summit of the distant peak, which dominated the view.

Guests at the Chateau who happened to be wandering the prominent path in front of the lake, taking in the exquisite views, probably wondered who those exotically dressed women were. As they passed by, they might have smiled, hearing the hushed, soft cadence of their Spanish.

Like all women who are in the forefront of establishing themselves in a male-dominated activity, they had their challenges: males doubting their climbing skills, disparaging remarks directed their way that questioned their lifestyle. "You should be at home raising the kids, cleaning the house and cooking meals." They encountered roadblocks deliberately put in place to challenge and hinder them – mostly in their own country. From a safety standpoint, some of the criticism might have been significant, but most of it was not. To put things in perspective, the first, all-women attempt to climb a serious peak in Canada didn't occur until 1976 with the First Women's Mount Logan Expedition. The first North American woman to summit Mount Everest was Sharon Woods in 1986. The

Mexican women were certainly groundbreaking pioneers, and they were undertaking a huge challenge, over two decades before the Logan expedition.

The Mexican Alpine Club, which the women had approached for some financial assistance, never contested the choice of Eduardo San Vincente as their guide. He was a very experienced climber who had been to the top of many of the big summits in both North and South America, peaks such as Alaska's Denali (Mount McKinley back then) and Peru's Huascaran.

However, the club did have reservations about the women who intended to climb. They had come together as a loose unit from different climbing clubs around the country and were a determined group. The men in control of the financial committee of the Mexican Alpine Club challenged the women's experience level and felt their objectives were set too high. They wanted them to lower their sights and look at some lesser peaks. This was hotly debated throughout the membership. They were eventually denied financial assistance, but through the efforts of San Vicente and his dedicated support of the women, a second, more understanding committee was formed.

The women were from different backgrounds. Some of them worked as professionals, and all were gainfully employed. Most of them were strangers to one another. Eventually the Mexican Excursionismo Federation approved the trip but withheld official sponsorship. With the money in order and the wrangling behind them, the barriers amongst them soon came down and the women settled into the serious training necessary for their expedition to Canada. For seven months they climbed and trained together all over Mexico, getting to know each other even as they tabulated their strengths and weaknesses. Finally, the departure date arrived and they boarded a Mexican Airline flight to Calgary.

As they debarked at the train station in Banff they were met with much fanfare and excitement. They were immediately approached by a reporter from the *Crag & Canyon*. He soon learned much about

Abbot's Pass and the Death Trap.
KATHY CALVERT COLLECTION

the women's objectives and how the group had come together. Their leader, an attractive woman of twenty-nine, who was also their spokesperson, conducted an interview with the reporter. The reporter learned that two compatriots of theirs had visited the area in 1953 and returned home with glowing reports of Banff's spectacular mountain scenery and the wealth of peaks that abounded in the area. She said the team hoped to climb Castle Mountain (back then Mount Eisenhower) on the way to Lake Louise, with their major objective being Mount Victoria and possibly Mount Lefroy. Mr. San Vincente followed up by saying, "An international expedition of this kind was the first ever undertaken on the continent."

There were huge challenges for the seven women and their guide in summiting Mount Victoria via the route they had chosen, particularly that year. They wanted to climb the East Face, which would take them to the south summit rather than the standard route to the main summit, which was much safer. The route they had picked had only been done once before, and owing to a heavy winter of snow and the late arrival of summer, the steep face was prone to avalanches. This and more was pointed out to them when they arrived in Lake Louise, by the Swiss guides employed by the Canadian Pacific Railway. One of the guides, Ernst Feuz told the party, "The high mountains are in bad shape from this winter. In all history we have never had such a hard winter, so much snow or so late a spring." He went on to say that if they were successful, they would be the first party to ascend the south summit that year.

The group had much to consider after talking to the Swiss guides. San Vincente, on hearing about the conditions, wanted to hire one of them to guide them up their chosen route, but the Swiss turned him down, saying it was too dangerous.

The group had made its first mistake in not heeding the advice of the Swiss guides. The next day as they headed out, they pushed aside any negative feelings, buoyed by the huge turnout of people who wished them well on their adventure. They probably got swept up in the excitement of the moment. The second mistake was made when they met Ernst Feuz's brother, Walter, below Abbots Hut on his way down. The hut is located in the high col between Mounts Victoria and Lefroy, a stone structure that added a Swiss alpine feel to the spectacular setting. He warned them that tomorrow they should stay on the rock ridge leading up to the summit and avoid the snowy East Face. The other point was that they should not be on the snow-covered face when the sun was at its highest at midday. Not only was the avalanche hazard high, the snow would be soft, adding to the likelihood of their crampons balling up with wet snow, making a slip probable. The clogged crampons would be useless and could become a hazard. The advice was disregarded.

They reached Abbots Hut without mishap and settled in for a comfortable night, perched precariously (especially the outhouse) on Abbot Pass, with stunning views down both sides, overlooking Lake Louise on the Alberta side, Lake Oesa and Lake O'Hara on the British Columbia side.

The next morning one of the women wasn't feeling well and decided to wait for the rest of them at the hut while they climbed the mountain. One wonders what created her condition: foreboding, an inner voice she listened to, or a real physical ailment. This changed the configuration of the rope mates. The first group took off as a rope of four, led by San Vincente. The guide led off with the two most experienced and in-between the least experienced woman. The female leader of the expedition then followed on a second rope with the other two members of the team.

They had good climbing conditions that morning as the summer sun slightly softened the frozen snow. They climbed up the East Face and reached the south summit in good style. After a half hour at the summit, snacking and taking pictures, they made their third mistake. In considering their route down, they had the choice of returning along the ridge, which was much safer, as Walter Feuz had pointed out, or climbing down the route they had just come up.

They choose the latter with fatal consequences. Because the snow had softened from the heat of the sun, they had to move in a steady and efficient manner. They had to move quickly before the snow softened to the point of becoming an avalanche hazard. This required moving in unison, without the protection of a belay, which taxed the members with less climbing experience. But their descent was slowed even further as their crampons were now balling up and the slippery footing hampered even the most experienced climber. Because of their tenuous purchase and the lack of a belay, a slip by any one of them would result in the whole rope being pulled down.

It was now 1:30 PM. The leader of the second group reported afterwards, "I saw position number three starting to slip and start to drag the others down, and then they tangled up together in a ball and rolled down very fast. When I saw them fall, I knew it was over."

Down at the Chateau, people were following the party's progress with fascination, through a hotel telescope. When the fall occurred, there was a gasp and shock that quickly passed through the crowd. "Oh, my god, they've fallen!" Then a hush settled over them. Not far away, at Brewster Transport, a mechanic just happened to be watching the party through his binoculars at the exact moment the slip occurred. He later said, "I saw them sliding down and it looked as though they started an avalanche. I could see them easily for about half of the way, then they were covered in snow and then [they] dropped behind [Mount] Lefroy." The fall happened only 300 feet below the summit.

Throughout the afternoon and evening spectators lined up to view the surviving women as they tried in vain to reach the safety of the ridge. They aimlessly wandered about, sometimes up to their waists in rotten snow while attempting to come to terms with the position they were in. No doubt paralyzed by fear, they made no cohesive attempt to gain the summit again and reach some temporary haven. With the sun passing beyond the East Face of the mountain, they were now in danger of freezing.

Ernst Feuz knew this was the worst mountaineering accident in Canadian history, and it had the potential to worsen with the three shocked women still up there. There was an urgency to get up there quickly for the sake of the surviving climbers. A handful of employees who were climbers from the CPR and Chateau Lake Louise – including a lawyer, two bellhops and a medical student – sprang into action. They met up with Ernst at the lakeshore, where he embraced them. After reviewing what was in their rucksacks, they headed out. A second party consisting of an RCMP corporal, the chief park warden and a Banff doctor (Dr. Titamore) followed a little later.

Once they reached the site where the fatal party had come to rest, near the edge of the moraine, below the last cliff they had sailed over, it was hard to tell how many were involved. At first it looked like only two but on closer examination there were four, hopelessly tangled up in the climbing rope. They had all succumbed to their injuries. They could do nothing now but carry on to Abbot Pass. Here they discovered the woman who had stayed behind and broke the news to her as best they could. Three of the rescuers stayed behind to prepare food for the survivors while the other followed Ernst up along the ridge to the south summit. They made the distance in half the normal time.

Once directly above the women on the ridge, Ernst lowered his fellow rescuer down to them, instructing the bellhop to cut good steps along the way so that the women would have good footing to get back to the ridge. It was now shortly after 8:00 PM. From here it took two more hours to get them safely down to the hut, their confidence crushed.

Ernst had planned to spend the night at the hut but with concern for the surviving women, he decided to take them down as soon as he got some food into them. He didn't want them to have the shock of seeing the bodies of their fallen comrades during daylight hours, so they passed by the fateful spot under the cloak of darkness. Today the spot is referred to as "The Death Trap," and over subsequent years it has lived up to its ominous name.

The rescuers got the surviving women to the Plain of Six Glaciers Tea House, which is located midpoint between The Death Trap and the Chateau Lake Louise, and there the four women spent the night. The next morning, they continued their journey back to the Chateau, while the rest of the rescuers moved up to where the bodies were. It took four hours to untangle them, and then they wrapped them up and hauled them to a point where the horses could get to them. Before the bodies were removed by packhorse and in honour of the guide, they wrapped San Vincente's body in a Mexican flag – a salute to a fellow mountaineer who lost his life, guiding clients in a foreign land.

Back in her hotel room, the expedition leader was reluctantly forced to take her thoughts back to that troubled and devastating experience on the mountain, while giving an exclusive interview to a reporter from the *Calgary Herald*. From the room's picture window, you could see the turquoise lake and in the background the glimmering mountain. Below the south summit, you could unmistakably see the telltale skid marks of death. Fortunately for her, weather soon moved in, obscuring the view. Through an interpreter she told her story. But

The rescue party bringing bodies down from Mount Victoria.
DALE PORTMAN COLLECTION

what never came out was why they made that fateful decision to go back down the way they had come up, instead of taking the safer and easier route back down along the ridge.

No one knows the intricacies that played out between the Swiss guides and Eduardo San Vincente. Was their conversation cordial or was it strained, because of the forceful nature of the Swiss in their response to the party's desires, to take the more hazardous route? There might have been some arrogance coming from the Swiss and some resentment developing in the Mexican guide. Ego might have entered into the decision to go back down the face. It would also be quicker. They had successfully climbed the route in good conditions, proving the Swiss wrong on that point and maybe returning the same way would prove their point even more so, but in the end, the Swiss were right.

There were several tourists milling about when they brought the bodies down. Suddenly a string of horses came out of the trees in front of the Chateau. Amidst the din of the horses' feet, you could hear clearly, repeated by a few people closer up, "Bodies," and then a hush fell over all of them. The only sound was the footfall of the

The four surviving Mexican women.
BANFF WARDEN OFFICE COLLECTION

hooves on the gravel. Across the lake, you could see the indifferent presence of Mount Victoria. They carried the climbers wrapped in canvas, one draped in a foreign flag. Someone said, "I think it's a Mexican flag." It must have sent a chill through all of them on that hot and sunny afternoon.

In an interview with the *Calgary Herald*, Ernst Feuz was quoted as saying, "The Mexicans should not have used crampons on the soft rotten snow on the sun-soaked east face. The crampons could not reach the hard snow underneath the slushy upper layer and only the unstable surface snow therefore held the climbers. Neither the Mexicans nor any other mountaineer should climb on the east face of Victoria. That's committing suicide in these conditions."

The Mexican tragedy was followed the next year by an even more devastating accident on Mount Temple, where seven boy scouts from Philadelphia were killed in an avalanche. The Canadian Pacific Railway and its hotels could see where the trend was leading. It saw that more parties were inclined to climb without a guide and that their Swiss guides would be called upon to perform more and more rescues. It was that year the CPR announced that it would no longer provide a guiding service for its hotel clients. Some of the guides decided to head back to Switzerland, but many settled in the neighbouring communities, and one of the most popular destinations was the logging town of Golden, BC.

Controversy surrounded both accidents. With regard to the Mexican women, many made it a gender issue and some even claimed that the sport wasn't suitable for women. Some went so far as to say it was too mentally and physically challenging for the "weaker sex." To me it was a mountaineering accident that just happened to involve women who had a male guide. The seven boys died on Mount Temple as the result of incompetence on the part of the male leader, who was never taken to task over it. His peers back in Philadelphia protected him. They actually blamed Banff National Park for not informing them of the avalanche danger. It was later established they had never even sought advice.

THE ICONIC WALTER PERREN

Walter was born in Zermatt, Switzerland, in 1914 to a relatively poor family with six children to feed. His father was a stonemason and climbing guide. Walter had little interest in schooling and would often skip class to climb, practicing on nearby cliffs. He climbed the Matterhorn when he was fourteen, while being employed as a porter. During his career in Switzerland, he would reach that mountain's lofty summit 140 times.

He worked his way up through the ranks from that of an underprivileged apprentice to that of a celebrated guide, leading some of the best clients Europe had to offer. During the winter months, he instructed skiing, and his skills soon attracted the attention of the Swiss Alpine Club. It was putting together an expedition, Switzerland's first attempt on Mount Everest, and the club wanted Walter on the team.

The war interrupted that adventure and Walter changed course. Switzerland's neutrality presented unique circumstances for someone of Walter's talent, and he soon became involved with the French Underground. He guided countless refugees and Allied soldiers from France over the mountains into the safe confines of the land-locked country.

His climbing exploits attracted the attention of the Canadian Pacific Railway, which offered him a climbing contract in Canada. It was 1950, he was thirty-six years old and unmarried. With nothing really holding him back, he accepted. When he arrived in Halifax, he boarded a CPR train and headed west to his destination, the home of the Swiss guides, Golden, BC. He was travelling with fellow guide and countryman Edmund Petrie. At a stop at Lake Louise, they went off to stretch their legs. For them, this meant climbing the Needle on Mount Whyte, before catching the next train.

Walter settled into his life as a Swiss guide, attracting and entertaining his many clients with his lively stories and engaging personality. In *The World of Lake Louise*, Don Beers, who authored several splendid guidebooks of the area, wrote, "Both Edward and Ernst Feuz had great respect for Walter's ability and judgment, especially in his route selection. Edward, a proud man who never gave unmerited praise, told warden Jim Sime that he was frustrated that he could not do as well as Walter." This was followed up with, "He was the last of the CPR guides and was considered the finest climber of all; he was the only one to do difficult technical routes like the Tower of Babel, Eiffel Peak or the overhanging East Ridge of Mount Whyte." His solo, first-ascent of Mount Whyte in 1951 was accomplished ten years before the advent of a new generation of climbers, a breed that would set high standards in rock climbing and attempt these routes unguided. All were impressed at the degree of difficulty of the many routes pioneered by Walter.

He finally married at the lofty age of thirty-nine. He met Pamela Hughes at the Chateau Lake Louise, and he needed to be persistent and determined to win her heart. Having her undivided attention on the summit of Mount Louis, he presented her with a single red rose and proposed to her. They were married in the small Roman Catholic church in Field, BC, in 1953.

The tragedy of the Mexican women on Mount Victoria was a

wakeup call for the Canadian Park Service. They needed to act quickly to put a mountain rescue plan in place in the mountain parks. The three Feuz brothers had retired in the fall of 1954. Walter Perren and Edmund Petrie's contract with the CPR had been terminated, and Edmund, who had come to Canada with Walter, had moved to the United States to continue guiding. It was apparent to a few guides and one or two park wardens that the mountains were going to be besieged by a hoard of enthusiastic, inexperienced and guideless people. Climbing as a middle-class sport had been brought over by the Europeans and the British after the Second World War. Many of them settled in western Canada – Calgary being a strategic spot – where the idea of climbing perked the interest of young Canadians. Soon, Calgary was a climbing hub.

The Feuz brothers wisely directed their concern about guideless climbers to Jim Sime, the chief park warden of Yoho National Park who had grown up with many of them in Golden, BC. They knew Jim, and he respected them, and if the Swiss were telling him something, he realized he'd better listen. He immediately started a letter campaign directed at Ottawa and brought his concerns to the attention of his fellow chief park wardens and the regional director in Calgary.

Jim had the perfect candidate to run a mountain rescue program. He knew Walter well, but he had to convince his superiors of Walter's value. However, once Walter's contract with the CPR expired, he planned to move back to Switzerland. A job offer had to be in place before the termination date, so Jim had to hustle. Of course, it was hard for some people in government to grasp the immediacy of the situation, given their unfamiliarity with the mountains. So instead of visiting Jim Hutchison, the regional director of the Canadian Park Service in Calgary, and trying to explain the urgency of the situation in his own words, he talked him into travelling to Golden and talking to Edward Feuz in person.

Edward was blunt enough to convince Hutchison to act promptly, and with little hesitation, Hutchison gave the Banff superintendent the authority and money to hire Walter. It was amazing how quickly everything fell in place. Fortunately for everyone, no better man could have been found.

After leaving the CPR in the fall of 1954 and taking up his new position with Banff National Park, Walter got busy training the wardens in climbing and mountain rescue. He was on the job for only a short time when seven boy scouts were killed on Mount Temple in an avalanche, and he was there to run the operation. He eventually developed a nucleus of men he could trust and a second tier that could help in most situations. From this second group would come his next generation of leaders.

Every summer he put on climbing and rescue courses throughout the mountain national parks (Yoho, Kootenay, Banff and Jasper, as well as Revelstoke–Glacier and Waterton Lakes). In the winter he taught students how to ski and travel safely in avalanche terrain. Other highly skilled, European climbers, such as Bruno Engler, Peter Fuhrmann, Toni Klettl, Tony Messner, Hans Gmoser, Willie Pfisterer, and Fred Schleiss, along with local Banff guide Ken Baker, ably assisted him.

In this fashion, the mountain rescue capabilities of the warden service progressed to the point that by the mid-1960s, when the wave of new climbers peaked, Walter was ready. Walter's rescue of Rick and me off the cliff at the end of Lake Louise proved to him that the cable rescue system he had brought over recently from Europe worked. Our rescue allowed him to work out the kinks in the system and its equipment. It was none too soon because in the summer of 1966, he, his men and the system were needed in an epic rescue on the Tower of Babel.

Soon after taking charge, Walter established standards, requiring guides to be evaluated for their climbing skills, route-finding abilities and client care. The first two to be tested were Hans Gmoser and Bruno Engler. Out of this came the formation of a guiding association (Association of Mountain Guides, or ACMG) that took over the responsibility for testing and training guides. When that happened, Walter could concentrate on the search and rescue end of things. Two who came out of this new program as guides were Charlie Locke and Brian Greenwood.

LOCKE AND GREENWOOD ON THE TOWER OF BABEL

Locke and Greenwood were attempting a difficult new route on the face of the Tower of Babel, which is overhung near the summit. They were near the top when Locke, who was leading, fell off. The fall was held by Greenwood, but on the way down, Locke badly damaged his wrist and could not climb. They managed to secure themselves on a ledge for two days before they caught the attention of some hikers below. When the hikers contacted Wally McPhee, the district warden in Lake Louise, about the accident, he shuddered for he knew which route they were on. He had signed them out days earlier. He sent his assistant, Jay Morton, to verify their position and get some additional information. Jay came back ashen faced to report that they were 400 feet below the summit, under an overhang, which made things look extremely tenuous for all concerned. If they were that high up on the mountain, under those black overhanging cliffs, Wally could not see how they were going to be able to get to them, let alone get them off.

Walter arrived soon after with several men from Banff. In the meantime, McPhee had gone and taken a look for himself. Using binoculars, he spotted them high up on the mountain. McPhee thought a rescue was impossible but the decision was Walter's call, and Walter had no desire to leave them there.

Walter had a few tools of his own at his disposal that had not been fully utilized in previous rescue work. It was all going to have to come together to get them off that mountain. He had the cable rescue gear, he had a helicopter and he had a willing and capable helicopter pilot in Jim Davis. He also had room near the summit to land the helicopter. To climb up from below and try to reach them was out of the question, much too dangerous, considering the objective hazards the rescuers would face. No, they would have to bring them up from the top.

They had successfully brought Crosby up by cable the year before, and the cable system worked well on that occasion. Since then, Walter had trained the men with the system at summer schools, and he was confident in its operation. The problem with this situation was that once the rescuer was lowered over the edge and past the overhang, he would be hanging free of the cliff, which Walter thought would present new problems.

In the end, it was an amazing and successful rescue, and it couldn't have been pulled off without Walter, and everyone knew that. It received national media attention. It was a compelling news story, after all, which involved two well-known, local climbers.

WALTER'S UNTIMELY DEATH

As an instructor, Walter was thorough in his teaching and relaxed in his delivery. He was also extremely personable in delivering his remarks and instructions, so much so that they became legendary in retelling. When things got tense and wardens were struggling with confidence issues or a particular climbing move, he would say, "You're doing fine. I could lead a milk cow up here." When they were climbing along on ridge crests, some of his pupils would be found crouched down, apprehensive about standing up on such an exposed ridge. That's when Walter would say, "Stand up. You're not going to bump your head up here."

Through the summer of 1967, Walter noticed he was getting oddly fatigued on climbs. This was unusual, considering his reputation for boundless energy. As Bruno Engler recalled, "Walter was a tiger." He was diagnosed with leukemia shortly after and sadly passed away in late December 1967. A true legend was gone at the young age of fifty-three. His son, Peter, was only twelve when his father passed on, and he later became a park warden in Banff. My wife, Kathy, who was doing research for her book, *Guardians of the Peaks*, heard a very interesting story about Walter from Peter.

Peter was a young park warden in 1973, climbing with another young warden, Terry Skjonsberg, on Mount Hector. On summiting, they pulled out the registry from the rock cairn to record their ascent. To his surprise he found an entry written by his father and dated on the day he was born in 1954. He told his mother about the note and

Walter and Pamela Perren on their wedding day in Field, BC.
PERREN FAMILY COLLECTION

learned that it still bothered her that Walter had missed the birth of
his first son because he had gone off climbing.

Later, Peter received another insight with regard to the day he was
born, when he attended a reunion at the Chateau Lake Louise. Here he
met someone else who had been on that same registry back in 1954:
the young bellhop working at the Chateau who had participated in

the rescue of the Mexican women on Mount Victoria that summer. He had been badly shaken by the event, as were some of the others who were on the rescue. They had all lost interest in climbing, and Walter decided to take them under his wing and re-introduce them to the joys of mountaineering by climbing Mount Hector together. According to the former bellhop, that climb, on the day Peter was born, rekindled their spirit for the mountains.

A WEIRD AND WONDERFUL TRIP THROUGH THE PACIFIC NORTHWEST

I tried to get as much skiing in as I could during the winter of 1967–68, and my progress was enhanced by the odd ski lesson. I tried to cram a few trips into Skoki to help out with the chores there. I enjoyed the exercise of travelling in and out on skis. It brought my fitness level up and honed my travelling skills. I returned to work for Timberline Tours that summer and went on the fall hunting trips. Hans Baumann returned that fall and got his moose. I was his illustrious guide, which helped me lose my moniker, "the kid."

I met my wife Barb at the Post Hotel that winter. She was working for Alfa Legace as a waitress when we started dating. She was a tall blonde with short hair, often teased on top, who had a fashion sense not commonly seen in the mountains back then. In May 1968, we decided to head south, travelling through the US Northwest. A lot of the trip was covered by us using our thumbs, hitchhiking. We thought it would be a good opportunity to get to know each another better and add a little adventure to our lives, which was spiced up by meeting some interesting people along the way.

Hitchhiking can be a dodgy way of getting around, but in those days, it was more acceptable. This type of travel would force us to interact more with the locals we met instead of insulating ourselves, as people often do in conventional travel. We had no desire to do the trip on the cheap and camping was out of the question. We did carry a couple of light down sleeping bags for an emergency, but they were never intended to be used for sleeping outside. Packed in their stuff bags, they took up little room in our packs. We wanted to stay in small hotels or motels and possibly at a relative of Barb's in Sacramento. Maybe the odd stranger's home if the opportunity presented itself. If the hitchhiking got tough or the weather became inclement, we could always hop on a bus. At least my partner this time was much better looking than on my last attempt to hitch south.

With that strategy in mind, we set out from Banff on a Greyhound bus for Vancouver. We spent a few days near English Bay, staying at a quaint boutique hotel called the Sylvia. It was not far from Stanley Park in a quieter, leafier neighbourhood not far from Robson Street and the downtown core. Virginia creeper completely covered its west-facing wall and the small hotel entrance, softening the exterior of the building. From our hotel window, we had an attractive view of English Bay and all the boats coming in and out of the harbour. Between the hotel and the shoreline was a strip of greenery that enhanced the setting and provided us with an occasional picnic spot.

The seawall nearby provided for a peaceful stroll during the sunny mornings and the early evening. It also led to Stanley Park. The park's brochure stated that there was over a half-million trees in the park, and we soon discovered a tall standing forest, which had numerous trails winding throughout. We took delight in exploring its interior, which had nuggets of interest here and there. Nothing was more noticeable than the counter culture that was blossoming there. Hippies were scattered about, selling everything, including jewelry and artisan ware. Most items for sale were spread on sheets but some had display boards. Connecting the park like a thread was a miniature railway that was fun to ride, even for adults. The zoo didn't disappoint, but it was the majestic Sitka spruce that impressed me the most.

We spent a couple of nights dining out in Chinatown's predominantly Cantonese style restaurants, filling up on egg rolls, deep-fried shrimp and various noodle dishes. We relished the warm spring weather that was so much more advanced here than in Banff. We strolled along Chinatown's main drag, taking in all the activity and the neon signs hanging overhead with their oversized Chinese lettering.

Herbalist and spice shops displayed their wares while racks of roasting chickens hung in several windows. We caught the wafting smells as we passed. It was a festive atmosphere to stroll through.

We were tempted to spend more time in Vancouver but that would've meant changing hotels. We were splurging at the Sylvia. We had spent more here than we expected, so we left on our third morning.

We boarded a bus to Portland, Oregon, a city that we soon discovered had bridges and overpasses that went nowhere. They hung in the air like incomplete thoughts. The city had run out of money and they were left half-finished. The bus station had more black people milling about than I'd ever seen in one place in my entire life. The only black people I had met at that time were from Digby, Nova Scotia, and they were either working for the CPR hotels or in the Canadian military. I thought this Digby must have been be a pretty interesting place with all these African Americans coming from it.

In Portland everyone seemed preoccupied, buying tickets, rounding up their kids and paying us little attention. There was very little opportunity to interact – we were almost invisible to them – and so we focused on the map up on the wall. Lincoln City became our first choice for a jumping-off point on the coastal highway. We purchased our tickets and just watched the bustle of the crowd while we waited. We arrived in Lincoln City in the evening and found a small hotel nearby.

The next morning saw us hitching south from Lincoln City on Highway 101. We weren't there long when we got a ride with a young couple heading for San Francisco. The back seat was covered in numerous containers growing bean sprouts. We had to constantly duck around them on our way in and out of the car as they stopped often to take pictures and stretch their legs.

They were chiropractors who were as hard-core hippie as you could find. They were involved in faith healing and practiced the Japanese art of Reiki, which they explained to us at length. They extolled the virtues of the process and told us the secret was the transfer of universal energy through the palms and fingers of their hands, which allows for healing. They said it develops a state of harmony and equilibrium in your body. In hand placement, they said, they relied on an intuitive sense rather than a systematic or organized approach. The energy that was transferred was referred to as "ki."

This universal energy they were referring to has many names. For example, Rosicrucians refer to it as "vital life force," in the practice of yoga, it's called "prana," and in the Taoist performance of tai chi, it's referred to as "qi." Today, Kathy and I routinely participate in tai chi for exercise. But back then, Barb and I were clueless.

The couple seemed to be in no hurry to get to San Francisco. They also drove exceptionally slow, about 40 miles per hour, and once in a while they would pull off to let the traffic by. Although this was turning out to be an interesting introduction to hitchhiking, as we got farther into the trip, it started to resemble not something out of the *Heart of Darkness* but the "heart of weirdness."

Our ride with the couple came to a climax when we got closer to the state of California. At a cliffy point that overlooked the Pacific Ocean near the border, we pulled off into a large parking area and viewpoint. I think it was called, San Sebastian. Everyone got out of the vehicle.

Barb and I were content to stretch our legs and look out over the expansive ocean to the west. At one point, we looked back over at the couple standing by their car. That was when things really became bizarre. They seemed to be polishing the car with their hands. We walked over and couldn't help but notice that their hands were positioned five or six inches from the surface of the vehicle. This was strange, and I asked what they were doing. They said, "We are cleansing the car. We're getting rid of the jagged edges of sin." In explaining it further, the woman said, "We have to go through a stop check for fruit and vegetables and we don't want any negative energy around us to complicate things as we pass into California."

Off to the side, I looked at Barb. I couldn't believe what I was seeing and hearing, and I suggested to her that we part company with these strange people at the next town. We stuck with them, though, and finally stopped for the night at a campground in a state park where they set their tent up. We slept in the car.

They were nice enough to share their supper with us, which turned out to be a salad with lots of vegetables, lettuce and, of course, bean sprouts. We were not surprised to discover they were vegetarians. Throughout the dinner preparation, which she busied herself with, her partner wandered around, seemingly in a daze, peering at different flowers, which he plucked and closely examined. He seemed to be in a meditative state but was probably just effected by the marijuana he had consumed. Barb and I kept busy gathered firewood. The following morning at the first service station we stopped at, I loaded up on some junk food, to tide me over for the day. Both of us were hoping they would stop and take in the Redwood Forest, but they kept on going.

At a place called Leggett we left Highway 101. We stayed on Highway 1, hugging the coastline. Time slowed while the highway winded and tucked into each side valley, following the contour of the many rivers and streams that came down from the mountains. At Fort Bragg, we left the ocean and Highway 1 for the interior, travelling up a small highway, which climbed into the forested hills that lay between the coast and Highway 101. Why the hell they didn't stay on 101 all along was a mystery to me. Everything about this trip was becoming enigmatic and weird.

As we drove through the hills, I couldn't help but notice how primitive the rural dwellings were. The small villages along the way were like scenes from the movie *Deliverance*. Most of the buildings we came upon were vintage 1920 and 30s, right out of a Steinbeck novel. My biggest concern was that the car would break down and we would be marooned in this seemingly primitive culture. It would not be a healthy place to be a hippie, asking for help. Finally, to my relief, we got back on the 101 and continued south. Everyone else seemed to be oblivious to the potential danger of being stranded in the backwoods of northern California.

We also couldn't help overhearing our hosts' conversation. They were talking about putting thought-proof bags around bombs so that no one could detonate them, and something about flushing them down the toilet. I asked, "How do you accomplish something like that." They looked at me like I was an idiot.

He said, "With your mind, man!"

As we got closer to our destination, they started talking about a book that apparently appeared decades earlier but was first published in 1955. I asked him who wrote it. He said there was no author connected with it. It was written by celestial beings. He said it was found in a metal safe, although he seemed vague about the safe's location. I presumed it was somewhere in California. Where else? The book, he explained, described the structure and hierarchy of the cosmos and the three major realms of reality. He followed by saying that trying to explain it to us was like trying to convince someone who believes the world is flat that it's actually round. People just can't comprehend. He pointed out that the sky we see on clear nights is a living entity and that Earth is just a speck in it all. The book also explained the history of our planet, which he referred to as Urantia. What was particularly fascinating, he said, was our human history. According to him, Adam and Eve were sent to our planet to biologically uplift the human race, almost 40,000 years ago. It was too much for my tired little mind, but he referred to the book by name. I found a copy of it many years later.

Early that evening, they dropped us off at the corner of Haight and Ashbury, and we soon found a small hotel, happy to be on our own again. That night we searched out a nice restaurant, and I treated myself to a steak dinner. The conversation soon turned to our strange travelling companions. We both agreed they were a bizarre but generous couple that added a new definition to the term "Space Cadets." Even today I can't shake the encounter we had with them. It all seemed to be part of a bigger puzzle that I couldn't put my finger on, just confusing at every turn.

The next morning we took a bus to Sacramento and were picked up at the station by Barb's cousin who was a captain in the US Air Force. We spent a couple of pleasant days visiting them. They showed us around the capital and some of its beautiful parks. The only downside occurred when Barb's purse was stolen out of the vehicle at one of the parking lots we stopped at. We found ourselves at the Folsom County Sheriff's Office, filing a theft report. Barb was being fingerprinted as a means of identification, which she didn't submit to very well, much to the consternation of the officer in charge. She just couldn't relax. The next day we thanked our hosts and headed east.

We got a ride with a guy who looked like a fifty-year-old James Garner with his well-defined features, a slight puffiness to his face. He had black wavy hair combed in much the same manner, back on the front and sides with a couple of curls falling casually over his forehead. He was heading to Reno for a weekend of gambling. He was a pleasant source of conversation, asking us who we were, where we were from, what it was like in Canada. He also told us how much he enjoyed the atmosphere and excitement Reno provided. I thought, no doubt he enjoyed the presence of all those Kino girls. He told us how much snow fell in the Lake Tahoe area in the winter and that he often had to chain up to get to the casinos. I was amazed to find out how much snow fell this far south. It was May, so much of the snow was still there to see. He dropped us off at a casino he recommended and wished us luck.

We wandered through a maze of slot machines with their accompanying bells, whistles and alarms. Smoke hung in the air as stoic housewives cranked on the handles. Finally, we arrived at the reception desk and checked in for a couple of nights. Everything in Reno was cheap, outside of the gambling. Rooms, meals and drinks were almost free and soon we were trying our luck with the slot machines. We later wandered around the downtown core, taking in the bright lights, and bought tickets to one of the evening shows. I can't remember who the entertainer was but it was good show. After two days of observing this hedonistic lifestyle, we took a taxi to the eastern edge of town and got dropped off.

The fellow who picked us up was driving a blue Plymouth Fury, and he skidded to a stop 50 yards past us. We ran to catch up and got in. We were now going down the highway like a bat out of hell, with him fidgeting at the steering wheel, while his eyes darted about. He seemed pretty wired, and I was wondering what he was on. He quickly glanced our way and said, "Have you heard of the Mustang Ranch. Do you have them up there in Canada?" I naively said we had lots of ranches up there, both cattle and sheep and also wild horses, which we sometimes refer to as mustangs. "No, no" he said, "Whore houses." I said I'd heard of the "Chicken Ranch" if that helped and he said, "It's the same thing but down in Vegas." He continued in this agitated manner until he pointed south, to a couple of buildings off in the distance. "There she is," he said. We saw a dirt road ahead, leading off the highway in that direction. He dropped us off at the junction and tore off in a cloud of dust. We found ourselves left in "nowhere land" with very little traffic on the highway.

After an hour or so, two guys picked us up. They were both retired railroad engineers in their late fifties, heading to their cottage on Bear Lake south of Montpelier, Idaho. This was fortunate for us, as it was on the way to Yellowstone, our planned destination. The route from Reno to Yellowstone is convoluted, having numerous route options to choose from and no direct way. We knew it was going to be complicated to hitchhike there so we welcomed the ride with the retirees.

Now that we had a ride to Bear Lake, this would put us directly south of Yellowstone. They invited us to stay with them for the night in their Pan-Abode cottage. From their porch, they had a great view of the lake and the dry hills on the far shore. After a steak dinner and a few rounds of Canadian whisky, we continued to talk well into the night. They both enjoyed a drink of rye and bemoaned the fact that in the USA, all you could get was blended whiskeys or bourbon. They decided before we went to bed that they would be headed to Jackson in the morning. They hadn't been there for a while and wanted to do a day trip. It was on our way and we were glad of the unexpected lift.

The town of Jackson is located in the Star Valley, where over a thousand head of elk winter. Their grazing is subsidized with hay during the long winter months. In April the elk drop their antlers. Later, the boy scouts go out and collect them. The antlers eventually end up in the town in an open park just off the main drag. Here they are stacked into numerous piles and each pile auctioned off to the

Antlers piled for auction at Jackson, Wyoming.
DALE PORTMAN COLLECTION

highest bidder. Many of the customers are from Asia, a culture that has used antlers for medicinal purposes since the earliest times. The boy scouts got a substantial cut of the profits, so the exercise was very beneficial to them.

Jackson's a cowboy town, my kind of town, which still had hitching rails and saloons with swinging doors. Everybody looked western, sporting silver trophy buckles on their belts and wearing various shades of Stetsons. Boot-cut Levi Strauss blue jeans were popular, and Tony Lama boots, some with tall roping heels, were common. Spittoons were in evidence and the culture was vintage 1960s cowboy, with fights breaking out in the saloons like they were hockey arenas. We took it all in, and then we decided to hitchhike out of town the next day and head for Yellowstone.

Despite liking the town, my appearance was not conducive to the surrounding culture. I was sporting a black, well-trimmed beard and it was just long enough to make me look like I might be a hippie. (In fact, when I think about it, it probably helped us get that first ride

Our cabin in Banff during the winter of 1968–69.
DALE PORTMAN COLLECTION

on our trip south with the young couple.) As we stood on the side of the highway, every vehicle that passed seemed to be a half-ton truck and every second one tried to run us down. A couple attempts almost succeeded. One thing we quickly learned was cowboys in the 1960s hated hippies. Sporting a beard or long hair in this part of the country was a very bad idea, and I even had short hair.

We lost our enthusiasm for hitchhiking and walked back into town in search of the bus station. We got on one headed for Great Falls, Montana, and watched the Tetons and Yellowstone National Park pass by through the bus window. A couple of days later found us safely back in Banff.

MY GOAL OF BECOMING A PARK WARDEN COMES TO FRUITION

That summer, Barb went to work for the Mickles in Skoki. She then found herself cooking on the fall hunting trips. We spent the first half of the winter in Banff in a small, one-room log cabin. It was located across from the Luxton Museum on the south side of the Bow River and just down from the park administration building. It was sparsely furnished, with a table and a couple of chairs, a bed in the corner and a propane heater up against the back wall. Barb fixed it up and made it cozy to stay in. Neither of us was working, so we had a good opportunity to get to know each other and experience Banff.

In February Barb went to work in Skoki as a cook's helper to Donna, the chef, and they got along well. I spent my time travelling back and forth between Temple and Skoki on my days off as a lift operator at the ski hill. I also hauled supplies into Skoki by snowmobile, and it allowed the two of us more time together.

Once the season was over, I had to make a decision on what I wanted to do with my life. Barb and I had decided to get married. She wanted me to stay working for the Mickles and Timberline Tours. I saw no long-term future in that. I wanted to get a job as a park warden and felt I needed to start working towards that goal.

I went to Banff and talked to the town warden, Ed Carlton, about available work for the coming summer. I wanted to apply for a seasonal warden position, as a first step, but those positions had already been filled. He said there were still some fire-lookout jobs open. He suggested I put in for one of those positions, just to get my foot in the door. I took his advice and filled out a job application.

Not long after that I was offered one of the fire-lookout jobs. Just before I was to report for work, another job opening came up as an assistant seasonal warden in Lake Louise. Someone had turned down the position. I jumped at the chance and spent the summer in complete bliss, as it was a great opportunity for me.

We got married on May 10, 1969, at Temple Lodge, and Bert gave Barb away. We had purchased a trailer in the Lake Louise trailer court and settled in. We then followed that up with the purchase of a vehicle, a used Acadia Beaumont. We went for a short honeymoon to the Okanagan and then continued north through British Columbia, ending up in Jasper. We were both back in Lake Louise for the start of my job on June 1.

Barb, 1969.
DALE PORTMAN COLLECTION

The day we got married, the ski hill had already closed down for the season, but a Canadian Ski Instructor course was being run and the Larch Poma lift was operating for the students' use. One of the class participants was Kathy Calvert, who wondered at the time why someone would want to get married on such a gorgeous day for skiing. When our paths crossed in Yoho during the summer of 1975, she found out from Don Mickle that it was I who had gotten married up at Temple Lodge back then. She looked at me and laughed, "I wondered who the idiot was, getting married up there that day."

The summer position in Lake Louise lasted well into the fall, and I was hoping the government would find money to keep me on through the winter. When that wasn't possible, I was faced with two other opportunities, spend the winter either at the Ya Ha Tinda Ranch helping ride colts or at Rogers Pass, working for the Snow Research and Avalanche Warning Section (SRAWS) as an assistant observer. Barb was all for going to the Ya Ha Tinda while I was leaning towards Rogers Pass. I felt that the avalanche work would look better on my resume and better for our future. I already had a reasonable amount of horse experience under my belt. We spent the winter of 1969–70 at Rogers Pass, while Barb made the best of living in an apartment in a snowbound world. She eventually got a job working as a waitress at the Northlander Hotel, across the highway from the apartment complex.

SEVEN

ROGERS PASS

A SNOWFLAKE CHASER IN ROGERS PASS: 1969 TO 1971

When Barb and I arrived at Rogers Pass for my six-month position, we were given an apartment to live in. We had very little furniture so it seemed pretty empty. That was the beginning of November 1969, and TV had not made it to this isolated outpost in British Columbia. Helping out with the monotony was a library in the basement of each apartment block. Both Schleiss brothers, who ran the avalanche operation, were voracious readers. Walter (my boss) was into science fiction, while Fred was into westerns. Louis L'Amour was his favourite. Hence, one of the apartment libraries was full of westerns, while the other was crowded with science fiction.

There was a lot of community spirit back then, and you always had a bingo game or whist tournament going on in the evenings. Most employees worked ten-day shifts and got four days off. Very few took them off in Rogers Pass, especially during the winter months. The saying back then was that Revelstoke or Golden, depending on your preference, was the asshole of the world and Rogers Pass was 50 miles up it. Most people on their days off made a trek to somewhere where there was a TV. One fellow, Reg, a snowplough driver, took his family to Calgary at every opportunity and checked into the Blackfoot Inn. There they watched TV and ordered in food.

Barb and I still had our trailer in Lake Louise, which was only a couple hours' drive east on the Trans-Canada. I worked a strange schedule. In a two-week period, I had a five and two followed by a four and three. We usually headed to Lake Louise on the week with three days off and stayed at the pass on the two days off. As the winter progressed and the snow piled up (and it does a good job of it there), you felt the cabin fever creeping in. By March we were looking forward to some kind of spring, which was always tardy in the pass. When the job terminated at the end of April, it seemed to me the snow had not receded a centimetre. We both made the best of our stay there, and we returned for a second winter in the fall of 1970.

At the end of the first season, I competed on an eligibility list for seasonal park wardens and placed reasonably well. And so, on June 1, when I returned to Lake Louise as an assistant seasonal warden, I was informed that the list had been activated. I was being transferred to Jasper.

The second season was made easier by Donny Mickle's arrival and a two-year stint working for Peter Schaerer and the National Research Council. He was there to take snow readings and set up devices that tested the power of the huge avalanches that came down. Another responsibility was conducting watercourse sampling throughout the Selkirk Mountains.

What helped augment our social life was an army canteen that was open twenty-four hours a day. I think back then it was mandatory for the army to provide an outlet for their men's confinement. It was also an outlet for us civilians, although we had the lounge in the Northlander Hotel to gather at, too.

There were a number of us who had started together as seasonal wardens in various parks. After our first season there, Bob Haney and Gord Peyto got permanent positions as park wardens in their respective parks, Bob in Jasper and Gord in Glacier National Park. The

Bob Haney skiing down from Mount Fidelity.
DALE PORTMAN COLLECTION

other wardens that first season were Randy Chisolm and Hans Fuhrer.

Randy, Hans and I returned for a second season. I was fortunate that Hans stayed for the winter before moving on to Jasper the coming spring. He really helped me improve my skiing. Watching him glide down through the deep snow, displaying so much grace and finesse, made me wonder if I could ever get to be half as good as him. He took the time to give me instruction, always reminding me to bend my knees and ski from the waist down. He had a movie camera and often filmed the group skiing together. This helped me make the necessary corrections. There was too much movement in my upper body. We carried heavy daypacks while working there, and that complicated our skiing technique. However, the heavy packs soon forced me to quiet my upper body movement. By the time I left, I was a pretty good powder skier.

A highlight of the job was getting a chance to make some turns in the deep powder off the summit of Mount Fidelity. Weekly trips up Mount Abbott every Monday to take weather readings and dig a snow pit were always perks we strived to be part of. We often had to use avalanche probes to locate the roof of the cabin and then dig down to its door. After lunch, we would dig a snow pit to ground level and examine the snow's different layers, taking readings and measurements. Many of these pits could be up to 5.5 metres down as we moved deeper into the winter.

The destruction of avalanches has been a problem in Rogers Pass throughout its history, and those who fought to mitigate avalanche threats in the early years had poor results. It wasn't until Noel Gardner arrived that this started to change. But along with his vision came a certain underlying volatility that he brought to the work environment.

A COMPLEX MAN OF VISION

Noel Gardner was the first to see the coming tide of social change in the Canadian Rockies. He was a cowboy with a ranching background, whose family spread extended along the south bank of the Elbow River north of Bragg Creek. Today the Boy Scouts of Canada's Camp Gardner bears the family name. He was the son of Clem Gardner, a world-class bronc rider, who along with Guy Weadick's dream, and financing from the big four ranchers (Pat Burns, George Lane, A.E. Cross and A.J. Maclean), created the Calgary Stampede in 1912. Clem was its first all-round champion.

Noel was well-known for being hard-nosed with staff, especially those outside his realm of authority. You would have thought the Schleiss brothers (Fred and Walter) would have had to put up with the same strict demands from Noel as everyone else, but that wasn't the case. Noel respected them because he knew they brought a great deal of knowledge from their work in the European Alps. He also had a good relationship with other old country guides such as Bruno Engler and Hans Gmoser.

He was born in 1913, the year the CPR started construction of the Connaught Tunnel in Rogers Pass, which was built to reduce the threat of numerous avalanches that threatened its route. These avalanches drew Noel to Glacier National Park and the work that would become his legacy.

He arrived in the mountains in the early 1940s and took up guiding dudes on horseback into Skoki for Lizzie Rummel. In the winter he often packed in supplies on skis with a big pack. He was also attracted to the lifestyle the mountains offered. Working in here also provided an opportunity to put some distance between him and his hard-as-nails father, who tried to mould Noel to his particular liking.

After that first busy summer, he had nothing to do and so he focused on learning how to ski. He ended up at the Sunshine ski hill near Banff and met Bruno Engler, who had recently arrived in the country from Switzerland. Bruno had landed a job teaching skiing there. He taught Noel how to downhill ski and then introduced him to ski touring. He was a strong and focused student who picked up the sport quickly under Bruno's tutelage. He eventually became a ski instructor, as well. The two of them were often seen ski touring together, and Noel absorbed all that Bruno passed along about avalanche awareness, route selection and safe travelling tips.

Don Mickle, who had worked for Noel, told me a story from that period. Lizzie Rummel (who was managing Skoki at the time and well-known in the Banff area) asked Noel to haul a woman out because of an injury. When he got her to Temple Lodge, she asked how much she owed. Noel looked her up and down and said, "How much do you weigh?" She was initially shocked by the enquiry then puzzled by his response. "I charge by the pound!"

For several summers, he continued to lead dudes and packhorses at both Skoki and Assiniboine. Now that he had acquired superb winter travelling skills and was a solid horseman, it wasn't long before he decided he wanted to become a park warden. He succeeded in 1948 and was stationed in Glacier National Park.

In the early winter of 1948, the head of the Swiss Federation Institute for Snow and Avalanche Research, Dr. Marcel de Quervain, came to Canada. He was the leading figure in avalanche research in the world. He was travelling across the country by train and arrived in

Glacier National Park to examine the avalanche problem the CPR was facing there. It's assumed he met Noel there. De Quervain commented on the snow profile chart he spotted on the wall of the building he was visiting. It was amazing to see such a remote location and so far ahead of its time, especially in a country trying to develop a new avalanche research capability.

Noel was a big man with a strong personality and a fearsome look, who tended to dominate those around him. He had a stern temper and, with his physical build, was an intimidating presence, which helped him get his way. This was especially apparent with his supervisors who were always being challenged by his rogue vision and strong personality. He was a freight train of will putting his ideas into action, which often led to rubbing people the wrong way, especially his peers and superiors. He saw the need for a rescue capability within the warden service long before anyone else did, particularly in avalanche rescue. This fascination with snow and avalanches set him on an important research path.

He conducted his first warden avalanche awareness course in 1951, by gathering five recruits to Glacier National Park where he drilled them with classroom lectures on the dangers of avalanches. This was followed by strenuous basic ski exercises on local slopes, near the CPR station. When these men originally joined the warden service, none of them were prepared for this aspect of the job, but they were also aware of how such training would help them in their future careers.

Noel was committed to the idea of wardens becoming involved in rescue scenarios that he felt would inevitably become the parks' responsibility. In this, he was considerably more far-sighted than some of his superiors, which must have been frustrating for a man of his temperament. He realized the task ahead was going to be monumental, and the training required was far beyond the scope of the small, yearly ski schools. His ultimate vision was to bring the district wardens to a high level of competence in rescue and skiing ability so that, should the need for a rescue party arise, they would be competent as second-party leaders. It would be Noel, though, who would be making the decisions at all times and be in command of the situation. He wanted effective support from these men in leading and conducting search and rescue operations. In this he had the backing of his park superintendent.

His courses increased in size throughout the early 1950s, and Walter Perren, who was working on a contract at the time, assisted him. Walter was never able to work easily with the more forthright, tempestuous Noel, even though Walter was a quiet, easy-going and patient man. The two men differed on where the rescue program should head, as well. Noel wanted most of the training to revolve around skiing and avalanche work while Walter knew that general mountaineering skills would soon be required. Noel, I think, was seeing a rising star in Walter and grudgingly had to accept it.

It was fortuitous that in 1954, Noel had this to say, "Ski and snow craft training for field personnel has made a fine start and will, I hope, go on to a fitting conclusion." He also committed to the next advance in the avalanche training program, which needed to include general mountaineering. However, he acknowledged it would have to be taught by someone more experienced in the field than he was. On the eve of Walter being hired by the Canadian Park Service, Noel realized he could not do both jobs. He quit the warden service and moved on to a job with the Department of Public Works where he focused on avalanche research.

The CPR had built their railroad through the pass in 1885. It ran through a corridor of avalanche paths that was often referred to as the "gauntlet through hell." It was this route that the Department of Public Works (DPW) highway planners were now looking at. Noel was tasked with finding the safest route through this treacherous terrain and into that he poured his heart and soul.

To alleviate as much of the threat from the "white dragon" as possible, the CPR had built a number of avalanche sheds over the worst stretches. Of particular concern to DPW was the stretch where the Connaught Tunnel protected the tracks. The highway would be forced to take a more exposed route through the pass, across some of the worst avalanche paths in the country.

The Connaught Tunnel had been built because of a devastating tragedy that occurred in 1910. It was unparalleled in the history of avalanche accidents in Canada. The circumstance surrounding the event is worth telling.

On March 4, 1910, a small slide came down from Mount Cheops at around 6:00 PM, forcing a large crew out to clear the tracks. Throughout the night, the crew worked in the midst of a huge snowstorm that steadily increased the hazard above. In the middle of the night, the crew heard the ominous rumble of an avalanche. Sixty-two men died that night and the CPR had no choice but to take drastic measures in their battle with the snows of Rogers Pass. In 1913 they started construction on the Connaught Tunnel in an attempt to eliminate 5 miles of snow sheds and 21 miles of track. Like the Spiral Tunnel, it was an engineering miracle that was completed in 1916.

NOEL'S RELATIONSHIP WITH MONTGOMERY ATWATER

The new program in Rogers Pass caught the eye of the US Forest Service in Alta, Utah, and they invited Noel down to attend a week-long avalanche course. It led to a meeting of two great minds on the subject of avalanches in North America.

Alta, Utah, became the centre for avalanche research in the United States because of the great amounts of snow that fell there. It also had a past. The ski area – previously an old mining town – inherited a history laden with miners killed by avalanches. The US Forest Service hired the first "snow ranger," who was given the responsibility of observing avalanches and collecting weather data. In 1945 Montgomery (Monty) Atwater arrived in Alta and got a job as a snow patroller. He stayed to pursue this new career, influencing not only fellow researchers in the United States but those in Canada, as well.

Noel accepted Atwater's invitation and came down for the course. Atwater would go on to say that it was amazing to discover someone from Canada who was doing the same important work on avalanche research. They got along well and many discussions went well into the night. Monty was so impressed with Noel and his operation that he invited a team of Canadians to come down and attend the course the following year. On returning to Canada, Noel passed the invitation on to the park superintendent of Banff.

The wardens chosen to take part in the course in Utah felt they had something to prove. The best of the best were picked: Jim Sime, chief park warden of Yoho; Bert Pittaway, assistant CPW of Banff; and Tom Ross, a park warden who was a very good skier and instructor from Jasper. They went with the expectation that they would use "spit and polish," be courteous (our national trait) and dignified and create a favourable impression of the Canadian Park Service. In accordance with those expectations, they were issued a previously recommended olive-green uniform, and as Sime said, "We were all decked out like a million dollars." They stood out immediately on the slopes of Alta not just with their uniforms but also for their style and ability. In fact, their new instructor, Monty Atwater, to test their mettle, put them through the wringer.

Atwater later wrote to the director of the Canadian Park Service, J.A. Hutchison, saying:

I hope you won't mind a little human interest story about these men. When they first appeared at Alta I recognized them by their uniforms. They were, of course, complete strangers to the area and everyone present. I took the opportunity to introduce myself to them, make them welcome and at the same time form some estimate of the kind of man Canada has as snow rangers. I suggested we take a little tour together of the ski area.

Snow conditions were a bit difficult for anyone unused to the heavy snowfall of Alta. The terrain I chose was the steepest and roughest we have, and I set the fastest pace of which I'm capable. You will understand that I thought this would be as good a chance as I'd have to "get my bluff in first," as we put it. The course was as familiar to me as it was unfamiliar to the

Canadian snow rangers. If you are a skier yourself, you will realize how great an advantage this gave me and I exploited it fully. Some of the other instructors who saw this performance later accused me of most unfair tactics, and they were justified. Nevertheless, no matter how I forced the terrain, every time I looked back, those Canadians were right on my tail. I knew then that your National Park Service was going to be well represented, and it was.

It was a good start for the two nations in their cooperation on snow research and avalanche control. And it has carried on to this day. But mountain rescue and avalanche research have taken different paths in North America. Avalanche research in the United States was a stepchild of the Forest Service and not a particularly welcome one, either. Hence avalanche research there has never had the whole-hearted support of the federal sponsoring agency. In Canada the federal agency in charge, the Canadian Park Service, took on the responsibility with enthusiasm.

Canada was now starting to become a major source of avalanche research, slowly garnering a credible international reputation. Many, who admired the facilities at Mount Fidelity near Rogers Pass, came to observe, while others came to learn. Monty Atwater was one who came to observe, for he envisioned the research being developed there. As he later wrote in his book, "The area of critical danger in Rogers Pass is 50 miles (80 kilometres) long, within which Gardner identifies seventy-four avalanche paths. Through this gauntlet of snow slides, the Department of Public Works proposed to push a four-lane all-year highway. All things considered – the density of traffic, the extent and severity of the hazard, the design of the highway – Rogers Pass qualifies as one of the most difficult problems in avalanche control ever undertaken. It is certainly the best researched and the most elaborately defended."

Noel and Monty had a friendly and professional relationship and respected each other's work. They had no desire to compete but to complement each other to further our knowledge of avalanches. As my generation, in their university years, contemplated Sartre and Camus, when these two got together around a table, they often contemplated a snowflake while sipping Irish whiskey.

Noel had his detractors back in Canada, amongst them some Canadian Park Service staff and management. But amongst the European mountain guides, he was always held in high regard. There was something about Noel that was agreeable to the Germans. He had little patience with senior management, who on occasion tried to stifle his creative and scientific mind. This led to well-documented encounters with his superiors. This was Noel's Achilles heel. He had a problem articulating his ideas and vision to Ottawa.

Art Judson, a snow ranger with the US Forest Service and a long-time friend, recalls arriving at the station on Fidelity for the first time. "There was someone doing ground breaking work in avalanche forecasting up there.... I was impressed with what I saw. He had a first class system. I have never seen anyone integrate snowpack profiles with weather patterns." He also remembers a man who was obsessed with avalanches. "He thought snow 24 hours a day, often waking up in the middle of the night with new ideas on research techniques."

DON MICKLE'S DAYS WORKING FOR NOEL

Don Mickle worked for Noel in the early 1960s, and he provided me with numerous stories about his experiences working for the man. Actually, he worked for all three of the men who had a major influence in developing avalanche research and forecasting in Canada: Noel Gardner, Peter Schaerer and Fred Schleiss. Don's father, Bert, knew Noel Gardner. They had grown up together as neighbours, and it was Bert who got Don a job with Noel at Rogers Pass. Upon receiving the job offer in the mail, Don wrote back immediately that he would accept. It was good money in those days and better than cutting fence posts for the winter near Millarville, like he had done the past few winters.

He was told to supply his own ski boots and they would supply the skis and skins. He had no clue what skins were, but he picked up some

Snowcat at Flat Creek, destination Mount Fidelity.
DALE PORTMAN COLLECTION

ski boots at the Hudson Bay Company store in Banff for $10 and headed for the Mount Fidelity parking lot, 15 miles west of Rogers Pass. He was picked up in a snowcat and taken up to the Mount Fidelity Research Station, high up on the mountain, where he had an opportunity to settle in.

The next day he was told they would ski up to the top of the mountain to the Round Hill weather station to take some readings and go over some of his duties. The next morning, his bafflement over what skins were was solved when Noel produced a pair to put on his skis. Don was handed a pair. The fur on the skins lay flat in one direction so that when they were strapped on to the skis, they could slide forward easily but could not slip backwards. Copying Noel, he soon had his skins on and they set off.

At the top he was quickly run through his duties, which included maintenance, taking snow measurements and weather readings. Then, offhandedly, Noel pointed to a skinny, 45- to 50-foot-high pole that had some revolving cups sitting on top. He instructed Don to climb the pole and clean the frost rime out of the cups. This was a test and Don knew it, and he had no choice but suck it up and head up the shaky pole. When he got to the top of the rickety thing, he really didn't appreciate the magnificent view he had of Schuss Lake off to the north, 2000 feet below. He was more concerned that his weight and the wind might snap the fragile pole. His perch at the top was precarious, and now he had to let go with one hand and try to clean the wind cups while hanging on with the other. This was a terrifying move and to accomplish the manoeuvre, he had to stop the rotating cups with the side of his face and use his free hand to get rid of the hoar frost. He was never happier to get off something in his life; a bucking bronc was a piece of cake compared to this.

Thinking he had survived the worst, he was then confronted with the ski down. I know personally that Mount Fidelity is not the place to learn to ski. The dope slope at a ski area is far better than acres of steep, untracked powder that takes the added art of equally distributing and balancing your weight on each ski. To stand, move and float down a steep slope in deep snow involved finesse that was well beyond him at this point. This was long before the arrival of fat boards, which has made powder skiing so much easier to catch onto.

When Noel started taking off his skins, Don asked if he should, too. "It's up to you," he said as he skied off. The fog rolled in, and all Don could do was follow his tracks down the mountain. He fell continuously and struggled to get back up on his skis each time in the endlessly deep snow. When he got to the bottom, he was exhausted, steam was coming off him from all the exertion and he looked like a snowman. He fell a lot that winter. Noel's wife, Gladys, took pity on him and decided to teach him how to ski.

As Don settled into his routine duties, he came to know the people he was working with, including Fred and Walter Schleiss. Unlike many others, he candidly remembers Noel as a really charming guy – really interesting to talk to. He also discovered that Noel loved to teach and, as such, he learned a lot about the avalanche program and the principles of avalanche behaviour. Noel came from the school of hard

Mount Fidelity Research Station.
DALE PORTMAN COLLECTION

knocks, reflecting on his childhood and his difficulties with his father, so he did not pamper people. He was tough, he had a temper, but he was fair. However, if you earned his wrath it was best to hide or be somewhere else. His nickname behind his back was "Old Snowflake," and he had a lot of power in terms of what was going on in the park. Don said people jumped when he said jump. He also felt that Noel was good to Fred and Walter, and he respected their skills as men of the mountains.

One humorous episode occurred that winter. Don was chewing tobacco in those days and he wasn't too careful about where he spat the excess. One day Noel said he had to take the dog to the vet in Revelstoke as he was having bowel issues. Don thought nothing of it but Noel was getting pretty concerned because it hadn't cleared up on returning from Revelstoke. When he took the dog to the vet a second time and, on returning, pointed out the most recent example of the dog's excrement to Don, Don became alarmed. He suddenly realized Noel had mistaken the tobacco juice for dog shit. In quick fashion, he quit chewing tobacco and the dog's bowels miraculously cleared up. He vowed never to reveal a word to Noel.

TALES ABOUT "OLD SNOWFLAKE"

Another humorous story that involves Noel's dog was an often-repeated one amongst North American avalanche personnel who would get together at international avalanche workshops. I indirectly got the story from Tim Auger, who in turn got it from Keith Everts, who worked in Rogers Pass. Tim said:

Anytime I'm swapping stories with other avalanche people who may not have heard this, I always have to truck it out. It's such a classic. Noel is up at Mount Fidelity and it's a dark and stormy night gripped in the jaws of a major blizzard. There is someone else there with him.... They're drinking Irish whiskey and playing cards...most likely crib. Noel has his dog there. It was a little mutt with long hair that looked like a mop without a handle. In the middle of this session, Noel calls the dog over to him. The dog comes over and Noel tips his chair back and scoops up the dog. Then he leans over and pulls the door open, heaves the dog out into the blizzard, closes the door and plays the next hand of cards – just like that. A few minutes later there is a whining and whimpering at the door, he opens it and the dog comes scampering in. He slams the door against the howl of the wind and the curtain of snowflakes, picks up the dog again and puts him in his lap. He reaches over the other shoulder to a shelf, gets his hand lens [magnifying glass], leans over and takes a closer look at the dog's back. Then Noel sits back and makes the pronouncement, "Yep...dendrites!" (It's a scientific term for star-shaped flakes of snow.)

Walter Schleiss who recalled Noel's encounter with a grizzly bear near Schuss Lake one summer told the following story to me. Noel's little dog caught the scent of a grizzly bear and took off to investigate, with a concerned Noel looking on. The meeting between the two animals was an obvious mismatch, and the mutt decided it was time to return to the safety of his master. On seeing this unfold, Noel immediately headed for the closest tree and started scrambling up it. He was making difficult progress through the maze of limbs but was aided by fear, adrenaline and a puckered sphincter. Suddenly the bear had him by the leg. He managed to shake loose from the bear's grip but not before he received lacerations to his leg and a significant bite on the heel of his foot. Finally, he got up far enough to be out of the bear's reach. The bear eventually got bored and ambled off. After a while, Noel cautiously climbed down and headed back up the steep slope to the research station. Warden Jim Sime recalled picking Noel up at Flat Creek and taking him to the hospital in Golden. Jim waited in the reception area, and finally the doctor came out and on seeing Jim, came over and said, "Jesus, Jim, you need to go back up on the mountain, you need to go back there and get Noel, you brought the wrong one in."

Jim chuckled saying, "That's how ornery Noel could get." Actually, one observer compared his crankiness to a "she cougar giving birth to a roll of barb wire."

When the Department of Public Works gave Gardner the responsibility of developing an avalanche safety program, it did so with the stipulation that an engineer should be involved designing and developing avalanche defences along the proposed highway. A Swiss engineer by the name of Peter Schaerer, destined to start the ball rolling on "Scientific Avalanche Research" in Canada, was loaned to DPW. Peter was a slight, gentle, easy-going man, who was a total contrast to the boisterous Noel. Again, personalities clashed. Much like his countryman, Walter Perren, Peter displayed a quiet self-confidence, tackling his work with single-minded determination. He had a great capacity to accommodate those around him both as teacher and mentor, always with an attitude of deferential politeness.

Noel, by contrast, was a tough taskmaster – a loner who grew restless with the confinement and restrictions of government bureaucracy. His moody disposition and independence often led to confrontation with his superiors, and he bridled at the position Peter had in his work at Rogers Pass. With Fred Schleiss in a position to take the reins from Noel in the avalanche program, Noel looked for greener pastures. He was an initiator and instigator but never designed to be a team player. That was not in his DNA. He eventually moved to Wyoming, bought a ranch and took up the position as chief avalanche forecaster at the well-known American ski resort Jackson Hole, located in the shadow of the Grand Tetons.

PETER SCHAERER: THE AVALANCHE SCIENTIST

Peter Schaerer was born in Berne, Switzerland, in 1926 and graduated as a civil engineer from the Federal Institute of Technology in Zurich in 1950. One of the courses he attended at the university was snow mechanics and avalanche control, taught by the world-renowned snow scientist Dr. Robert Haefeli. He had a strong interest in ski mountaineering and had taken courses in that field to hone his travelling skills. After graduating, he served as research assistant with the professor of road engineering at the Federal Institute of Technology. He carried out tests on snow removal and ice control on roads. His work brought him in contact with the Snow and Avalanche Research near Davos, where he acquired a good knowledge of snow physics. In 1965, while visiting his brother in Ottawa, he learned that the National Research Council was looking for snow researchers. Two months later he had a job in Canada.

According to Peter they offered him several projects, but the one that interested him was working on the avalanche control program at Rogers Pass. And so began his illustrious career in Canada. It was capped off in the autumn of his life with the Order of Canada.

Peter remembers his first discussion with Noel about snow. "On my second day at Rogers Pass we were out doing a snow profile, and Noel asked me what methods we used to forecast avalanches in Europe. I thought – what methods? We did not have a system. I realized quickly how things should be done." Until then the transfer of knowledge travelled north–south between Canada and the United

States instead of east-west from Europe. Though Peter recognized the value of the work Noel was doing, he soon learned at this stage of their work that little could be done to mitigate the avalanche hazard along the proposed route of the highway. So in consultation with Noel, he made adjustments to the location of the proposed Trans-Canada Highway wherever possible, as well as the size and location of the concrete snow sheds that were going to be put into place.

FRED AND WALTER SCHLEISS

During our working hours, we observers and assistant observers conducted countless patrols along the highway, observing downed avalanches and recording their size and frequency. The rest of the time we tediously recorded telemetry data and transferred it into huge books. My boss was the Austrian Walter Schleiss, the brother of Fred Schleiss who ran the Snow Research and Avalanche Warning Section up at Rogers Pass. Walter was the easy-going one, but you never wanted to take advantage of that. He had a memory like an elephant. Fred was a firecracker who had the potential to blow up one minute then forget all about it an hour later. As a group, we seemed to continuously test the patience of them both.

On New Year's Eve that first winter, I tested Fred's tolerance to the limit and felt his wrath first-hand the next day. Because of my Polish background, I had a collection of ethnic Polish jokes that I could draw on. I felt it was warranted from a self-deprecating standpoint, and I never hesitated to roll one out when appropriate. Fred's wife Edie was Canadian, as was Walter's wife Jerry, and when Edie found out I had a repertoire of Polish jokes she dared me to tell a few but convert them to Austrian. By now I'd had a few drinks, and with flawed logic, I thought that was a pretty good idea, so I indulged her. There was great applause from everyone, especially Edie who always wanted one more. I was certainly in the mood to oblige. I ended with, "How do you know an Austrian has been through your backyard? Your garbage cans are tipped over and your dog's pregnant." Everyone contributed to the uproar over that one, except for Fred, of course.

I woke up the next morning, my head feeling like cotton, wondering how the hell I could have done what I'd just done. When I got to work that morning, Fred was there to greet me. Not many words passed between us, but they were to the point. I never left the office for a month. I spent my penance recording telemetry data while gazing longingly out the window as the boys loaded up the Suburban for another ski trip to gather avalanche information and snow data. It was early February before I got on a day trip up Mount Abbott and a chance to enjoy a nice ski down.

Fred could be a hard taskmaster, and you sometimes felt like you were in the Hitler Youth with all the mistakes we were reprimanded for in our first season and the standard we were supposed to uphold. He was from an alpine nation with a great mountain tradition, and he had brought that culture to Canada. All of them had. They felt they were above Canadians when it came to the mountains, and they were probably right. Even so, it was easy for us to resent the superior overtones. We eventually came to realize that we had a lot to learn. Today, I look back with gratitude for and fondness of what those pioneers from the old world taught us.

Fred had come to Canada in 1956 from Austria and settled in Jasper for a few years, teaching skiing and ski racing to the local kids, as well as honing his climbing skills in the summer. A couple of years later, he sent for his brother Walter, telling him he should come to Canada as there was a position available for him at Rogers Pass. Soon Walter was working for Noel Gardner, as well. Both Schleiss brothers got along well working for their new boss. There was mutual respect, and the brothers learned not to challenge Noel on his ideas.

Back in the late 1950s, howitzers were being looked at as a means of bringing avalanches down before they got too big and threatened the highway. Trials were carried out using 75mm and 105mm guns, with good results. Because of the consistent positioning of the howitzer at the various gun placements, a set of bearings and elevations could be recorded for each placement and target. With this established, the gun could be fired with a high level of accuracy during storms without

A 75 mm field gun at a gun position near Rogers Pass.
The weapon was a relic from the Spanish Civil War, which dates back to 1936..
DALE PORTMAN COLLECTION

the targets needing to be visible. This also allowed them to shoot at night and during storms. The weapon of choice became the 105mm howitzer, and artillery crews from Shilo, Manitoba, were assigned to spend their winters stationed at Rogers Pass.

As noted before, Noel quit in 1965 because of the volatile and toxic work environment he'd created with his superiors, and Fred was hired to replace him. Fred stated that avalanche forecasting at the time wasn't an exact science, and one man had to make the final decision – it was not arrived at through committee, although Fred often consulted with Walter. Predictions were arrived at half through science and half through intuition, or by the seat of your pants. The goal in developing avalanche forecasting was to eliminate as much of the subjective component as possible even as you remained appreciative of that inner voice.

Fred observed, "I always said forecasting was 60–65 per cent technical and the rest intuition. Now I would say personally [when] I was in my prime and I went out a lot in the field – this is one thing that is very important – I would get to 80 per cent, I would think at times. When I was a manager and not able to get out into the field as much and spent more time in Revelstoke, I lost a lot of that feel, and it came down to 65 per cent, which was definitely accurate but I would normally say with most forecasting, if it's not done on the right lines...it's 50/50."

One factor that was always a concern for any boss in government back in the 1950s and 60s was protecting your turf or someone else would poach it. A lot of energy was expended by managers in the Canadian Park Service doing what was referred to as "empire building." There was a tendency among managers to try and enlarge their spheres of influence, to increase their responsibilities, for the sake of ego, power and more money. It usually had nothing to do with effective management. Fred found himself challenged in such a work environment. The general works manager, who oversaw snow removal and the maintenance of equipment, wanted control of the avalanche program, and a power struggle ensued between the warden service, which Fred worked under, and general works. He found himself caught in the middle.

During his first winter as the boss, Fred found managers around him jockeying for new territory, especially that general works manager, now that the hard-ass Old Snowflaker was no longer there. In the other mountain parks, wardens had been working in avalanche safety for a while now. The skill set brought to the table with a highway maintenance background was not consistent with grasping and grappling with the subtle and elaborate world of snow physics and avalanche forecasting. There was a noticeable tug of war going on between the warden service and general works as to who should manage these responsibilities. To balance out the workload, senior management decided that SRAWS should be under the control of the general works manager. This was becoming a huge challenge for Fred.

According to him, it was January 6 or 7, 1966, when the roof of his trailer blew off. It was at night and he was in bed when the wind hit. When he got to his office, he found the wind measured 160 kilometres per hour. Walter had his crew out on an avalanche shoot that night.

He had reasonably good success but with a real tempest blowing and with no visibility, they decided to close the highway. They shut both east and west ends, but there was still traffic caught between the gates. The only thing they could do was send a warden in a truck through to sweep the highway. A half-hour after closing the highway, an avalanche came down just west of the pass. Without knowing where the cars were, wardens had to assume a vehicle might be caught in the slide. In desperation, they called out all available staff to search the deposit. Wardens set up roadblocks on either end to prevent anyone from ploughing into the frozen wall of snow. The wardens had their hands full parking oncoming traffic in areas safe from other slide paths. The pass was still under the onslaught of high winds and heavy snowfall. Meanwhile, the searchers probed the deposit, which had crossed the highway and run partway up the other side of the valley. All were aware that fresh snow was accumulating in the nether regions of the steep slopes above.

All of a sudden, Fred spotted a front-end loader and grader heading to the slide. He was alarmed and demanded on the radio, "What the hell are you guys doing out here?" He found out the wardens had let them through. Fred asked the wardens why they had let the machines through and the response was, "Well they have the authority [general works] to go through to plough slides and make that important decision." Their foreman had sent them out. Fred retorted, "Nobody gets to go through the check points out here – there's danger of another slide!" After failing to reach the foreman on the radio or anyone with authority in general works, he jumped in his truck and drove to the compromised road block. He yelled at the wardens, "Look, I don't care what, nobody goes through!...and I want those two guys off the slide." As he turned back towards the site, he could hear the low rumble, as haunting a sound as you can get in the mountains, especially that night. With a sinking feeling, he radioed to his own crew to get off the slide path. They had pre-established an escape route and they followed Fred's cry of alarm – all except the two machine operators who had no escape plan and no communication with those who had. They were both hit by a wall of snow and killed.

It was unfortunate that it took an accident like that before Fred got the authority to run his own operation. After that he had the say-so over both general works and the warden service when it came to operating his avalanche program. From that point on, Fred dictated when and where things happened and inveigled the warden service to operate the roadblocks. With the authority of a badge and the National Parks Act through the warden service, he had the necessary staff to enforce closures and keep unauthorized people out of danger. That left general works to plough snow, fix graders and maintain the park's buildings and facilities.

A FREIGHT TRAIN OF AN AVALANCHE

One incident that winter stands out in my mind. I was an assistant observer at the Lens gun position on a storm shoot. It was a typical night shoot with the Canadian Army. The gun location was about a hundred yards up the road from the Lens avalanche shed in the middle of the slide path. It was not originally located in direct threat of being hit by avalanches but over the years the path had been widened by these large slides until the gun position was exposed. The practice at night was to shoot the gun and then everyone remain silent, as the only indication that the shot was successful would be the sound of the muffled detonation high up on the mountain and possibly the subsequent avalanche. Because it was so dark and the danger involved, everyone's senses were heightened. We had no idea how far the slide would come or if it would come at all.

The first audible sound in the encompassing darkness was the woof of the exploding shell. After a short, indeterminable time, the next sound we heard was the distant bellow of rushing air, followed by a slight hint of stirring trees higher up. At this point we started to run. A low rumble followed and we could hear the sharp sound of snapping branches. On this last revelation, we put our heads down and ran like hell for the protection of the shed. All I could think of as I ran was whether we had lingered too long at the gun site and missed the subtler sounds of the impending avalanche. When we got to the shed I had a sense of exhilaration that we had cheated immi-nent death. Suddenly, there was the sound of the avalanche roaring overhead, like a freight train. When we got back to the gun position we found everything covered in snow and pushed around like Dinky Toys. That summer, Fred relocated the gun position farther up the road, out of the path of the slide.

MISSING THE MOUNTAIN

I remember one particular avalanche shoot when I was in the back seat Fred was driving and Walter was in the passenger side. The army corporal had just passed on to the gunner, the elevation and bearings to the gun crew and the necessary adjustments were being made in preparing and sighting the gun. When all was ready, Fred gave the OK to fire and with a big bang, off the round went on its way. In the truck, we listened closely but heard nothing. The gun crew checked their settings and they were off just enough to miss the mountain. Then a call came on the radio asking, "What the hell is going on?" A round had exploded near the caller, much to the alarm of those working on the highway located on the other side of the mountain.

Fred looked at his brother and said, "With a goddamned army like this, Walter, I don't know how we lost the fucking war." They forgot I was sitting in the back seat. It was pretty funny telling it to everyone afterwards.

On a more serious but humorous note, this next story needs to be told for its visual setting. Both Fred and Walter liked to park in the middle of the slide path during a shoot to observe the avalanche coming down and then drive away at the last moment as it approached. They were there for scientific observation, but it was also like playing chicken with the avalanche. On one occasion, Fred was alone while he observed the slide coming down. In his fascination watching the wall of snow rushing down, Fred realized he had lingered too long. In his haste to leave, he stalled the vehicle. The truck was suddenly buffeted around and covered in snow, and Fred found himself trapped in his vehicle. He got on the radio and excitedly let the dispatcher know his predicament and his location – followed by, "Please hurry!" After a short time, a road foreman approached Fred's truck and opened the driver door to confront a shocked Fred. The truck had only been hit by the windblast from the avalanche, which left a wet layer of snow, several inches thick, coating the entire vehicle. Fred sheepishly stepped out into a normal, snowy and overcast day. To him alone it was gorgeous. After that, he ordered vehicles with automatic transmissions.

HOW TO GET A JOB IN AVALANCHE WORK WITHOUT KNOWING HOW TO SKI

There was a guy who went to work for Fred who had no skiing ability but who really wanted to work for SRAWS. Don Farrell was better suited to be a desk clerk then an avalanche technician. Just before he went for his job interview with Fred and Walter, he borrowed someone's skis in town. After the lifts had closed, he climbed up the Revelstoke ski hill and found himself well above the Nels Nelsen Ski Jump, at which point he took off on his borrowed skis, rocketing towards the uplift of the foreboding jump. After hitting the lip, he sailed through the air, in a most un-aerodynamic fashion, like a wounded duck being shot out of a cannon. When he landed, or should I say hit, there was an explosion of used ski apparel and snow. Out of this carnage, he suddenly popped up like jack-in-the-box, slapping his extremities. Gratefully acknowledging that he hadn't broken anything, he collected his gear and walked down to the parking lot. At the interview the next morning he was asked by Fred if he knew how to ski and Don Farrell said, "Hell, I've jumped off the Nels Nelsen Ski Jump." Fred was so impressed he hired him on the spot. Fred had done some ski jumping back in Austria and knew the skill and courage required.

We called him by his last name, Farrell, and he did some goofy things over the years while working for SRAWS. More for the entertainment value than anything else. I was witness to the following well-repeated story about him. Farrell was the observer at the Ross Peak gun position while Fred and Walter were headed to Flat Creek to pick me up and then they planned to head back to the gun position.

No one could shoot until the Canadian Pacific passenger train passed and they had final clearance from Fred. Farrell was sitting in his truck while an army corporal was observing the railroad tracks from the top of a large snow mound. Fred asked Farrell to let him know as soon as the train passed. Suddenly he got word from the spotter that a train was coming. Farrell speaking into the radio mike said, "265 to 261 on A channel, there's a train coming – 261 to 265, what kind of train?"

So Farrell poked his head out the truck window and yelled to the spotter, "What kind of train?"

The spotter yelled back, "A choo-choo train."

So Farrell got back on the radio and said, without hesitation and possibly tongue in cheek, "It's a choo-choo train, Fred."

I had just skied down from Mount Fidelity, and Fred was picking me up. As I was putting my skis in the back of the Suburban, I hear Fred's reply, "Look, you fucking idiot, I need to know whether it's a freight train or the Canadian passenger train. What's wrong with you?" Then while I climbed into the back seat and Fred was no longer on the radio, he looked at Walter and filled the cab with blue smoke. You could imagine all those descriptive adjectives and verbs coming out with a German accent; Farrell's ears must have been burning back at the gun position. It was right out of Colonel Klink and *Hogan's Heroes*. It must be noted, SRAWS had their own "A" channel frequency that the rest of the park had no access to, you didn't have to be so discrete in your choice of words, although as proper radio protocol it failed miserably.

Years later I was attending an international snow science and avalanche symposium in Revelstoke, held at a local hotel, and the desk clerk was none other than Don Farrell. A bunch attending the symposium wanted me to tell them the story of Farrell and the choo-choo train. I told it and then said, "If you want to meet the guy just go downstairs and check out the desk clerk. That's him." Farrell got off work at 8:00 PM and I invited him to a social gathering in one of the rooms. He was a huge hit with this mixed group of scientists, technicians, avalanche forecasters and mountain guides from the Western world. He captivated them for hours with his own unique take on working for Fred and Walter Schleiss in Rogers Pass.

THOSE BIG WET ONES

After I left Rogers Pass, Don Mickle spent one more winter working for Peter Schaerer and the National Research Council. It was the heaviest winter for snow on record, both in the Selkirks and the Canadian Rockies. He remembers one of the worst storms, which brought down a new slide at Cougar Creek. "It had never been down before – there was one-hundred-year-old timber up there. It was amazing." The huge avalanche came down and covered the highway as well as the railroad tracks on the other side of the valley. Don shuddered, remembering that he and Paul Anhorn had just been there the day before, taking measurements from an NRC snow gauge, thinking it was one location they did not have to worry about. Because the slide was natural and not the result of a stabilization shoot, there had been no road closure in place, so once again, there was no way of knowing if any vehicles were buried. One of the wardens, Gordon Peyto, was freed up to help Don check the slide for vehicles. Before they arrived, a cat operator had been cleared and sent down to begin the removal process. The operator, happy to see someone else in his lonely vigil, came down on foot to meet them, leaving the machine on top of the slide, now some 6 yards above the road. There was also a CPR crew working to clear the railroad tracks across the way, and they had their hands full.

They began searching with a magnetometer (for detecting metal) when to their horror they heard the timber cracking and snapping well up the creek valley, trumpeting the rushing onslaught of another slide. The three men stared at each other for a brief moment of paralyzing panic, and then they realized the slide deposit was over 900 yards wide and they were in the middle of it. Fortunately, only the small amount of dust from the windblast settled on their shoulders, sparing them the wall of wet snow above. All they could feel was relief

Gord Peyto on a ski trip in Kluane National Park.
DALE PORTMAN COLLECTION

as they listened to the groaning of the compressed and tortured air within the slow-moving beast above them. It came to rest about a hundred yards away.

Gordon immediately shut down all work on the slide. Anyone buried would have expired by now, and it was now too dangerous to search. They retreated to the sanctuary of the Northlander Hotel at the summit of Rogers Pass. On arrival they were unceremoniously received by a pack of angry motorists trying to get through the pass that night, not enthralled by the delayed journeys. The two men were both so pumped full of adrenaline from the slide experience that when a kid's toboggan accidently fell over, they both nearly jumped through a window. Since they were now off duty, they ignored the crowd, changed shirts and made their way to the hotel bar.

Everyone working in Rogers Pass at one time or another had a close call with avalanches. Everyone had stories; whether it was the speed plough drivers or grader operators, snow flake chasers or park wardens, hog heads on the CPR trains or the crews that kept everything running. It was a tight-knit group that united under the aegis of the avalanche. For me it was immersion into metric measurement, the study of snow and the mystery surrounding avalanches that kept me there. Watching them come down on a clear day was like seeing a white symphony of power and motion. The slides evolved as you watched the airborne snow, billowing out as it expanded down the face of the mountain. Avalanches were often backdropped by azure skies while dark stands of age-old spruce and fir lined the way. They were captivating events.

I remember one huge wet avalanche, much like Don and Gord experienced, slowly move down onto the highway, displaying so much mass and energy, groaning and moaning like a drugged animal. A wall of snow inched onto the road and crept across only to encounter a guardrail, constructed of solid posts and metal – that rail burst like buttons on a shirt. Slowly the mass settled into a frozen wall of depleted inertia.

EIGHT

EARLY JASPER

AMETHYST LAKE AND THE TONQUIN VALLEY

When I arrived in Jasper after my first winter in Rogers Pass, I was one of three park wardens transferred from Banff. It was all part of a reclassification of our positions and a subsequent promotion. I stayed; the other two weren't happy with their work situation and transferred back to Banff. I got assigned a backcountry district for the summer while they got stationed in the townsite, which neither of them wanted. They were accepted back in Banff with open arms and even kept their new job classification. They were much maligned in Jasper and that bad feeling seemed to linger for some time in the park's glacial memory. Even though I'd done nothing outstanding or meritorious, I was welcomed warmly when I decided to stay. Jasper always played second fiddle to Banff. Being the first national park in Canada, Banff always seemed to get most of the attention and money.

What helped in my decision to stay was being assigned to the Tonquin Valley. I had a great summer that year working for Toni Klettl. When Barb came up to visit on some of my days off, we would often get together with Toni's four kids – Linda, Howie, Loni and Robbie – for some pickup baseball. Their mother Shirley often joined us. She was a stay at home mom, which was pretty common then, with four kids to bring up. I remember she was also a very good baseball player with a good arm and an even better glove hand. They lived at a rural station, about 12 miles south of town so there was lots of room to play. It was the Cavell District, which included the Tonquin Valley, Amethyst Lake, as well as the Whirlpool Valley and historic Athabasca Pass.

The summer went by quietly. I found myself checking fishing licences, patrolling the trails and supervising the campgrounds. This included hiking up into some of the basins, checking on the caribou herds. I would sometimes head over to the Alpine Club of Canada hut near Eremite Valley – the Wates-Gibson Hut – to touch base with the hikers and climbers there. There were several trails in that area, and it received a lot of visitors. The campgrounds were busy throughout the valley, and I visited them often. I got to know the people who ran the two small fishing lodges on the lake. They both had horse riding concessions and brought their guests in on horseback.

One day Doug Lamond showed up on the porch with a group of people looking for the campground. The mosquitos have always been bad in the Tonquin and he had a cloud swarming around his head, probably staved off by copious amounts of repellent. He had come in with his clients for a few days of climbing, so I invited him over for coffee. When he got everyone settled in, he dropped by. It was nice to have some company for a change, have someone to talk to, even someone I meagrely knew from the past. I caught up on his solo backpacking trip up the Clearwater and how the cat made out. He asked me if my singing had improved. We had a number of mutual friends, which kept the conversation lively and animated. I lost touch with him when he moved Atlin, BC, near the border with the Yukon.

Amethyst Lakes has some of the best rainbow fishing in Jasper, and it was a big draw for the clients staying at the two lodges. Coming off Mount Clitheroe in the early summer are numerous small streams and brooks that are fed by melting snow. They are perfect for the rainbow to spawn in. You could see the females in the clear water, ripe with eggs, swimming upstream as far as possible then laying their eggs on the gravel beds next to their male counterparts who would fertilize them. These big males, four and five pounds each, deeply rich in colour, couldn't be missed as they flashed by, displaying their prominent hooked noses and red sides.

ANOTHER AUSTRIAN BOSS: TONI AND THE KLETTL FAMILY

The summer went by quickly and my boss, Toni Klettl, came in on a couple of occasions for a visit to check on things. He was a mentor to many young wardens in Jasper throughout his career. He and Warden Gordon McClain took many of us under their wing and guided us along. They made sure we felt welcome at various government parties and functions. If you needed a question answered or advice on a park matter, they were there for you. At the time Toni was involved in mountain rescue training during the summer and avalanche forecasting in the winter. He often assisted the alpine specialist for Jasper, Willi Pfisterer, in teaching us the skills we needed to become good team members on search and rescue operations.

The first thing I noticed about Toni was he had a heavy accent, and I found him hard to understand early on. He liked to tell a good story – embellished a bit by his enthusiasm – but it was often challenging for him to make his point. My favourite all-time Toni story is the one that took place up the Whirlpool valley. He told it to Al Stendie and myself one night in the Athabasca Hotel. His story went like this. He arrived at the Middle Forks Warden Cabin up the Whirlpool valley in the summer, and he found camped nearby seven beautiful women and they were all nymphomaniacs. How he knew that I have no idea. But the oldest woman was the most stunning of all and he also told us how nice her breasts were. He didn't say it in a lewd manner, but respectfully, commenting on her beauty. What stood out about her, though, Toni said, were her steely blue eyes. Then he said, out of the blue, "I will always remember them for they resembled Hitler's when he gave me my Iron Cross."

This story was so remarkably exaggerated all Al and I could do was look at him in stunned disbelief, not sure we even understood it because of his heavy accent. I wondered if he really thought we believed him or if he was telling us a Jim Bridger whopper to shock us. Hitler and the Iron Cross were doable but seldom would you run across anybody up the Whirlpool, let alone a beautiful woman with six companions. The only thing I could think of was he did it for the shock value, to test our gullibility and amuse us at the same time.

Jim Bridger, the legendary American frontiersman and fur trader, was famous for telling outlandish stories to perfect strangers. One of his best was being chased on horseback by one hundred Cheyenne warriors who managed to trap him in a box canyon. At this point Bridger went silent, just like Toni would often be after telling his stories. Bridger intentionally did it, sucking his listeners in until one would finally ask, "What happened next Mr. Bridger?" Jim would reply, "They killed me." Then he'd laugh like hell.

With Toni, sometimes you thought he had ended his story and you missed something. So, you would bring your own story forward and start telling it. When you finished and without blinking, he would continue with his story from where he had left off as if you had said nothing. I often felt like an idiot when that happened.

Toni was born in Neukirchen, Austria, in 1927, the youngest of seven children. All of them had faced extreme hardship and poverty growing up during the Depression. There's no better training ground for a war than hardship and adversity. Joining the army seems the best way to escape for some, but in the end, it often merely extends a hard life. In 1944, at seventeen, he joined the 6th Mountain Division and found himself on the dreaded Eastern Front, fighting the Russians. He said he was part of a commando-style unit that was involved in some historic battles. Towards the end of the war, his division was stationed in Finland, part of the Axis army fighting the Russians. They eventually retreated into Norway where they surrendered to the British forces.

Toni immigrated to Canada and became one of the first Europeans to bring alpine skills to western Canada. Despite carrying the bitter burden of war, he embraced his new surroundings and the prospects it provided, opening his heart to this new country. He thrived and flourished in the fresh freedom of his new land. He started out by working as a logger in various lumber camps across Canada. He eventually got a job as a powder-man, working on the Trans Mountain Pipeline, which was being built through Jasper at the time. He soon met Shirley, and they settled down to raise four kids.

He joined the warden service in 1955 in Jasper and became a true pioneer in the field of mountain rescue, avalanche safety and conservation. He made many innovations and lasting contributions to the outfit. His years as a backcountry warden in Blue Creek, the Tonquin Valley and the Whirlpool were according to him, "The best years of my life."

He was comfortable with everything the job tossed his way. He had solid wildlife-management capabilities and superb travelling skills, on skis, snowshoes or horseback. He was a strong mountaineer with mountain-rescue leadership skills and ran the avalanche control program at Marmot Basin. He was a very capable all-round warden and a committed family man.

Toni was also a wood carver or "whittler," and I have three of his carvings in my home today. He carved the animals he loved, the grizzly bear, the cougar, the elk and the bighorn sheep. They were prized by many locals and countless individuals across the country, and many ended up being sent to various people around the world.

Shirley and Toni's four children grew up with an incredible and unique childhood and a fierce addiction to open spaces, solitude and wilderness. Something I also had the privilege of experiencing.

TOM AND FAYE MCCREADY AND ATHABASCA PASS

Part of the extended Cavell District was the Whirlpool valley and Athabasca Pass. This was the route the fur traders crossed at least twice a year – spring and fall – carrying the beaver pelts they had acquired in New Caledonia, which is now British Columbia. They travelled by canoe up the Columbia River and from Boat Encampment they made their way by land over Athabasca Pass to Henry House, near the present town of Jasper. From there they continued by canoe down the Athabasca River. Trips were made in both directions, at least once in the spring and once in the fall. It was also a route employed by others in getting over the mountains. It was a rough trail over tough country, which could be hard on both horses and men. There is evidence that dog sleds were also incorporated crossing the pass during the winter months. I saw the pass for the first time with Tom McCready and his wife Faye. Tom was working for the warden service at the time, and we were sent to clear the trail of winter deadfall. Faye was excited to see the valley again, getting a chance to sleep under the stars and nodding off to the soothing sound of horse bells in the meadow near the pass.

Tom was an outfitter from Jasper, short in stature but big in reputation and respect. He was kind and helpful individual while his attractive wife Faye was personable and complementary to his life. She raised three children, two girls and a boy who grew up in a mountain environment that provided the foundation for interesting careers later. Chrissie joined Loni Klettl, Toni's daughter, on the Canadian Alpine Ski Team. Todd became a heralded helicopter rescue pilot that our generation of park wardens came to trust and admire for his skill and sound judgement.

Tom had spent his whole life in the mountains around Jasper and the Wilmore Wilderness to the north. He got his start as a teen working for his uncle, outfitter George Hargreaves. Years later he put together his own string of horses and started his own outfitting business. Seven of those horses were willed to him on George's death. Faye and Tom spent all their summers out on the trail. In the winter, Tom ran a ski school at Marmot Basin with his business partner, Joe Couture. He eventually sold the business, retired and built a beautiful house in Jasper, turning it into a popular bed and breakfast. In his later years, he worked for a well-known outfitter in the area, Eddie Regnier. Temporarily working for the warden service was the perfect solution for Tom to get out on the trail, and Faye would often be by his side.

On this trip, we left the Meeting of the Waters, an old fur-trade name for where the Whirlpool enters the Athabasca, and travelled with the horses in a stock truck up a gravel fire road to Moab Lake. The lake was as far as public transportation was allowed. From the gate, we continued up valley until we arrived at Tie Camp Warden Cabin, located at the end of the road, a distance of about 6 miles. There we unloaded our duffel, camping gear, tack, food and horses. We had six head comprised of three saddle horses and three packhorses.

Once we were packed up, we followed the trail into the bowels of the timbered valley dominated by giant Engelmann spruce. It wasn't long before we had the chainsaw out and removed a large tree that was across the trail. One and a half miles farther on, we passed Tie Camp. This site was built in the early part of the century. There were still several rotting log buildings scattered about and even an old wooden boat. It was here that the timber was harvested, then floated down the Whirlpool into the Athabasca River and retrieved at Jack Ladder about 7 miles east of town. There was a mill set up at the location, and the logs were cut into railway ties for the new railway construction.

By late afternoon, after a 7-mile ride, we arrived at Middle Forks Warden Cabin. It's located in a manmade clearing that held a countless array of plants, lush enough to make you think you were in British Columbia. The open area was dominated by false hellebore standing four feet tall and cow parsnip towering even taller. These plants verified that we were in a moist habitat, and though the cabin had seen better days, it was a welcoming sight for us. There was little grass about so the ponies wasted no time hobbling up the trail a ways to a meadow next to the river.

We spent two nights there, sharing the cabin with a pack rat that we finally dispatched after numerous attempts. Besides enduring the pungent odour emitting from his nest on the upper bunk, his droppings were everywhere. He had to go. The rat was cornered in the woodpile rack along the inside wall. To force him out into the open, Tom had a mop handle that he was pushing in and out of the space between the wood and the wall. He wasn't looking at the woodpile but

Scott Flats looking west with Tom and Faye McCready.

at me, wondering when I would verify if he was having any success in this effort. Every time he pulled the handle out, the pack rat was standing on it. He must have done this three or four times before I could stop laughing and let him know what was happening. It wasn't long after that we finally succeeded in discouraging the rat's attempts to make the cabin a home.

With Faye along as cook, Tom and I enjoyed some great meals and all it cost us was the cleanup afterwards. We spent the following day cutting trail as far as we could up valley and then returning that evening to a great steak dinner. We packed up the next morning and headed out. We had cut as far as Scott Flats the day before so we made good time and arrived there after a couple of hours. These gravel flats are in a magnificent setting that provides spectacular views of the Scott Glacier and the Hooker Icefield.

Near Ross Cox Creek at the start of the flats, in a stand of thinned timber, which edges onto the gravelly dryas vegetation, we found an old cabin built with square-headed nails. A team of surveyors under

Walter Moberly erected it in 1872. The roof had rotted away and fallen in long ago, but the walls were still standing. We didn't linger long as we still had 6 miles of cutting to complete before we got to Kane Meadows and our planned campsite. A few miles past Scott Flats, deep in a forest of mature timber, we crossed the river to the other side of the valley. It got so heavy with deadfall we had to leave what we could step over or ride around, figuring we would clean it up on the return trip. If we had tried to clear it all, we would not have made camp until well into the evening.

Kane Meadows is named for Canadian artist Paul Kane, who travelled over the pass in November 1846 with the fur brigade headed west. He spent the winter and summer on the west coast, painting the coastal Natives, then in October 1847 he left Boat Encampment for the Athabasca Valley, on his way home to Montreal. Throughout his epic trip, he detailed the landscape and the Native peoples who inhabited it. In innumerable paintings he etched their features, their impressive clothing, and their everyday life. Later he wrote one of the most fascinating of Canada's early travel books, *Wanderings of an Artist*.

We set up camp near a small clump of trees in the meadow not far from a silt-laden creek coming off a glacier, high up on mythical Mount Hooker. The location provided us with spectacular scenery in every direction, with abundant firewood and fresh water close by. It would be our home for the next four days as we hacked and cut our way to the pass.

After a hearty breakfast the next morning, Tom and I headed out on foot with a can of gas, the chainsaw, saddle axes and bagged lunches. We left Faye behind with a good book as we battled our way towards Committee's Punchbowl and Athabasca Pass. It was 5 miles to the summit and the trail was ill defined in places with lots of boggy stretches and the biggest stand of Engelmann spruce you could imagine. The canopy, though, was less dense than you would expect, providing enough light to allow all kinds of shrubs and plants to flourish. It was a botanist's heaven. As we neared the pass we were cheered on by many small meadows, brilliantly covered in a host of wildflowers. Radiantly red, Indian paintbrush; yellow, heart-shaped arnica; tall, bodacious, blue and purple larkspur, along with the muted blue fleabane – all competed to cover these small clearings. They even infiltrated the forest floor, encouraged by a warm and sunny summer.

It was slow going, as we sweated away well into the late afternoon until we ran out of gas and had to return to camp. That night we sat around the fire, and Tom entertained me with some stories of his early years in the mountains. He was tremendous axe-man, and I think prouder of that skill than his reputation as a gentle and sure-handed horseman with stock. His axe was always sharp, and he often honed it at night around the fire, immersed in meditative thought.

Of the many tales he conjured up for me over the years, the one he told that night around the cozy fire stands out. He was a young man in his late teens working for George Hargreaves and they had left the Tonquin Valley with a couple of clients for Athabasca Pass. I think he was trying to emphasize that back then there was often no trail to follow and you had to cut your own way to get anywhere. (Much like what we had gone through over the last few days with the big exception that we had an old trail to follow.) They had nothing more than a Swede saw and, of course, their trusty axes to make their way through unchartered bush. What we were doing here was minor compared to what they had to endure.

Their route was over Tonquin Pass into the upper reaches of the Fraser River in British Columbia and then south up to Fraser Pass. From there they dropped into the densely timbered Hugh Allan Creek before heading east again up to the Alberta boundary at Whirlpool Pass. Once there, they travelled down the middle fork of the Whirlpool to where it meets the main fork near the present-day warden cabin at Middle Forks.

I can't imagine anyone taking horses over Fraser Pass then down into Hugh Allan Creek and then coming up over Whirlpool Pass. Many years later I hiked up the middle fork of the Whirlpool and over the pass with a bunch of mountaineers from the Grizzly Group.

Tom and Faye McCready in camp at Kane Meadows.
DALE PORTMAN COLLECTION

I discovered Whirlpool Pass to be one of the most rugged, timber-choked, moss-covered, rock-strewn place in the mountains. It had the makings of an ideal place to break a leg – human or horse.

Tom said that one of the main challenges on the trip was finding a place to camp with horse feed nearby. When they did set up camp they would go off and cut trail for the remainder of the day. They cut all day, returning to camp at night, exhausted. They would repeat this every day until they found another suitable campsite, hopefully before the distance between the two camps became too great. They would then move everything up to the new site and repeat this leap-frogging up and down the valleys.

Inspired by Tom's tale, the next day I returned to the job of clearing trail with renewed vigour. We again enjoyed the small meadows cropping up here and there, as we inched towards our goal. Finally, we broke out of the timber about half a mile from the pass. We had a traditional drink from the Committee's Punchbowl, toasted our efforts and saluted the fur brigade of bygone days. I went over the pass and looked down Pacific Creek into British Columbia and the lush vegetation it harboured. The fur traders called the route down "La Grande Côte" (The Big Traverse). I felt sure it would be an awful trip to Boat Encampment, beating your way through dense masses of trackless timber.

The next day I hiked up to Canoe Pass, directly behind our camp, while Tom and Faye had a day in camp. It provided me with grand views north towards Fraser Pass and the jungle of trees choking the valley of Hugh Allan Creek in the foreground. To the south I got a clear view of Mounts Hooker and Brown. Hooker to the east was the more spectacular with the Hooker Icefield tumbling down towards our campsite. On the way back I reflected on how much I had enjoyed the trip with Tom and Faye, who for me now symbolized this rugged and wild land.

It was a splendid time reliving the history of the fur-trade days in the evening, but it was finally time to return to Jasper. This wouldn't be the last trip I spent with Tom. Years later, he would accompany Kathy and me on a number of commercial horse-supported hiking treks in the Jasper area with outfitter Ed Regnier.

"I'M GOING TO HAVE HER HIDE HANGING ON MY WALL." – PERCY GOODAIR

While stationed in the Tonquin Valley I became intrigued by a story from the past. The warden cabin in the Tonquin is located on a shallow bench overlooking Amethyst Lakes. It was built in 1965. The old cabin sat on Maccarib Creek at the edge of a long meadow that stretched as far up the valley as Maccarib Pass, almost 4 miles away. Not far from the old cabin site is the grave where Warden Percy Hamilton Goodair is buried. It sits on a hillside north of the cabin with a view looking east towards Maccarib Pass. Through his cabin log and diary entries, we know that Percy was fatally mauled by a grizzly bear on September 12, 1929.

Percy was born in Preston, England, in 1877. After a British military career, he came to Canada, settled in Jasper and became a park warden. His district was Amethyst Lakes and the Tonquin Valley, and he was a member of the Jasper Park Masonic Lodge, number 143. He loved his district and took pride in maintaining and looking after one of the most beautiful places in the world.

Throughout that fateful summer he searched for a grizzly bear that was causing damage to his cabin when he was away, either patrolling or out on days off. He wanted her hide hanging on his wall as payment for the harm she was inflicting. It was the grizzly that won out in the end.

He was cutting logs for his winter fuel supply on September 12. The trail to the logging site was up a hill, and he was probably travelling with his head down and making little noise as he approached his work site. The four wardens who found his body filed a report that suggest Percy probably turned off the trail and walked into the bush to reach his work site. It was likely there that he met the bear. She had a cub, which made her automatically defensive and protective. It had to have been a sudden encounter, for he had no opportunity to climb a tree or lie down in a submissive fashion. They were probably too close to each other to allow the sow to get her cub out of harm's way.

The report assumed that Percy was left with few options but to stand, face the bear and hold his ground. It appeared that he tried to fend off a blow from the grizzly by raising his right arm to protect his face or to ward off the strike. He took the strike to his chest just under the armpit, exposing some of his ribs and severing an artery. The bear seemed to have left him on the ground and ran off with her cub while he lay prone. Before leaving, she put claw marks on the side of his neck, on his lower jaw and along his chest. But the worst was under his arm where her claws had severed the artery, causing him to bleed to death. He tried to staunch the flow of blood by using a sash he often wore around his waist. He attempted to reach the cabin located about 490 yards away but after 30 yards, he knew it was over and he met his death with solemn dignity. He laid down on his back across the trail, crossed his arms and waited to meet his maker. The *Edmonton Journal* reported, "…He closed his eyes and died as he had lived – a man."

On September 26, four wardens – two of which were Frank Bryant and George Wells – rode in looking for Percy as it had been a while since he had reported in. As they approached the scene, there was little evidence of the attack as the land was covered in fresh snow. It was Wells's small dog who found Percy's body lying under a foot of snow. Three days later they had a Masonic burial near his cabin that was attended by sixteen of his brothers. Six months before, in a reflective mood, he had made a request to his fellow masons that if he should die he wanted to be buried here in the Tonquin Valley, overlooking the Ramparts and Maccarib Pass. At the head of his grave were placed the words of Robert Louis Stevenson:

Under the wide and starry sky
Dig the grave and let me lie.
Glad did I live and gladly die,
And I laid me down with a will.

This be the verse you grave for me:
Here he lies where he longed to be;
Home is the sailor, home from the sea.
And the hunter home from the hill.

The *Edmonton Journal* summed the man up saying:

He is buried, as was his wish, on the hillside north from his cabin. The summit of Maccarib Pass and the gigantic mountains of the Tonquin Valley that he loved so well can be seen from the grave.

Jasper Park has lost one of her best wardens, an honest, out-spoken, conscientious man who was devoted to his duty, and carried out the meaning of all regulations to the best of his wonderful ability.

The wardens have lost a brother and a friend, who has raised the standard of the service of his actions, conduct, and the plain fact that he was a member of the service.

An old timer, a gentleman and a man has gone from our midst. We miss him and mourn our loss.

What makes this event even more interesting is that on September 12, 1992, a grizzly in the same area mauled two tourists from Britain, a man and his wife. He was killed while she was left seriously injured and disfigured. Both attacks happened not far apart. It occurred on the same date, September 12, while the years are reversed from 29 to 92. Percy Goodair and the fellow mauled were both from Preston, England, and they were both Freemasons. It certainly makes you wonder about the two events.

POACHING PATROL IN THE BRAZEAU DISTRICT

My season in the Tonquin Valley ended early in September, so they sent me to Poboktan Creek. It was a larger warden station with a few houses, an office and an enclosed garage/work area. The wardens called it "45" as it's located at Mile 45, south of town on the Banff–Jasper Highway. I arrived with two weeks' worth of grub and was immediately shown my saddle horse and two packhorses. The food I had with me was for two people, and the fellow I was going to be working with stepped forward and introduced himself. His name was Jim Macintyre and he informed me he had never been on a horse before so everything was going to be new to him.

After he was assigned a saddle and a horse we left early that afternoon and trucked the horses and gear up to Camp Parker, a few miles south of the Columbia Icefield in Banff National Park. It took a while to get our gear sorted out and our packhorses loaded. I knew very little about the trails in Jasper outside of the Tonquin District and nothing about this part of the park. Jim had just recently arrived from Prince Albert National Park in Saskatchewan, and he knew even less than nothing about the country.

A half-hearted attempt was made to explain where the trail went over Nigel Pass (we found out later there were two trails) and how it dropped into an open river flat and that the trail was to the right. The

Brazeau District Warden Cabin with outbuildings.
DALE PORTMAN COLLECTION

Poboktan warden said you can lose the trail once you come off the pass. He also said that we should head for Isaac Creek where we would meet up with Wardens Alf Rabbis and Norm Woody. The instructions were helpful, and at the end of the flats, we crossed the stream and entered the trees, as the terrain dropped down into a side valley. We eventually came across a cabin (Four Point) that was near the trail junction for Jonas Shoulder. Its porch was a superb place to have a late lunch as the cabin sat on a grassy bench, overlooking a good portion of the valley. Because of our late departure, we had to decide whether to stay here or carrying on to the next warden cabin on the Brazeau River.

After a quick bite to eat, we decided to keep going. It was 10 miles to the Brazeau Cabin. Most of the trip was spent in the trees. The trail crossed to the south side of the valley for several miles, which provided some nice views from a couple of big meadows. We finally crossed back to the north side, into a dark stand of spruce and balsam fir as dusk settled in. The trail was now hilly and windy, with jumbled, rock-strewn stretches as it skirted an extended section of canyon.

While working our way through the rocks, the night arrived suddenly, and I gave my horse his head as he picked his way along the bony trail.

We were forced to cross the north fork of the Brazeau River in the dark. I could only put faith in my saddle horse to know the way. Shortly after, we arrived at what seemed like a trail junction, and my horse swung sharply to the right and soon approached a gate. Off in the distance was a welcoming light coming from the Brazeau Warden Cabin. As we approached, Bob Barker, the district warden stepped out onto the porch and welcomed us. Once we had unpacked and unsaddled our horses, he instructed us to turn them loose in the pasture. We were told his wife Barb had supper on.

It was a big cabin, the largest in Jasper, and it was well laid out with a dining area, a long counter that ran across the front wall with cabinets above and below and a double sink in the middle. In the middle of the cabin was a wood-burning Ashley heater and the cook stove. Past the heater was an open area with a bunk. The woodpile and the water stand were all set up against the west wall. Opposite on the east side next to a window was a table with four chairs.

Behind the heater and stove was a plywood wall, cutting the cabin in half with another similar thin wall separating the back area into two bedrooms. After washing the dishes, we sat down with Bob so he could explain what had happened and why we were here.

Apparently, two poachers, each carrying a sheep head on his back, had been spotted well inside the park on Isaac Creek by Warden Norm Woody. It was around 11:00 AM when he saw them crossing the dry creek wash a hundred yards above him. Norm was on horseback; the poachers were on foot. On realizing they had been spotted, the guys took off running into the bush with Norm in hot pursuit. Somehow the poachers slipped away.

Norm related the incident to Bob via the forestry phone that night. The day before, Bob had spotted footprints inside the park, heading up Aztec Creek, which provides access to Isaac Creek over a high pass. He followed these tracks up into the rocks near the head of the valley but lost them in the barren terrain. There was no doubt in Bob's mind they belonged to hunters trying to access the sheep habitat of the upper Isaac Creek valley. The creek enters the Brazeau River near Arête Warden Cabin, halfway between Isaac Creek and Brazeau.

After hearing Norm's report, Bob headed out the next morning and rode the provincial side of the Brazeau River, checking out the different outfitter camps. One of the people camped along the river was Dennis Weisser, a conservation officer with Alberta's Fish and Wildlife out of Hinton, Alberta. He told Dennis the circumstances surrounding the poaching, and before long Dennis had a provincial helicopter on site and Bob and Dennis were flying up Isaac Creek. In a sheep basin on the north side near the upper end of the valley called Sawtooth Basin, they spotted ravens. On further examination, they found two sheep carcasses with heads and capes missing. Then, they saw a large, cube-shaped rock that would have been the perfect blind from which to shoot the sheep. Here they found six shell casings from a 30.06 rifle.

At Jerry Verhegge's outfitting camp Dennis seized a sheep head. There was no sign of the other head, but one of the weapons seized was the guide's 30.06 rifle. Both guides at the camp were charged under both provincial and federal regulations. Also removed from Sawtooth Basin were the two sheep carcasses. Most of the investigative work was now left in Dennis's capable hands.

After Bob's lengthy briefing, we went to bed and left in the morning for Isaac Creek, getting there in the late afternoon. We were slowed by Jim, who often had to get off his horse to walk and stretch his legs. He had been issued a very ill-fitting saddle, one that fit the horse but not him. The seat was too small for his stocky size and thick legs, and his thighs were forced tightly up against the front swells of the saddle. This eventually resulted in bruising and much discomfort. Any trotting put him in ever-increasing pain, so I maintained a slower than normal pace. He was in noticeable discomfort when we got to Isaac Creek. I had to help him off and I suggested he head into the cabin and let Norm, Alf and me deal with the horses, which he quickly agreed to.

Morning came early as Norm was accustomed to getting up at

4:00 AM to get the stove going and the coffee percolating, while lighting his first cigarette of the day. He said the rattling of the pots was unfortunate but I think he intended to roust up some company. That way he would have someone to sit around the fire with, smoking, drinking coffee and waiting for dawn to arrive a couple of hours later and provide enough light to go out and get the horses.

One of the things we brought in for Norm was a can of Export tobacco and some rolling papers for which he was very grateful. I later found a can, partly full of used cigarette butts. He must have realized he was going to run out and started saving his butts. Alf told me later that he ran out a few days before we arrived and he had started taking the butts apart, salvaging the unused tobacco and then re-rolling. Then he ran out of papers and settled into being a grumpy old warden suffering from withdrawal.

Bob said our job would be to head up Isaac Creek and install a fly camp near the head of the valley with close access to Sawtooth Basin. There were a few basins that needed to be explored while there. Bob wanted us to keep track of the sheep and where they were located and look for any further sign (footprints, horse tracks, etc.) of additional poaching. Until the case wrapped up, they wanted us up there. Woody and Rabbis were heading out to the highway over Poboktan Pass as their shift was over. Barker was going to leave his family at the Brazeau Cabin and move up to Isaac Creek for the next several days and conduct day patrols out of the cabin, keeping track of the hunting camps on the provincial side. Jim and I soon found ourselves headed up valley with our fly camp gear, food and duffel.

We departed early the next morning, leaving the cabin clean-up to Alf and Norm. The trip was uneventful, and when we got to a willowy meadow under the shadow of Chocolate Mountain we set up camp. We found a nice grassy clearing on the edge of the meadow with lots of horse graze and water from a spring. It was a cozy spot that held our horses well over the next ten days. Every day was full of activity, both on foot and on horseback, as we checked out most of the side basins. We saw a lot of sheep, up in the neighbourhood of a hundred head.

Complicating our situation was a grizzly bear spotted several miles down from our camp. We hoped there was a lot to keep his interest there in the large grassy meadow so he wouldn't come up the valley to check us out. Thankfully, he never did.

The meadow we were camped in had two streams coming in from either side of Chocolate Mountain. We wasted little time exploring these two valleys. We explored the branch to the north, and after an hour's walk, we broke into a clearing where we could see the approach to the backside of Sawtooth Basin. I set out the next day to climb over and into the basin from the back side, while Jim spent the day getting in firewood and tending to things in camp. It was relatively straightforward for me to make the 2,000-foot climb to the top of the ridge from that side. I followed along the summit to where you could look down into the basin. From there I glassed as much of the country as was visible to me. From this vantage point I spotted ten rams at the eastern end of the basin, high up on its west-facing, grassy slopes. After recording the sheep observation in my notebook, I looked down into the basin. I walked out onto a prominence of land that jutted out over the basin and I got a better view of the terrain. On the south side, directly across from me, were almost forty ewes and lambs. I saw a narrow scree slope to my right that started from the crest of the ridge and ran down into the willowy terrain below. I took this route and soon found myself trying to wade through chest-high willow in an attempt to reach the main part of the side valley. This way I could connect with the old trail on the opposite side. I could see it led out to the Isaac Creek valley. After struggling for what seemed an eternity through the cursed willow, I finally made the bottom of the basin. I then climbed up a few hundred feet and found the trail. I was tired of struggling through the unyielding willows.

Jim and I were enjoying ourselves in our cozy fly camp and looked forward to the remaining days there. The weather stayed sunny and seasonally warm, and time went by quickly. Finally, our shift was over. We left the tent standing, with lots of split wood stacked up nearby for the next shift. The kitchen gear was stored, and we headed

Isaac Creek Warden Cabin just before heading up country.
DALE PORTMAN COLLECTION

out for a few days off. We got to Isaac Creek that evening and on to Brazeau the next night, where I had to help Jim off his horse again. He couldn't lift his right leg over the back of his saddle. Barb provided us with another excellent meal, and we left our remaining food – including some precious cans of butter and Tulip brand bacon – for the coming winter. The following day we got to the highway and left the horses in the corral with hay and water. I spent my four days off in Lake Louise with Barb.

I found myself heading back in on my own, as Jim had been assigned somewhere else. It was dark when I got to Isaac Creek but the cabin was all lit up, and I could see Barb wandering about inside making supper. Bob came out to help me unpack. It didn't take long, as Bob flew about like a whirlwind, grabbing a rope here and a tarp there and carrying on a conversation at the same time, about something the government had screwed up on. I turned the horses loose, while he continued to vent. His nickname was "The Bear," and I could sometimes see why. He had worked as a guide for a few years with both Ray Legace and Bert Mickle, and he had a western drawl that was hard to put a finger on. He could yodel as well as Wilf Carter, and he could often sound both serious and light hearted in the span of a few sentences. He was great company on the trail and good to work with and for.

After supper, we did radio call and there was a message for me. I was to head up Isaac Creek with Bob and pull the camp out then head back out to the highway. I was supposed to be at work in Rogers Pass the day before. What that meant was that they didn't have money for me to work through the winter in Jasper, but Rogers Pass did. So, Bob and I headed up Isaac Creek in the morning, packed up the camp and brought it out to Isaac Creek. Once the camp was unloaded and stored, I packed my horses and headed to Arête Warden Cabin. The following morning, I headed for Four Point Warden Cabin. That night I set up a pickup time for Camp Parker and met them at noon the next day. The horses and I were trucked back to "45," where I picked up my vehicle and headed for Lake Louise. Two days later I was in Rogers Pass, trying to prepare myself for another winter, chasing snowflakes.

In preparation for the court case against Jerry Verhegge and his guide, Dennis Weisser sent the confiscated cape and hide (from the carcass) off to the crime lab in Edmonton where technicians proved a match between them and the sheep heads. They fitted together perfectly. It was the first time a match like this was undertaken by a Canadian crime lab and used as evidence in a court case. The six shell casings also matched the guide's 30.06 rifle. Both men were convicted and fined heavily. Bob said that Dennis did 95 per cent of the work in investigating and putting the case together and did an exceptional job. Barker later discovered the trails the poachers had been using over the years, which gave them access into the numerous basins of Isaac Creek. Sawtooth Warden Cabin was built a few years later, at the edge of the meadow at the base of Chocolate Mountain. It was hidden from view and not far from where we had our fly camp.

NINE

ALFIE AND GINGER

A SUMMER AND WINTER AT ATHABASCA FALLS

I returned to Rogers Pass for the winter of 1970–71, which finished in late April. Barb and I sold our trailer in Lake Louise and moved to Jasper. I was assigned to Athabasca Falls District, working for Bert Rowe, taking up accommodation in a hay shed that had been converted to seasonal quarters. It was less than ideal, and Barb was not impressed. I could understand her concerns, but the job was more important and the rent was almost nothing. Unfortunately, it was situated near the electricity plant, which generated a lot of noise.

I had been working for Bert for about a month when he decided to retire to Creston, BC. I was sorry to see him go, as he had been a great guy to work for. Whenever we did a truck patrol I was always captivated by his many stories of his younger days. He had been a trapper in northern Manitoba and had some great tales of his life then, but for me his most interesting stories came from his time in Winnipeg during the Second World War. He tried to enlist in the army but was turned down for medical reasons, so he got a job as a bread man in Winnipeg. During the war, there were two jobs that had great side

Barb and Dale at Don and Grace Mickle's wedding in 1971.
DALE PORTMAN COLLECTION

benefits: bread man and milkman. Bert wasn't married at the time, he explained, and in his shy manner, he told me about some of the compromising positions he was put in by lonely women who met him at the door and invited him in.

My first rescue as a park warden occurred that summer. Rafting had just started up in Jasper, and the rafts were large, carrying up to twenty-five people. One raft, almost at full capacity, hit a pylon on the Five Mile Bridge, located just south of Jasper. It had managed to wrap itself around the closest pylon on the west bank of the Athabasca River. The current kept it pressed in place and while seven were dumped into the river, seventeen remained standing on the inflated gunnel of the raft. The ones tossed in the river all managed to get safely to shore and walked out to the highway where they were picked up. It was amazing that only seven ended up in the water and were carried down with the current, and even more amazing was that the seventeen were able to cling on for as long as they did.

After we reconnoitered the situation, Willi Pfisterer, our rescue leader, decided that the best solution was to rig up a secure station on the bridge above the abutment and lower a man down with a rescue harness and haul the victims up one by one. When we got there, the people on the raft were terrified they were going to lose their perch and slip into the current. I was the lightest and nimblest, so they sent me over the railing with a harness on, attached to two ropes.

I was lowered directly over them, and room was made for me on the gunnel. I had an extra harness, which I gave to the closest person and helped him put it on. Once the harness was secured, I attached the second rope to it and they hauled the person up. By now there were several wardens who had arrived to help haul each person up, hand over hand. It was the quickest method, as time was a factor. The harness was lowered to me repeatedly, and soon we had all of them safely on the bridge.

THE TRAGIC DROWNING AT MALIGNE CANYON

Another rescue soon followed the first. On a hot summer day in mid-July, things were running as usual at Maligne Canyon, but that changed in an instant.

Six bridges span the 6 kilometres of the Maligne River that runs from the start of the canyon to the river's confluence with the Athabasca. All but one is a footbridge, and three are suspension bridges that hang high above the torrential water, carving its way through the canyon. The canyon itself is so narrow in spots that if you had a running start and lots of nerve, you might be able to jump it. The trail that follows the edge of the canyon, crossing from side to side as the bridges dictate, is one of the more spectacular trails in Jasper National Park.

Things look rather non-threatening at the start of the canyon near the tea house. As the river passes under the highway bridge it flows over a smooth stretch of rock that seems benign. Just before the first suspension bridge, though, it disappears. It falls directly down into a punch bowl in front of the footbridge, which provides a spectacular view for tourists. The flat upper stretch of the river above the canyon is relatively calm and inviting.

That day, a nine-year-old girl stood before the river, while her parents directed her to step farther back for a picture of a lifetime. Whether they lost their depth of field through the lens of the camera or were distracted by the distance as they focused on their daughter, we don't know. She moved back one step too far and slipped in. The deceptively strong current grabbed the girl's small, light body, and in a flash, she was carried over the lip of the falls and into the walled confines of the canyon. Within seconds she disappeared.

Once the alarm went out over the radio, wardens responded from all over Jasper. As we straggled in, some of us were sent out to look for her along the canyon while others were assigned to stand in place on one of the six bridges, acting as spotters. Others mobilized rescue gear. The RCMP arrived quickly to interview the parents and determine what had happened. Everyone was coming to the same conclusion: her chance of survival looked next to impossible. I was told to patrol the canyon walls in case she was clinging to some wedged piece of driftwood or perched on a ledge. Peering into the abyss of churning back eddies, roaring falls and turquoise ponds, I knew it was highly unlikely that she would survive such a traumatic journey. This was one of my earliest rescue/recovery situations. Tragedies of this magnitude so early in your career tend to stay with you longer than usual. To this day, I remember all the vivid details.

As the hours of the day evaporated in the heat of the sun, hope diminished. By the end of the day it was now a matter of recovery for everyone involved. Alfie Burstrom, the park's dog handler, was puzzled that no one had called for him and his dog. He hung around the radio all day waiting for that request for help. Late at night, the phone rang. They wanted Alfie on site early the next morning, but there was no mention of the dog. Alfie and Ginger were the first and only trained dog team in the park system. Before them, RCMP dog teams provided assistance, if they could be spared from their detachments. It was a constant battle for Alfie to remind people of the dog's worth. He had hoped that the phone call indicated people were buying into the dog program. He was hugely let down. Actually, he wasn't just let down; he was pissed off.

To make a point, he showed up at first light with Ginger, eager to go. The rescue leader wanted him to rappel into the canyon at strategic locations to look for the missing girl. He saw no use for the dog in this search and was surprised when Alfie barked, "Screw your search if you don't want to use the dog!" At that, he marched off, determined to do things the way he felt most effective. There was no sense standing there arguing.

Alfie was determined to use Ginger in some capacity. "He was trained to search for God sakes," he yelled. He decided to search the river's edge below the sixth and final bridge, the stretch before it enters the Athabasca. This was a flat section that could be accessed from both sides by Alfie and the dog. Once he determined his game plan, he went back to the rescue leader to inform him of his intent. The rescue leader shrugged his shoulders and, as an afterthought, scanned the surrounding wardens until his gaze fell on me. "Here's a man, use him wisely!" he yelled as Alfie stormed off again.

I happily scooted behind him. I was, after all, the fresh-faced seasonal warden eager for anything and everything. I felt like a hostage in a wilderness soap opera as I caught up to the handler and his dog. He was spewing out a cloud of profanity to no one in particular, words that would have been the envy of any cowpoke pushing stubborn cattle. I took up the rear, scuttling along, trying to be as inconspicuous as possible. Not a word came from my lips, which some would say was uncharacteristic of me. Alfie wasn't a tall man but he was big, like a lumberjack, Skookum and tough, and he had an amble to his walk. I certainly didn't want to get in his path.

We finally got to his search area. I was looking along the east bank of the river between the sixth bridge and where it entered the Athabasca, a distance of maybe a half kilometre. The bank was deeply undercut with lots of roots, which made it difficult to see anything. Max Winkler was searching on the opposite shore. He was also a big bear of a man who was as proficient a warden as you could find. He was equally at home climbing, skiing or on horseback, and was as strong and capable as any in the outfit. Alfie and Ginger were working along my side of the river when Ginger stopped and peered into the translucent water. Alfie inspected the site but couldn't see anything so he tried to move on, but Ginger would have nothing to do with it. Ginger returned to the spot and again looked into the moving water. He stared at the surface then looked over at Alfie, then again stared at the water. Alfie got down on his hands and knees and peered beneath the bank. He thought he saw something white below the surface, which could have been a hand waving in the current. Alfie called Max, who crossed over on the bridge above, as I quickly approached. When Max got there, he offered to investigate. Alfie secured a rope around him and Max backed into the river. He was soon up to his chest in icy water. He probed around until he felt clothing, then an arm and, after a bit of a struggle, he managed to free the body from a tangle of roots. Ginger had found the girl.

Although it was only a recovery, Alfie was hugely buoyed by the success. The mission was a victory, not only for the dog but for him, as well. Ginger had proved why a dog was needed and now Alfie had an good example of the worth of a working dog. In the early years of any dog program it is important to demonstrate what a dog can and cannot do. This incident would be the first of many bodies I dealt with over my career, related to highway accidents, mountain rescues or dog cases, homicides, suicides, accidents, falls, and missing persons cases.

I often think back on the events of that day. The parents must have been devastated by what had happened, and I could only imagine how helpless they must have felt as she slipped over the top of the falls. I only hope that they somehow could get some form of closure from their child's recovered body and her subsequent funeral. Not all bodies are found in these unrelenting mountains.

Ginger's success was also important because it was the first time in Canada that a dog had found a body under water. Before long, the RCMP Police Dog Service Training Centre in Innisfail, Alberta, began exploring this possible new component of a dog's searching ability. They found that warm, stagnant water tended to mask human odour, while cold, clear water allowed the gases from the body to rise to the surface, where they are more readily detected by dogs. Because virtually all water in the Canadian Rockies is cold and often clear, the use of dogs on river searches quickly became an important tool. Eventually, dogs were also employed in lake searches, with them positioned in the bow of boats.

My experiences working with Alfie and Ginger over the years was the clarion call for me to later become a dog handler. This river recovery was followed by a search of a very different sort in the following winter season. It again proved the mettle of both the dog and his handler.

THE WHISTLER FIRE AND THE HIPPIE FREE CAMP

Before that terrible event on the Malign River, on a hot day in early summer, when the fire hazard was extreme, we had an active evening of dry lightning. The next morning was my day off, and after a leisurely breakfast, I went outside to stretch my legs. What I saw, looking down the Athabasca Valley towards Jasper, was smoke rising from the shoulder of Whistler Mountain. It looked like it was coming from a spot directly across from the Marmot ski area above Whistler Creek. It was 10:00 AM, so I assumed that the fire hall and warden service knew about it. I was wrong. I called the fire hall on the forestry phone line and asked the dispatcher if she knew about the fire on the south side of Whistler Mountain. She hadn't heard any report of a fire, so someone went outside and looked south and saw the smoke rising above the ridge. When the fire lookout positioned on Signal Mountain across the valley was called up on the radio, the conversation went something like this:

"Signal Mountain lookout from Jasper fire hall."

"Signal Mountain here. Good morning."

"Jasper fire hall. How's your view this morning? See anything unusual?"

"No, it's looking pretty good out there."

"How's the view west?"

"Holy shit! There's a fire."

It was pretty funny to hear this conversation on the radio; it looked like the lookout was caught sleeping.

I was called out for the fire, and I remember spending a week on it. I was a crew boss on the fire, and I was up every morning at four and found myself and the crew walking to the fire by 5:00 AM. We would get back down by 7:00 PM and have supper in town. I wouldn't get home until nine. We eventually got a fire line around it, had it under control and were mopping it up after a week. I don't think I had ever worked as hard as I did on that fire.

We had a free campground set up for the transient people (hippies) hitchhiking through the park. It was a safe and secure place where we could keep an eye on them. This was much preferred to having them camped in the woods, usually with an illegal fire. The campsite was located not far from town, and it provided our fire boss with lots of fire-fighting recruits. Every morning a bus would pull up and load up campers to take them up to a location where they could walk in to the fire site.

In subsequent years, the free camp became so notorious for its drugs and sex that people came from all over to take (part) in the action. We would check out the parking lot from time to time and there would be Cadillacs and Lincolns parked there with plates from all over Canada and the USA, particularly California.

ONE MAN'S EPIC AND HEROIC ENDEAVOUR TO REACH HELP

Because of my previous work experience in Rogers Pass, I was kept on that winter in the avalanche control program at Marmot Basin. I really enjoyed the work, and I had free skiing on my days off. Barb and I moved into an annex that was connected to the garage at the Cavell Warden Station that winter. We found it exceptionally cold at times, even though it had a propane heater. It was also an extremely cold winter. Cavell had a weather station that recorded temperatures. One night that winter, the temperature dropped to an amazing −56°F. The next morning, I got into the warden truck, tried to push in the clutch and it just shattered, it was so brittle.

I had a minor role in a major rescue that occurred on Mount Edith Cavell that winter. As I look back on my early exposure to working dogs, it seems that whenever a dog is performing well, displaying a good search pattern or following a tough track, nobody is around to see the result or they quickly forget about it. When a dog has an off day, maybe not as focused as he normally would be, more easily distracted, everybody seems to notice and they don't forget. There comes a time when you and your dog must prove yourselves to everyone involved. Each team has its defining moment, and that moment for Alfie Burstrom and Ginger was when Ginger found one small dime in the chaos of an avalanche accident.

On February 19, 1972, a party of four from the Edmonton Chapter of the Alpine Club of Canada headed out on skis for Mount Edith Cavell. They planned to climb the mountain by the East Ridge, which they felt would take three days, putting them back in Jasper by February 21. The two nights would be spent in a snow cave as high up on the ridge as they could get on the first day. They had planned to meet a local outfitter with a snowmobile at the trailhead, located at the start of Cavell Road. As they arrived and parked their car they were relieved to see the outfitter and his machine already there. The four were towed the 15 kilometres along the unploughed road to the Cavell tea house located at the end of the road. From there they headed towards a col to the left of the East Ridge. They skied under the mountain's imposing Northeast Face, which was to their right with Angel Glacier snuggled into her cirque, spreading her wings above the moraine below. A prominent lateral moraine rose steeply to their left. Just beyond the moraine was a timbered ridge, its summit covered by the beautiful and expansive alpine prairie known as Cavell Meadows, a popular hiking destination in the summer.

The party reached the head of the valley, below the steep slope that leads up to the saddle. The snow was hard and more easily gained by kicking steps, so they left their skis behind but took their ski poles. Once they reached the saddle, they swung to the right up a slope that grew increasingly steeper. They continued up a broad, snow-filled gully that would put them in proximity of the East Ridge proper.

It was 5:00 PM when they neared the top of the gully. The snow was still deep there, so they thought it a perfect place to dig their snow caves. A warm front had moved in during the afternoon, raising temperatures above freezing, and soon they were shrouded in cloud.

Peter remembers finishing the cave and crawling inside with his gear. The others were in various stages of unpacking, some inside and some outside their snow caves when there was a collapse of the surrounding snow. Air escaping from the snow pack was audible, and everything started to move as one consolidated piece. Peter remembers a loud crack sounding out before the snow cave, collapsed on top of him. He was knocked flat on his face by the weight of the roof, and he found himself pinned to the hard snow beneath. He was sure his chest would be crushed. Suddenly he was in motion, and he thought, "What a horrible way to die," as he moved headfirst downhill. He tried to bring his head up by digging his elbows into the snow, but nothing worked as the debris picked up speed.

The snow was travelling downhill over a hard layer in the snow pack, speeding up as it started to disintegrate. There was nothing anyone could do as the snow continued to fragment. The four climbers were being carried down towards the saddle, 600 metres below. Anyone witnessing the event would have heard the whump and whoosh of the escaping air from the crumbling slab as it rumbled down the mountain. As the avalanche reached maximum speed there would have been the sound of air rushing out and a billowing cloud of airborne snow.

Peter remembers coming to rest after flying over a rock buttress in the middle of the gully. When the snow stopped, he found himself pinned, head first, facing downhill. He was suddenly aware of the snow settling around him like concrete. He fought desperately to free himself before he was imprisoned in the rapidly forming cast that was surrounding him. With his head and torso covered and his legs on the surface, he made on last frantic attempt to wrench himself free before the snow stopped moving. He then found himself pushed to one side of the main avalanche debris, near a large rock. He was alive, on the surface of the snow, but when he tried to stand up, he realized one of his arms was broken near his elbow. He remembered numbness but no pain.

As he moved about on the avalanche debris, Peter realized his climbing partners were not so lucky. He found Jim, who cried out, "Help me! Dig my leg out and I'll help you look for the others." Once he dug Jim out, Peter realized that the leg was broken and he was not going to be able help in any search. The avalanche deposit was about 100 metres long and 70 metres wide, a substantial area to search. He covered the avalanche debris in a cursory fashion, finding no sign of Wayne and Chris, and then he returned to Jim. He needed to go for help, so he splinted Jim's broken leg to his good one and slid him into a sleeping bag that had been in a pack lying on the surface. Peter piled packs, clothing and snow around Jim and told him he was going for help.

Night had settled on the mountain as Peter surveyed the carnage around him, suddenly realizing what a desperate situation he was in. All of this added to his growing feeling of isolation. He found some liquid honey and a headlamp in a pack, which he took with him. He only took one ski pole because of his broken arm. He looked at his wristwatch. It was 8:00 PM. With some difficulty, he followed the route down from the saddle to the skis. Because of his broken arm, he decided not to ski out, but to walk.

He was hoping that when he got to the deserted tea house he might find a telephone, but he didn't. Sitting in the pit toilet for shelter, he swallowed some honey, and then he continued his trek to find help. It was a dark night, and in the gloom, he missed the road out and took a side road that led down to Cavell Lake. Progress was slow in the deep snow and often he moved forward by lying on his back with his broken arm resting on his thigh and pushed himself along with his legs and the ski pole. Time was of the essence, and while the detour didn't add much in distance, it took its toll on his energy and added an hour or two to his miserable trip out.

When he finally gained Cavell Road, he was still 13 kilometres from the car. The going was much better if he stayed on the snowmobile track, but in the inky cloak of the night he had difficulty maintaining the perch, and he often slipped off, sinking to his hip in the deep snow. He forced himself to keep going through the night, but the physical exertion and the pain from his arm caused him to occasionally collapse from exhaustion. He also found himself falling asleep as he walked. His mental toughness and determination to get help for his friends kept him going. Finally, dawn broke. Now he could see the way ahead.

He reached the car shortly before noon, and thankfully it started. It had an automatic transmission; if it had been a standard, he might have been hooped. He headed for the Cavell Warden Station a few kilometres away. Shirley Klettl was surprised to see him standing at the door, looking haggard and spent. She brought him into the warmth of the kitchen and sat him down. She gave the handle on the wooden forestry phone one crank and was soon talking to the dispatcher in the Jasper fire hall. She was immediately transferred to Bud Armstrong, the chief park warden, giving him the details. She also phoned the Avalanche Hut at Marmot Basin and talked to Willi Pfisterer, the park's alpine specialist. Willi then talked directly to the survivor over the phone and asked to meet him at the trailhead.

The warden service put the alarm out over the park's VHF radio and leapt into action. In all, twelve wardens from several districts throughout the park responded, and by 1:15 PM, all had gathered at the staging area, were geared up and ready to go. They were waiting for the helicopter that had been dispatched from Hinton, Alberta. Willi later recalled of Peter, "He was really bashed up with a broken arm, and I asked him some questions and he answered them precise.... He gave clear answers and I knew exactly what had happened and where it was. So, the thing to do was to get there as fast as possible – because of the light."

The helicopter arrived but was grounded until 2:30 PM because of bad weather. When things started to clear, the helicopter lifted off with Willi and two wardens on board to do a reconnaissance. A rescue party, led by Hans Fuhrer, had already been dispatched and was heading out on snowmobiles to set up an advanced rescue base at the tea house parking lot. When the helicopter finally reached the accident site, Willi could see a prone figure on the surface of the avalanche deposit. There was room to land on the slide debris, and at 3:00 PM they confirmed that Jim was deceased. He had been dead for some time as rigor mortis had set in. He appeared to have expired from internal injuries rather than exposure. Willi was concerned that Peter might have felt he could have saved his pal if he had reached help sooner, so the information about Jim's death was passed on to Peter, who was now in the hospital in Jasper. It was hoped it would help him come to terms with the ordeal he had gone through.

The next step was to get the dog team up to the site, as well as RCMP Sergeant Al Moore, who would act as the coroner. While waiting for Alfie and Ginger, Willi and the two wardens started a hasty search of the deposit, looking for signs of the other two victims. All the climbers' personal effects scattered on the surface complicated this. While they conducted their search, the weather deteriorated. The helicopter with its two passengers and the dog waited at the tea house. Willi would reflect later that it was a mistake not to have the dog team on the first flight in, but he rectified this in all future avalanche operations.

At 4:00 PM the weather lifted and the helicopter could land its valuable cargo at the site. Alfie wasted little time putting Ginger to work, and on being released to search, the dog immediately went over to investigate the body. It was a natural thing for a dog to do, especially on his first avalanche search. When Alfie caught up to the dog, the first thing he heard was, "Get that goddamn dog out of here." As much as the comment upset him, he didn't want to start a row – he needed to get the dog back to work.

All dogs have a natural inquisitiveness, but not all dogs have the confidence to approach a body. Some are repelled by it. It was a good sign that Ginger responded so positively to the presence of a deceased person. Alfie allowed him to satisfy his curiosity, then he moved him farther up the deposit to search for the victims under the snow. The dog's search was also complicated by the four climbers' gear and equipment. Outside of explosive and narcotic dogs, most search dogs are trained to indicate anything with human scent on it. Here there was an abundance of things that smelled like people: pots, clothing, dishes, toiletry, climbing equipment, bivouac sacs, sleeping bags and so on. Ginger would go out, fetch an article and return expecting praise for a job well done. Alfie would give Ginger a less than assertive "Good boy" before sending him back to work. This process took time, and in avalanche searches, time is critical. Soon, Ginger ignored the surface articles, which didn't elicit much response from Alfie, and he started sniffing for something beneath the snow. This was the first search of an avalanche with a dog team in Canada, which pushed the learning curve for everyone involved. In subsequent avalanche searches that employed a dog, if time permitted, the articles would be marked with a wand, recorded and removed, before the dog was sent in.

Willi had his own concerns as time was running out. If they didn't find the two climbers in the next hour, a camp would have to be flown in and set up. With the current weather conditions deteriorating and a poor forecast, he couldn't rely on getting back in to the site the next morning. This was the first time he had to solely put his faith in the dog team. He certainly hoped the dog came through soon, for everyone's sake, though there was only a remote chance someone could still be alive.

He was also concerned about Alfie. He knew this was the team's first avalanche search and he had to be feeling the pressure. The longer the team searched without results, the higher the stress level. That would also be conveyed to the dog, as search dogs are sensitive to their handlers. No one knew how Ginger would respond to Alfie's concerns.

As a search tool, a dog needed to be promoted and sold to those in the search and rescue field, and there were many skeptics amongst the wardens. Alfie had some early success with the RCMP in the criminal apprehension and law enforcement profiles and had established credibility with them; he now needed to do the same with his fellow wardens. If he didn't succeed here, he knew it might set back the entire dog program.

He certainly felt the scrutiny. He knew there were two people left in the deposit, unless they had been thrown clear of the debris or lodged somewhere above in the gully. As he peered up into the mist-obscured gully, it seemed unlikely that neither had happened.

It was 5:00 PM and Ginger had been searching for 40 minutes without any sign of finding a victim. Trying to hide his concern, Willi called up, "How's the dog working Alfie?"

"Oh, fine," he replied in a relaxed fashion not befitting the situation. "We found the first one a half hour ago." This was a surprise – and – relief to Willi.

"That's great, Alfie, really great," he called back. "Thank the dog for me."

When Ginger found Wayne's body, he didn't need a coroner to tell him he was dead. He had kept silent because he didn't want the other searchers tracking up the area and creating a distraction for the dog. But there was another reason; he didn't like being told to get his dog off the avalanche as if he was someone's pet. He was upset and he was feeling little warmth towards his fellow searchers, outside of Willi.

Soon after this conversation, in another part of the debris field, Ginger started pawing the snow and came up with something in his mouth, which Alfie retrieved before he had a chance to swallow it. He didn't know what it was until he dropped it into his hand. It was a dime. Ginger's nose was definitely working.

Alfie felt he was having no success on that part of the avalanche, so he moved the dog back into the area were Wayne's body was located. Suddenly the dog started digging frantically, his tail wagging. Shortly after there was a bark and then some growling. Ginger had recovered

Alfie Burstrom and Ginger about to be slung under the helicopter.

Chris's body, and by the time Alfie got to the dog, Ginger was tugging on the victim's sleeve. Alfie responded with customary encouragement: "Good boy. That a boy. You get him out of there."

Willi gave a sigh of relief that the dog team had come through. It was 5:45 and everybody it seemed would be off the mountain that night. The evacuation started at 6:15 with personnel and bodies being removed first, followed by the camp gear. The helicopter brought the final load down at 8:30 PM, terminating the rescue operation.

I came to know the survivor, Peter, who now lives in Canmore. The loss of good friends is never easily forgotten or dealt with when you were part of the accident that led to the loss. You carry a specific kind of burden when you're the only survivor. This burden, however, had not held him back over the years.

With this search and recovery, the warden service entered a new era, with the dog becoming an integral part of search and rescue in the Canadian Rockies. The national park's long-term success in the dog program has in large part been due to this team's early successes in the field. Establishing a search and rescue dog team in Banff National Park might never have happened if not for this search; after it, two new dog teams were ensconced in the park.

HOW ALFIE AND GINGER BECAME A TEAM

Alfie Burstrom was a mentor to me, but he was also someone you couldn't help admiring. He dealt with personal adversity trying to carve out a niche for himself in a world that was not always inviting and supportive. How he became a dog handler is an inspiring story.

He was the first certified avalanche dog handler in North America, and to get there was no small task. He's retired today, living on a sizeable acreage near Valemount, BC, with his wife June, surrounded by family and lots of animals, especially horses. Ginger is a legend in the annals of mountain rescue. On a page in his scrapbook is the 1964 dime that he found, searching for those two buried climbers on Mount Edith Cavell. The dime is a symbol that indicates how good a canine's nose can be, and it also reminds everyone of how good Ginger was.

This story starts in August 1969, at a time when Alfie was searching for a new role in a dynamic and evolving period for the warden service. He had a speech impediment, a bad stutter. It had hindered his comfort in dealing with people and took a toll on his self-esteem. Success as a dog handler mitigated most of that later in life. After fifteen years as a park warden that summer, he was at a low point in his career. When Ginger came along, he reached for the brass ring and held on to it for dear life, for it gave him the opportunity of a lifetime. When I reminisce with old timers, if Alfie's name comes up, you can see the sparkle instantly appear in their eyes, and their chests puff out, for he was the best example of what wardens should be, and we all knew it.

He acquired Ginger from fellow park warden, Gordon McClain, whose female dog had just had a litter of eleven pups. It was amazing how it came about, as if Gordon were connected to Alfie's destiny in some manner. Gordon spotted Alfie's oldest son Ed, walking near the post office in Jasper. He had the last remaining pup, the runt of the litter, in the truck with him and on impulse parked the truck and walked up to Ed. He plunked the pup into the pocket of Ed's winter jacket and said, "Take this home to your dad." When Ed got home, he said to Alfie, "Guess what Mr. McClain gave me."

At the time, the Burstrom clan lived at De Coigne Warden Station, just west of Jasper near the Continental Divide. Familiarization is an important component of any dog's upbringing but even more so for a potential working dog. The Burstrom kids, all five, helped immensely by taking him on all their adventures. They especially liked fishing, and Ginger always went along – until he started eating the bait. To eliminate the problem, before heading out on a fishing trip, the kids would lock Ginger in a shed on the property. Often hours later, their mother would come outside, hear the dog whining and turn him loose. He would instantly search around, looking for the kids' tracks. To the children's consternation, Ginger would soon be in their midst, wagging his tail and looking for bait. The desire to search and track was inspired by these outings, honing Ginger's tracking skills at an early age, for it wasn't training, it was fun. And so, his working talent was developed early on by happenstance.

One of the games Alfie often played with his kids was a kind of hide-and-seek. He would send them out, upwind as far as they could run and have them hide. After a period of waiting, he would turn Ginger loose, and inevitably the pup would find them all. Alfie was unwittingly developing the dog's searching capabilities. Ginger's father was a big German shepherd, but his mother was half-coyote. People wondered how that would play out in his development and capabilities. There were some questions about his heritage, and the main one was whether the coyote in him would reduce his capacity to accept discipline.

For a few months, the idea that Ginger would make a good search and rescue dog was coalescing in Alfie's mind. When the dog was about eight months old, Alfie approached the chief park warden, telling him that he felt the dog had great potential as a working dog.

The chief, Mickey McGuire, promised to look into it, planting the seed of their future together. It even perked the interest of other parks in the organization. They also started looking into establishing a dog program.

Jim Sime, the resource conservation coordinator who was now the warden service's representative at the regional office in Calgary, probably understood the need for an avalanche search and rescue team better than anyone. Jim was a chief park warden back in 1955, and he saw the need to establish solid mountain rescue and avalanche control capability within the mountain national parks. He was the one who pushed for hiring Swiss guide Walter Perren to head up both programs. Noel Gardner, the father of avalanche forecasting in Canada, assisted him in the avalanche safety program.

Jim had already approached the mandarin in Ottawa in 1969 with the idea of developing the program. He was aware of Alfie's speech impediment and the ridicule it brought him but he also noticed that Alfie never missed a word when he talked to Ginger – his stutter was magically gone. As Jim put it, "Alfie was a man who had an opportunity and was seeking that opportunity, which was being downgraded and downtrodden because of his impediment, yet had a tremendous capacity to bring forward."

Once Jim got approval to establish a search and tracking dog component to the program, his next step was to find a place to train the team. He talked to the head trainer, Staff Sergeant Terry Kehoe at the RCMP Police Dog Service Training Centre in Innisfail, Alberta. Once they met in person, Jim explained his vision, "The difference between your dogs and what I'm talking about here is that when our dog comes, it means help. It doesn't mean it's going to grab you by your backside and rip your pants off. Any dog that we have must never be trained to attack." Kehoe decided to try out Jim's idea by accepting a park warden on their training course and evaluate him. Jim did not hesitate to volunteer Alfie.

Jim was gambling on Alfie and Ginger. He could surely have submitted a couple of names but Jim had faith in Alfie, and besides, he already had a dog. Both men knew the future of the program depended on their success. So, in the fall of 1970, Alfie went to Innisfail to qualify on the quarry course. Quarry courses have two benefits. First, they provide the RCMP dog teams with people who role-play criminals laying tracks, and stand in as subjects in search and criminal apprehension scenarios. These courses also expose people to dog work and give the trainers an idea of how quarries relate to dogs and how well they interact with the other dog teams.

Every day seemed like a month to Jim, who kept in touch with Kehoe, hoping for some word of encouragement. Jim was there on the last day to watch the proceedings. At one point, Jim could no longer contain himself. "How did it turn out?" he cried.

"How did what turn out?" Kehoe asked.

"You know goddamn well what I mean! How did Alfie make out?" Jim repeated.

Kehoe replied, "You don't have another one like him, do you?"

Alfie had passed with flying colours. "You know," Jim said later with a sigh, "there was so much involved here."

When considering a dog for training, Ginger had three strikes against him. First, only one out of eighty dogs can become a trained RCMP dog. Second, he was relatively small for a working dog in police work. And third was the question of Ginger's coyote heritage. It was now the dog's turn to be assessed in Innisfail. His breeding remained controversial throughout the training. His pedigree wasn't in keeping with RCMP standards for potential candidates. Coyotes were viewed as sneaky animals obsessed with prey, not loyal life companions like a domestic dog. How dependable would Ginger be in the wilderness? Would he track a human if he scented a fresh deer track? Would he be too timid and shy of load noises and big bangs? Courage is always a factor in evaluating a dog.

"Where in the hell did the dog come from?" Kehoe boomed. He decided to be up front with Jim when they sat down to discuss Ginger, a few days after Alfie entered the training program. Jim became defensive and subdued at Kehoe's brusque manner as he began to whisper the dog's history when Kehoe interrupted. "It's all right," Kehoe assured, "he's in the program."

What Jim didn't know was that the kennels had dreamed up a special test for Ginger because he was going to be trained as an avalanche dog. In a test, set up right from the get-go, they tried to simulate that environment in a search. They dug a pit at the far end of a large field where a few people were placed under branches and debris. When Alfie brought Ginger out, Kehoe instructed him to turn the dog loose. Off to the left in the agility field, several dogs and their handlers were going through the course. Alfie was worried the dog would run straight to the other dogs. Ginger, however, took off like a shot, working the wind straight to the pit and dug out the quarries. That was enough for Kehoe; Ginger was a natural. Kehoe didn't know about all the searching Ginger had done as a pup with the kids.

In September 1970, the two found themselves at the RCMP trailing facility for the four-month course. Their group included two American sheriffs. Ginger may have been a natural, but he still needed a lot of training, obedience and discipline. Alfie required training to properly read his dog in all the different scenarios they would encounter. He also had to properly maintain the training regimen when they got back to Jasper and keep up the dog's obedience. In a sense, he needed to catch up to the dog's natural ability.

In keeping with Jim's wish, the team was trained in all RCMP dog profiles except criminal apprehension or attack work. The training would also include the new avalanche profile, which would be conducted after the main training was concluded that winter. Because the RCMP had embraced this new avalanche profile they were eager to also train a few teams of their own in the field, particularly in British Columbia.

By the end of the year, Alfie and Ginger successfully graduated from the training program. As soon as they got home, Alfie started doing demonstrations, broadcasting Ginger's capabilities to one and all, especially his fellow wardens and the RCMP. They soon blossomed into an effective unit, but it took a while to get people on side within the warden service. The idea of using the dog in search and rescue operations or poaching cases was new to everyone in the organization. While some readily embraced the concept, others doubted the dog's abilities.

The RCMP, which had had working dogs in the field going back to 1935, had no such doubts. The closest RCMP teams were at Stony Plain near Edmonton, one at Prince George to the west and one team in Kamloops, British Columbia. They were all at least 300 kilometres away. As Alfie said, "They had me chasing god knows who. They were used to working dogs." One of Alfie's first calls was from the local detachment that needed help with a hostage situation – someone was holding an RCMP officer hostage with a rifle. It was a sink or swim situation. Ginger had no attack capability, so this was going to be huge test.

The bluff was on. The team cautiously approached, until they were a reasonable distance from the hostage taker and the Mountie. Suddenly, the rifle was trained on Alfie and Ginger. "This dog will tear you to pieces," Alfie said as Ginger, seemingly on cue, lunged and barked. "All he wanted to do was lick him," Alfie said later. The hostage taker yelled he was going to shoot him. To which Alfie replied, "If you do that, the dog will tear you apart, and if you shoot the dog, you won't get another round in the rifle." It was an amazing situation to be in, pretty well on your first call out. What was also amazing was there was very little hint of a stutter. Alfie was unarmed but he had an RCMP member as backup with his gun cocked and ready. In fact, he said, the gun "was damn near resting on my shoulder." The bluff worked. The team's reputation grew amongst the RCMP that day.

With the success Alfie and Ginger were having in the field, it wasn't too long before Banff decided to join the program. In 1973 the park sent candidates to the training kennels for evaluation. There where soon two more dog teams working in the mountain national parks, Earl Skjonsberg was stationed in Banff while Jack Woledge took up residence in Lake Louise. Because Alfie was getting so many calls from the RCMP, the teams were later trained in the criminal apprehension and attack profile. Since then, the program has successfully spread to other national parks in Canada.

Alfie Burstrom kneeling beside Ginger.
ALFIE BURSTROM COLLECTION

Jim Sime said that one of the biggest rewards in his long career was helping Alfie and Ginger get started. He also said it was one of his biggest gambles. Jim believed that the program's success across Canada rested on that team. He reflected years later, "It's just such a gift, that dog. The guy and the dog had been brought together, and they deeply respected each other. It was like their moment in time had arrived, and nothing was going to change their course."

They worked together for eleven years and Ginger remained fit and active to the end. In his last few years, his only weakness was his hearing, but he was so well-versed in what to do in different situations, he didn't need to have Alfie tell him. Their story has appeared in elementary school textbooks across Canada, and they've been featured in numerous newspaper articles. In the early 1970s, the team was featured in a CBC TV special. When Ginger retired, he became the family's pet, and Alfie went on to train a new dog, Hiko. In 1986, when Alfie retired, I replaced him with my dog, Sam.

TEN

JASPER TALES

THE LEGEND OF SAKWATAMAU

At the end of the winter of 1970–71, I moved back to Jasper where I would stay until I got a permanent position. In the meantime, I began to meet the locals and learn much about the history and folklore of the park. While living at the Cavell Warden Station during the summer of 1972, I came across many stories that perked my interest. One legend particularly intrigued me.

An old timer passed along a Native legend about a long-forgotten burial site located in the Jasper area. An old Native woman was buried there, and her name was Sakwatamau (which means The Surviving One). Before she died she had had a vision; an unusual tree that grew nearby would mark her burial site. It would look like a single tree but really was a combination of several trees that resulted in an unusual shape. She said the site would be lost for many generations before being rediscovered. Once found it would be a signal to Indigenous peoples that the despair and repression they had long endured in trying to meet the expectations of an evolving world, would end. They would grow strong again.

The story began in 1829 when a group of Assiniboine people massacred a group of "Snake Indians" near the future site of Jasper House. According to the story, the Snake are said to be part of the Carrier (Dakelh) people, whose territory is to the west of Jasper, in the interior of British Columbia.[1] (I later found out that these people may have been misnamed in the story.) Apparently, a small group of the Snake people, thirty-seven in all, was camped on a point of land immediately upstream from the mouth of the Snake Indian River. Not far away was a larger camp of Assiniboine, long-time enemies of the Snake. On the pretext of making a permanent peace, the Assiniboine people invited some of the Snake men to their camp. On arriving, the men sat down around the fire in good faith, while Assiniboine warriors snuck up behind and killed them all. The Assiniboine then rushed over to the Snake camp and slaughtered the young men, women and children in camp. While ten managed to escape, three young women were taken as slaves.

The Assiniboine began to worry about what the Hudson Bay Company would do about this act of violence, and so they travelled out of the area, downriver about 200 miles, and set up camp near the present site of Fort Assiniboine. They had reason to be concerned. On learning of the massacre, the HBC moved the location of Jasper House from the east end of Brule Lake, farther up valley to a large meadow near the river were the savage attack had occurred. In this way, the company thought it could better enforce peace amongst the various Native peoples who came to trade.

For some years a Metis family named Bellerose had lived in the Fort Assiniboine area. When the senior Bellerose noted the arrival of the Assiniboine people, he also learned that the three Snake girls were

---

[1]   I later found out that these people are misnamed in the story. In J.G. MacGregor's *Overland by the Yellowhead*, he calls the people the Snaring Indians. Most references suggest that the "Snake" people referred to in this story are Carrier (Dakelh) First Nation. It's confusing, because Henry Moberly also refers to the main character in this story, the surviving woman, as having lived with a group of Shuswap people. I have kept the names of the peoples as I heard them when I heard the story so I don't introduce further errors.

lying naked and bound in one of the teepees. That night he snuck into the teepee, cut their bonds and turned them loose. All he could give them was a knife and his fire-bag, containing a flint, steel and some dried peat (a fire starter).

The women fled up the Athabasca River and within a few days had reached the mouth of the Berland River. Here the women quarreled and separated. Two of them, taking the fire bag, continued up the Athabasca River and were never heard or seen again. The third girl, naked and armed with only a knife, worked her way up the Berland, living on berries and squirrels. With the sinew from the squirrel tails, she made snares and caught enough rabbits to feed and clothe herself. She kindled a fire the old way, using friction by revolving the point of one dry stick rapidly in a hole made in another, eventually igniting tinder-dry moss. With a club, she hunted porcupines and marmots and then dried their meat. Her preparation for winter was so successful that she spent the entire winter at that one location, 30 miles up the Berland.

In the late spring and early summer, she moved farther west to a little lake, 25 miles east of where Highway 40 now crosses the Berland. That fall, an Iroquois man from the Grande Cache area came upon her tracks. They mystified him, but he decided that they must have been made by a weetigo, that is, a Native person who had run amuck and was banished from society. They were often thought to eat human flesh.

The next summer, after the girl had lived alone through two winters, the Iroquois man and his friends found themselves working their way down the Berland River, again hunting game. When he reached the vicinity of the tracks he had seen the fall before, he searched around. To his surprise he saw set snares, trees that were barked, and the same strange tracks, still fresh in the mud. Following them, he came to a cave-like hole in a high bank. In front of it was a stack of brushwood beside a still-smoking fire. Hiding himself nearby, he waited. Presently a wild creature in a skirt of rabbit skins came up bearing a load of rabbits. As he jumped up to catch her, she screamed and ran. While he soon caught her, she fought him so fiercely that he had great difficulty subduing her. Finally, he made her understand that he meant her no harm.

When he brought her back to his camp, the women were kind and accepting of her. She eventually fell in with their ways and lived with them for two years. Colin Fraser, the Hudson Bay factor at Jasper House, and his family then took her in.

She settled in and helped with domestic duties. She lived there for two more years. One day a family of Carrier people came in to trade at the fort, and she recognized them from her past. Feeling kinship with her people, she went off with them.

In 1846, after baptizing many Native peoples in the Jasper area, Father De Smet set out for Athabasca Pass. Near the junction of the Miette River he met a small Carrier party. Amongst them was a woman known as The Survivor or Surviving One. She told Father De Smet about her survival and subsequent ordeal in the wilderness. The story was pretty close to what he had heard from others, for her story had become well-known amongst the local people.

In *When Fur Was King*, Henry Moberly further adds to the story. While travelling through the Tête Jaune Cache area in the fall of 1861, he stopped to visit a group of Shuswap Natives and there met a most interesting old woman. Upon hearing that he was the factor of Jasper House, she told him her story of the massacre and her subsequent survival in the wilderness.

In Henry Moberly's unpublished journal notes that formed the basis for his famous book, he refers to the woman and her story and a dream she'd recently had. In the dream, she was told when and where she would die and she described it to him.

She dreamt that when death was close, she would travel east with a hunting party headed for the Athabasca Valley. In her dream, she died and was buried at a spot that had been used as a camp by Natives for hundreds of years. A peculiar tree would mark her gravesite. She said the tree would not appear for many generations after her death. From the woman's description and knowing the area well, Moberly felt the site was just west of the Snaring River, on the north side of the

Athabasca River, somewhere near Jacques Cardinal's old horse camp. Jacques was an employee of the HBC and looked after the company horses wintering in the valley.

In 1861, upon learning that Governor George Simpson had passed away, Henry Moberly, a Scot, decided to retire. He left his Native wife Suzanne Cardinal (Kwarakwante) and their two children, John and Ewan (as was common in those days), and headed west to the coast where he took up a different position. Suzanne and the two boys settled near the Snaring River on the north side of the Athabasca River, on a stretch of montane grassland. When John and Ewan grew to be adults, Ewan remained near the original site, while John built his home on the south side of the Athabasca River east of were the Maligne River comes in. Ewan often talked about an old Native gravesite nearby.

In 1995 I went looking for the tree and found one matching the old woman's description near the area that had been Ewan Moberly's homestead. I've never gone back to look for the unusual tree, but it is on my to do list the next time I visit Jasper.

JIM GIFFORD: HE WHO WALKS INTO ROOMS VOICE FIRST

I met Jim Gifford in the summer of 1973 although we were aware of each other a few years earlier. He worked for the CNR (Canadian National Railroad) as a lineman. A few years later he trained in Gimli, Manitoba, to become a train engineer. When he first came to Jasper in 1965, he got a job working for an outfitter from the Brule area just east of Jasper National Park. He was originally from Ottawa, and from what I could gather, had little horse experience. But as he was very outgoing and persuasive, he lined up a job as a guide and wrangler. He had lots of confidence in himself, had a high-octane work ethic and I could see why Leonard Jecke hired him.

He had a booming voice, and when he got excited, his laugh could almost shatter glass. He was often way over the top in telling a story, almost manic, but he was such a good storyteller that you hung on every word. I often accused him of entering a room voice first, which always raised a response from him. Bob Barker, who also worked for Leonard at the time, often referred to him as the Ottawa Valley cowboy. When I mentioned that to Jim, his booming laugh would explode and he would say, "That fucking Barker. Wait till I see him." He had a thick hide and this kind of stuff never fazed him. Because of our joint interest in horses and a good party, our friendship grew over the years. It would ebb and flow depending on which stage we were at in our lives and where we lived, as both of us moved around.

JIM'S AMAZING VENTURE INTO THE UPPER BLUE CREEK VALLEY

In the fall of 1967, Jim was kept on as a guide, wrangler and packer, to help with the hunts that were being conducted in the Wilmore Wilderness. He told me one story that caught my interest, so much so that I fleshed it out with him in an interview many years later. It was late in the summer and Leonard and Jim were putting in a hunting camp just off the South Sulphur River in anticipation of clients arriving for the fall hunting season. One morning they decided to scout the terrain above their camp.

At the edge of the vegetation zone there was a stretch of soft scree leading up to a col no more than 300 feet above them. Because the distance getting to the col was short, they went up to see what was on the other side. When they got there, they spent some time looking around. Spreading out below them was a beautiful valley that ran north–south. At the north end, situated in a low and gentle pass, was a deep blue lake. To the south, the valley stepped down quickly almost a thousand feet into a stretch that showed a long, velvety meadow. This field of green filled the valley bottom and stretched for miles to the south with a fine stream winding through its centre, like a ribbon of blue. The valley was flanked on either side by dark green coniferous forests. The mountains to the west were amazingly red in colour, so bright and dramatic it almost seemed like a garish painting.

This was the only side of the valley they could see. In the south and coming in from the west were numerous side valleys that flowed into the main valley. All held the potential for further exploration and discovery. Directly across from them was a broad side valley that

Jim Gifford at Caribou Inn.
DALE PORTMAN COLLECTION

held two large lakes, the lower one a deeper shade of blue the upper one a paler turquoise colour. To the right was a wall crowned with jagged peaks or small spires that hemmed in a high bench of land, littered with large boulders and interspersed with small, dark alpine tarns. Looking directly down, the descent route was covered in large talus boulders that defeated any idea of going that way on horseback. Leonard pulled out his binoculars and scanned the valley. The meadow below was expansive with clumps of coniferous trees lining each side. In the middle was where he saw the caribou, about ten head.

They managed to descend the steep talus slope on foot and headed south to where the valley dropped to the meadow below. Just above this is where the heavy stand of Engelmann spruce, white pine and balsam fir started. Once they reached the bottom of the slope, no more than 800 feet in elevation, they entered the large grassy meadow. It was a dry meadow with good grass that would hold horses for weeks.

They headed south following a trail, at times walking close to the stream. It meandered along, gurgling cheerfully in sections of fast water interrupted periodically by deep-blue pools. The east side of the valley was lined by timber that crawled jaggedly up the mountainside, no farther than 800 or 900 feet. Above the timber, grassy slopes thinned out as they swept up towards the rocky peaks. Looking southward as far as they could see along the eastern side of the valley, a mountain chain extended unbroken for miles, making an impenetrable barrier on the eastern side.

After walking for about a mile they stopped to glass for game at a point where the meadow broadened to accommodate a steep and shallow side valley. They didn't need the binoculars to see the sheep halfway up the side of the mountain. They were all rams with some displaying huge curls. There were about twenty of them, and just below them was a small watercourse that dropped steeply down towards the valley. What really caught their attention though was a substantial natural arch that bridged the stream channel; on the slopes above this bridge were more sheep, this time ewes and lambs.

They headed in the direction of the arch, and where the grass turned to timber they found what looked like an old camp. They continued to a point where they had a much closer view of the arch. It was huge, and the sheep grazing on the grass under it seemed small in its presence.

Jim took some pictures of the arch and the sheep, and then they turned and left. They had a long way to go to get back to the point where the high col was. They wanted to get back before dark so they could turn their horses loose in daylight. They decided to take a shortcut down through the trees, angling westward but up valley. When they hit the valley floor at the edge of a small willow-choked meadow, they discovered a small cabin.

It wasn't a tall cabin, in fact, they could look over it while standing up. It was maybe 8 feet by 8 feet square, a foot or so dug down into the ground. The floor was made of earth, and a small bed, made of local wood, was in one corner. A small table was placed under a small window, and near the front door was a small wood stove. There were a few primitive shelves that held a couple of old cans, some dishes and various other things. No one had stayed there since Curly Philips in the late 1930s.

Jim first told me the story that winter while we huddled over beer in the Athabasca Hotel in what the locals referred to as the "dead animal room" because of all the head mounts on display in there. Across from where we sat was a mural by Christy Keg that stretched across the length of the room. After hearing the story, I knew I would one day try to gain access to that valley and explore it. It triggered a vision of a lost paradise, a mountain Shangri-La that embodied a land of beauty and harmony. Little did I know that the opportunity to visit this magical kingdom would present itself a couple of years later. Many surprises and the odd mystery would confront me when I ventured into the remote Blue Creek valley.

WILDLIFE OBSERVATIONS

One of the things you usually have the good fortune to meet in your backcountry travels is the grizzly bear. Encounters with this animal can be nervy at times, especially if you're on foot, but you appreciate them even more afterwards. There is something about the heightened awareness you experience being in the presence of such a magnificent animal. Most of my encounters have been on horseback, but on occasion, I've stumbled on bears hiking, too.

I have built up a repertoire of interesting sightings over the years, which I always drag out at social engagements with friends and family. Usually most encounters are uneventful and a normal part of the day, but sometimes they can be interesting, intriguing, enticing, stressful and fascinating all at once. I never take an encounter for granted and try to take as much away from it as I can. All such experiences added to my growing awareness and understanding of the species and the landscape. Though many wildlife attacks are the result of poor decisions on the part of people and not the bears, some aggressive encounters are surprising for both parties. Accidentally interrupting a bear feeding on a recent kill is a good example of being in the wrong place at the wrong time. One of the biggest things a warden must learn early in his career is how to interact with wildlife in general, and bears specifically, though there is no guarantee of never encountering trouble.

As a park warden, I accepted being a solitary presence in the wilderness, and this led to a feeling of comfort amongst my surroundings. Yet we have no final control over the setting, and safety cannot always be taken for granted. In the end, the small risks we take in life are the ones that matter most.

If you've see a few grizzly bears, countless more have watched you amble along the trail without you knowing it. Once you realize the power of quiet observation, it becomes a tool at your disposal, and a wealth of wildlife sightings will be your reward for using that tool. It fosters a connection to the land that is less physical or objective and more subjective or mystical. When you work in the wild, there evolves a relationship between you and nature, a harmony and balance that is ever developing, that spiritual connection many of us seek in solitude and wilderness. This relationship leads to greater self-reliance and confidence in conducting yourself in that environment. I've never felt that I needed to possess a firearm for protection while in a backcountry setting. Those who do will probably never understand what I've written here.

I had a cougar encounter that was intimidating as it unfolded. I was checking the phone line near Shale Banks Cabin on a stretch were the cutline was long and straight. As I walked along I felt a presence next to me, off to my right; something was watching me. To my surprise it was a cougar crouched in the bush next to the right-of-way, looking at me in a curious manner that slowly transformed to a predatory gaze. I assumed it was an adult female and she was watching me intently, gathering interest in me as I passed. I ignored her by avoiding eye contact and continued walking as naturally as I could. She stood up and came out behind me, slinking. She was obviously sizing me up, wondering if I was too big for her to take down. Instinctively, I started trying to make myself look taller by standing up on my toes and spreading my arms out. I was looking for a club or piece of wood that I could defend myself with but spotted nothing suitable. I continued walking, knowing the fire road was only a few hundred yards away. She continued to follow me twenty feet behind but eventually her posture was more upright and less threatening. When I got to the road and started walking along it, she slowed her pace and the distance grew between us. Then she ran off into the trees, leaving me in a heightened state of shock and wonder.

In my formative years in Jasper, I had the opportunity to hang out with three well-known wildlife photographers – Tommy Thompkins, Bill Crawford and Bill Smaultz. From these three, I learned a lot about observing wildlife and their behaviours under various circumstances. Thompkins had a wildlife show on CBC back then but started out shooting still photography. He was famous for having a tamed wolf as a pet. Crawford did a lot of work photographing wildlife for magazines. He walked everywhere, and often we would pick him up in our warden trucks and give him a lift. Thompkins had a truck and camper and sometimes the two would travel together. Smaultz was a filmmaker. He was doing a documentary for the National Film Board on bighorn sheep in Jasper at the time. He was the most natural of the three and harmonized well with his surroundings and his relationship with his subject.

The biggest wildlife lesson I learned was from Bill Smaultz. It was on a minor peak called Little Athabasca near the Columbia Icefield. He was setting up his camera to film a herd of bighorn ewes and lambs. They had only recently lambed and were grazing off in the distance. Bill told his assistant and me, "We will set up here. Stay quiet and remain calm; soon they will accept us and approach." After about fifteen minutes they slowly moved up to our position. Soon they were in our midst, grazing within five feet of us. Some even came over to sniff the camera equipment and us. I got some amazing photographs that day.

After that experience, I became more involved with wildlife photography. One day at the Mount Kerkeslin viewpoint, close to a

Bighorn lamb at Little Athabasca near the Columbia Icefield.
DALE PORTMAN COLLECTION

goat lick south of Jasper townsite, I spotted some goats on the side of the road near the parking lot. I saw my opportunity when tourists started pushing some goats farther down the road edge into the ditch in their eagerness to get a photograph. I went farther down the road, below the herd and sat on a rock in the ditch with my camera. Within minutes the goats were all around me, so close I could touch them if I wanted. Some of the males were even closer at hand. The tourists were amazed, while I became concerned about my safety. Any small movement on my part might frighten them, and I did not want to appear as a threat, so I tried to calm down. It was a somewhat uneasy ten minutes for me, but the goats remained relaxed, trusting I would do nothing hasty. Finally, they moved away, grazing farther down the ditch. Some of the tourists thought I had some magical power over them. I left them with that impression as I drove off in the warden truck.

The opportunity with the goats made me much more aware and relaxed when encountering wildlife. I have sat quietly many times since, having lunch in some quiet spot, overlooking a nice stretch of scenery, when the local characters would suddenly appear in normal pursuit of their daily life. It might be a weasel chasing a ground squirrel or a pine marten after a pack rat, but in every case these creatures were either oblivious to my presence or just ignored me. Willi Pfisterer was sitting on his pack one day having a quiet lunch on his own next to his skis, when a rabbit ran up and huddled between his legs. A pine marten was chasing the rabbit, which decided Willi was less threatening than the martin. Willi threw pine cones and snowballs at the martin, finally driving him away. After a while, when he felt the coast was clear, his new friend hopped off. The power of observation – paying attention to your surroundings – while being as unobtrusive and quiet as possible are important factors that lead to these kinds of events unfolding.

The Starlight Range, which is on the boundary between Jasper National Park and the Wilmore Wilderness, found a group of us walking its ridgeline. I and a handful of clients spotted twelve head

Willi Pfisterer riding into Blue Creek in Tyrolean fashion.
DALE PORTMAN COLLECTION

Mountain goats at Mount Kerkeslin salt lick south of Jasper.
DALE PORTMAN COLLECTION

of caribou as we came over a rise. We stopped as their heads turned in our direction. On person instantly put her hands up over her head in the shape of antlers, and we all followed suit. They became very curious and advanced towards us in a less than cautious manner. When they were about 30 yards away they stopped and sniffed the air. When they finally concluded that we were not another band of caribou they trotted off.

During the winter of 1972–73 a pack of twelve wolves came out of the Brazeau River via Nigel Pass and into the upper Sunwapta, below the Columbia Icefield. Wolves had been observed throughout Jasper's backcountry that winter, but there had been no sightings in the Athabasca Valley. By the time the wolves got to the Beauty Creek flats they were in hunting mode. Bill Crawford was in Jasper looking for wolf pictures, and he had hiked up the Chaba River on an overnight trip.

While Bill was up there, some German tourist came across a fascinating scene in the Athabasca valley, near Beauty Creek, and got some amazing filmed footage of nine wolves taking down a cow moose. The entire episode took twenty-four hours. He filmed the nine wolves circling, developing a strategy to attack the moose. One wolf finally jumped up at the moose's nose, sinking its fangs into the soft tissue. The moose was now swinging the wolf back and forth off its feet. The moose was so forceful in swinging her head that the wolf was vertically extended outward. While this was taking place and she was distracted, others came in from behind and hamstrung her. Now that she was mortally wounded, the wolves backed off, laid down some distance away and waited for her to die. Twenty-four hours later she expired and the wolves in unison jumped up in a group celebration, standing and licking each other's tongues. Finally, the alpha male and female started feeding, followed by the others in order of rank.

Bill Crawford came out of the Chaba the next day with no photos of wolves only to hear about the luck this tourist had had in filming a sensational wolf kill. Barb and I had Bill over for dinner a couple of nights later, and he said it was really demoralizing to hear about the incident as he worked so hard at his craft with little financial reward for his efforts.

·A MOST UNUSUAL AND GIFTED PARK NATURALIST

I have already written about Bob Sandford in the context of hospitality training (see Chapter Two). Bob and I originally met in 1973 when he was a Parks Canada interpreter. He did not fit the mold of a park naturalist. We hit it off right away, often in the company of another mad Parks Canada employee, Bill Moffat a seasonal warden, and Gord Irwin, a fellow interpreter. Often once a week, the two of us would make the rounds of the many Jasper watering holes, trying to get into trouble. We didn't have to work at it. Trouble just seemed to follow us. I had never met anyone quite like Bob. He certainly wasn't the stereotypical studious, academic and reserved naturalist I had come to know in my young career. He was a breath of fresh air to a national park system that could often be staid and boring. He was enthusiastic and robust in his personality and character. There was never a dull moment around Bob, and he attracted the less-traditional naturalists in Jasper to his circle of influence. Jim Renny and Gord Irwin come to mind. In his tenure as a naturalist in Banff, the wild Pierre Comte also comes to mind; he now works for the Calgary Board of Education. Warden Gordon Maclean wondered, often out loud, if the two of us could survive each other and not disappear in a puff of spontaneous combustion.

I thought Bob was brilliant at times, very creative, especially when I look back on some of the interpretive programs he put together. Of course, next to me, anyone had the potential to be brilliant. He put together a mountain-building program that was part vaudeville, part comedy and grounded with just the right amount of scientific fact. That dash of objective knowledge kept it authentic without dampening the entertainment. Bob would slowly build the mountains out of a pile of sand he had on hand. As they rose to their ultimate height, he would douse them with a bucket of water, to demonstrate the effects of erosion. Then he would apply whipped cream to create glaciers and icefields. I was present on one occasion, when he performed this demonstration in the ballroom of the Jasper Park Lodge. When he threw the water, parts of his creation were sent sailing towards the spectators. Women wearing evening gowns got splashed, and they had reason to be offended, but the result was spontaneous applause from the crowd. No one other than Bob could have gotten away with something like that. He had that connection with the audience that gave him the authority to not hold back.

In 1971, Don Mclean released his song "Vincent (Starry Starry Night)," about Vincent van Gogh. Some time later, to create a new interpretive program, Bob got hold of an art book on Van Gogh's paintings and photographed several them to put together a brilliant slide show. It opened with a painting of a Paris street scene with a starlit sky. The title of the song and Bob's interpretive show were inspired by Van Gogh's painting of the night sky from the window of his asylum room. It was a very thoughtful and stunning program with Mclean's song playing throughout.

I was in Jasper's backcountry most of that summer and so I saw little of Bob until early that fall and segments of the following winter. After that my career aspirations were in flux just like his, and he found himself leaving Parks Canada and starting his own business. He was ambitious, and he often chaffed at the stifling bureaucracy his new boss subjected him to. The biggest constraints were the bounds the chief interpreter tried to put on Bob's more exuberant creations. Bob quit Parks Canada in 1976 and started his own interpretive company. He took a contract that found him in Pacific Rim National Park for a couple of years. Then in 1978, he ended up in Field, BC, and his company, Interpreters of Natural and Human History, started to take off.

He became the unelected mayor and his home with his fiancée, Vi, became the social and intellectual centre of the Yoho Valley. Through Canada Council Grant funding, he brought in noted poets and writers such as Al Purdy and W.P. Kinsella. At this time, he also created a slide show of the people in the community, called *Faces of Field*.

Bob hooked up with Brewster Transport in 1980, introducing hospitality training to its somewhat reluctant staff. As I mentioned in Chapter Two, his was the first such endeavour in Banff's history. He married Vi in 1980, and then in 1981, because of his increasing workload with Brewster Transport and other potential clients in Banff, they moved to Canmore where they remain today. Their life now has far exceeded the simple and rewarding times they spent in Field. Bob's role in human and natural history has climbed to the top of the industry, first nationally and now internationally.

MAC, THE ELDER STATESMAN

Mac Elder was stationed at Maligne Lake with his wife Cathy and two children, Craig and Fiona, when I first came to Jasper. There was nothing elder or old about Mac; he seemed endless in retaining his youth. He often talked of working for an outfitter and being on the trail north of Jasper in the mid-1940s. How could that be? It seemed he always look so young. Even today, retired in Cochrane, Mac and Cathy both seem far younger than their listed ages, and still light-hearted and good-natured about life.

Mac had a unique understanding of his surroundings and an enlightened way of putting things into words and perspective. His career spanned thirty-five years, culminating in the position of chief park warden of two newly established national parks: Pukaskwa, on the north shore of Lake Superior, and Pacific Rim, on the west coast of Vancouver Island.

Mac's experiences in the Canadian Rockies can be broken up into four parts. First are his pre-warden service days, when he worked as a guide and packer for an outfitter on hunting trips and later on geological surveys. Second are his years as a backcountry district warden in Jasper. Third is the time he spent as district warden at Maligne Lake and then worked out of the town of Jasper. Fourth were his two positions as chief park warden, before he retired in 1991. His time in Jasper is highlighted here, in his own words, as he spoke them to interviewer, Christine Everts.

Let's start at the beginning. I was born July 22, 1928, in Bassano, Alberta. I lived down there east of Calgary when I was small. My mother raised four kids by herself. My dad died the year that I was born. So, my mother was a pretty hardy and industrious person, you know. She did a wonderful job. We grew up through the Depression, but we had a good farm and my mother was quite a strong, pioneer person.... But later on, we lived near Olds [southwest of Red Deer and north of Calgary] and my mother was married again. I always wanted to work in the mountains. I worked horses. I rode a horse to school and everything.... So, I was breaking horses before I quit school. I always wanted to do that and go and work in that business because I had worked around ranches.... I went to work for Jack Hargreaves. Jack Hargreaves was a big outfitter at that time.... The first year I worked for him was 1947; we had over eighty head of horses on our hunting trips. He had three early trips and two late trips. Our trips were thirty days.... I worked in that business for quite a few years.

I had worked with two or three different outfitters at different times on these hunting trips and then the geological work after the Leduc field [oil discovery], we worked the limestone. You know the Devonian limestone is that grey rock that you have near Banff and around the cement plant [at Exshaw].... Once they had the Leduc field going the companies and the geological people were interested in studying the limestone because the Leduc field under the ground was very similar to what is standing up horizontal in the mountains, in the Rocky Mountains.... You got to remember we didn't have helicopters or anything. We didn't have any roads in the country in those days either. The Red Water field was in the Mississippian and it came a couple of years after the Leduc field. The Mississippian is also limestone. Then the Pembina field, which is the field at Drayton Valley, is in the Cretaceous. The Cretaceous is an older rock and it is outside of the mountains on the east side and for a couple of years, three years we worked the Devonian, up and down the mountains. I worked all the way from the Ya Ha Tinda clear north almost to Hudson's Hope, BC, with geological work over the years.... We did the Devonian and then we did the Mississippian and then in 1954 after the Pembina field we were out in that east country and out in the low country, what I call the low country and that was a much different kind of place to work because you were in a lot more mud and muskegs. Tough country, [there's] not too many trails. [I'm talking about] that country north of Entrance, north of Hinton and around where Grande Cache is today. It was just a small little settlement with about six Indian houses. When I've been [there] since those days, I'm lost because...they put in roads and houses and a railroad.... I can't even find my directions there anymore, it's so different!

In the winter months Mac worked for a small logging contractor near Sundre. Here he got some good experience in construction and operating machinery. While out on the trail with the hunters, he met the future chief park warden of Jasper, the district warden Mickey McGuire. Later when Mickey became the CPW, he often mentioned to him, "Mac why don't you come work for the parks. You are out there in the bush anyway!" Here, Mac observes:

> That was suggested to me for a few years. But I was smart enough to know that…if you are going to go out there and live in the wintertime like the guys did in those days you got to be pretty mature. I knew enough about that and I knew enough about living in isolation that I didn't want to do that when I was twenty-three or twenty-four years old because it is quite a life…. I was twenty-eight when I went to work for the parks. I was mature enough, old enough and experienced enough. I feel really sorry for the young people today that try to do that because they don't have the background and they don't grow up the same as we did…. We had a whole different background. Living in logging camps and things, you have a whole different world. Very adapt-able to whatever surrounds [we] found ourselves.

Mac spent the first few years on the north boundary of Jasper Park, building warden cabins and new trails. Parks Canada knew that a wave of backcountry visitors was coming, and a lot of them didn't ride horses. He then ended up in the Brazeau district again, constructing new facilities and improving the trails. Finally, it was back up north in the Willow Creek district.

> That north boundary of Jasper is nice country. When I was there, there was a lot of wildlife. We had, along with the horses, a hundred or so elk living there. We had some sheep ranges there. We had some goat ranges. There was a nice bunch of goats, about thirty that moved back and forth from a winter

range to a summer range. I used to see them and there was quite a bear population, a grizzly population, also caribou. We had some interesting times with the bears.... I was there [Willow Creek] until March 1964, up in that country. I enjoyed that country and I enjoyed the work because it was a place where I could ride a lot and there was lots of wildlife in those days. There was the odd [horse] party and there were quite a few hikers in the country in those days.

Bears were an issue throughout the mountain national parks back then, because of poor garbage and food management. As Mac observed:

After we built those first cabins, well there were old cabins in there because this [was] an old established place, but we replaced some and built some. But we got a bad bear in there. I think in 1962–63...a grizzly...in November he moved in. He got into about five of these different cabins. Climbing in through the window and broke everything. [He] tore the place apart. He even tore up the floor in one of these cabins. There was a young guy that was in there that was a warden. He'd been away for a week or ten days. He was married and had a couple of kids in town. He'd been out there for a while. Anyway, when he came back this damn bear was living in his cabin on the Blue Creek district. The poor guy didn't have any experience dealing with stuff like that. He was pretty spooked about it all. He really couldn't handle it.... I got him a new window from town.... I went down with a packhorse and got this window and brought it up to him. I had to take this window 20 miles for him! He didn't even want to stay there.... Well, anyway, the bear hibernated that winter and the next spring he was still around there. This guy that was there, he left. He didn't like living there with that damn bear. That bear was a problem. Of course, I was busy with the crews I had and stuff...the closest this bear came to me was 16 to 18 miles. Anyway, I eventually had to go up in there, I think about June or July I got up there and I was a little luckier than the bear.... He wasn't a nice bear to deal with, but he is history now.

When Mac transferred to a highway district at Maligne Lake in 1964, his experiences with bears only intensified.

In 1965, in late August, I had a young guy that was staff at one of the concessions there, it was a Brewster concession.... This guy and girl had walked into this damn [garbage] dump. I surmise that probably she or he, one of them thought they would like to see a grizzly bear and they did. This guy was mauled very, very badly. She wasn't. She claimed she fainted and they ran out of there and the bear caught him, nailed him.... I was at Maligne Tours Camp playing cards and it was raining and cold. It was the last two or three days of August. When I got this message it was dark, probably seven or eight o'clock at night.... I had an old Fargo truck and...I didn't have any warden to help. And I said to this guy that was there who managed this Maligne Tours Camp... by the name of Stan Kitchen; he was a guide and outfitter for most of his life. I said, "Stan, you better come with me because I got a phone call from the other place that they couldn't find this Fred." They didn't know where he was and they thought something had happened to him with a bear. They didn't have any information.... I went up there in the dark with a flashlight and Stan Kitchen was driving my pickup around the little bit of space that was there and shining the [trucks] lights around. I didn't find the bear, but I found the guy and he was in bad shape. I found people that were dead that weren't hurt as bad as he was.... He stayed conscious. He told me, "I was trying not to pass out because I was hoping that you would come to find me." He didn't know anyone else that would be able to find him up there in the jungle in the night. Anyway, I was able to go and get a stretcher and pick him up, and we came to Maligne Tours

Camp, bandaged him up as best we could. There was a dentist there because they had overnight accommodation in there at the time. The dentist helped me prepare him to be transported. There were about sixty people between the two concessions that stayed there overnight. [There were] about thirty at Brewster's and about thirty at Maligne Tours, plus all the staff. We bandaged this guy up...and loaded him up through an emergency door in a bus and I sent him off to Jasper. I phoned Mickey [Chief Warden Mickey McGuire] and said, "Do you think that you can send me up some kind of fast car to meet him on the road...I've got this mess here. A bear has mauled this guy and I'm sending him out of here, but it would be better if you had someone come up and meet him because they are not going to make much time here on this rough road with that bus."

A few months later I was talking to him [Mickey], and we were involved in this thing for quite a few years. I said to him, "I often wondered when I phoned you if I was excited." He said, "God, no you were as calm as can be. I was amazed!" Anyway, Bill Ruddy, owner of Maligne Tours came up with his station wagon. He knew the road and could come fast and we got this guy out of there. Then I hunted around and found this girl. She was in [the] Brewster Chalet. In the evening, they used to serve coffee and cocoa, cookies and everything to these guests. She got into the middle of these thirty guests probably and twenty staff, and it was just a horror show there! Her [there] telling about this bear chewing this guy up and everything. So, I grabbed her and got hold of one of the boys that was working there, and I said, "Let's get a damn car and we'll take this girl to the hospital and get her out of here. We can't handle her here and she needs someone to put her to bed." I couldn't do that there. I didn't have anybody to do that. So, I drove her to town and to a doctor.... He thought I might have another one that had been chewed up. The doctor was kind of upset because I had brought her in here and he said, "Why did you bring her in

Grizzly damage at Moraine Lake Lodge's pantry near Lake Louise. "Trying to get into the cookie jar."
DALE PORTMAN COLLECTION

here? I don't need her!" I said, "Well you got her!" But anyway, I had a couple of incidences where I took people [into the Jasper Hospital]...in not too good of shape.

That was an interesting time. The father of this guy [who had been mauled] was a used car salesman out of Edmonton. He was pretty upset, and that was understandable. I would have been too if my kid had got chewed up or somebody I knew. I was upset, anyway, and he wasn't related to me. But his father was pretty hysterical about it all when he did come... and I could tell [by] dealing with him that he was going to try and sue somebody. So anyway in a few months, we had a lawsuit against us. They sued me as the area manager and the supervisor of the place for negligence and my chief warden, Mickey McGuire, and Bruce Mitchell who was the superintendent, and the Queen. We all got sued. Our names were all on the thing. Because there wasn't any precedent, nobody had been sued over a grizzly bear at the time...so they were quite a while getting anything done. But they did eventually have an investigation for discovery [of evidence] and they, the bureaucrats did a poor job of it because they should have sent my chief warden to that investigation for discovery [pre-trial], but they didn't. They sent a bureaucrat. Of course, he had no experience, and of course, they made a mess of it. But that is the way they do things. The lawyer that I had at the time, he became a judge and had given me another good lawyer from Edmonton. He was a prince of a guy. I see him occasionally yet. He is a really nice guy and a really sharp guy. I was so lucky because...when you go to court with these government lawyers, most of them can't defend a traffic ticket, let alone deal with something like a bear mauling. But he was an excellent guy and he had an excellent helper. We went through that. Eight and a half years after the thing we were in court. It took that long. Mickey McGuire had retired and died. Bruce Mitchell had retired and he was in hospital in Victoria, and Stan Kitchen had died. The father of the young fellow who had instigated the law suit had died. So, when we got to court, there was Fred and myself, and he was a good guy. Fred was a real decent young man. Nobody deserves what happened to him. He had no animosity against me. He gave me full credit for saving his life. He even came and saw me. I had been to see him in the hospital. He was in the hospital in Edmonton for probably six months.... His attorneys and his father [before he died] and the rest of them, they didn't want him to come near me, but he did anyway. He was a nice fellow. We were in court for a week and it turned out all right. I told a couple of my supervisors in later years that I was found competent by a high court judge, and that was more than they could say! I don't know any other public servant that had been found competent by a high court judge.... anyway, I have that to brag about!

Most wardens have an arsenal of good bear stories accumulated over their careers, and Mac mentioned a good one in his interview.

Another one I was going to tell you.... When I was in town... looking after the high use area not too long before I moved out of there, I got called that there was a grizzly on the golf course at the Jasper Park Lodge. It was in the middle of the afternoon, I think it was in July or August. They had such a thing as a "Totem Pole" golf tournament. So, this grizzly was over there.... I jumped in my vehicle and went over there and called Norm Woody. He was in town working, he was an experienced guy. He met me over there. This big grizzly was right around this portable kitchen and they had a hip of beef and had buns and pickles and coffee and this kind of stuff. It was on a trailer sort of thing. This bear was around...as close as that bronze over there [20 feet].... He was a great big bear in good condition and he had a tag in his ear.... He wasn't furious, he wasn't mad yet, but he was very curious.... I didn't particularly like the look of him and, heck, there was fifty people there around that bear...You know how crazy people are around something like that. They thought they would pet him, I guess. But anyway, a couple of young wardens came along. We kind of worked this bear away from that picnic thing and away out there. I had a vehicle out there and a couple of times I worked him with my pickup.... Norman had a tranquilizer gun. He loaded it and he was good with a gun. He knew his business and one of the young guys went and brought a bear trap [a portable culvert trap on wheels] in there. We didn't get this bear moved very quickly...we were going to ease this bear out of there. There is a fence on one side of the golf course to keep the elk off it in the wintertime. Norm had gone over there and opened the gate.... These young guys were kind of staying away, they didn't get too close and I was working this bear and I think I had a broom or something.... I eased this bear up a little ways towards where Norm was, within 150 feet, and the bear got mad. He took me and I was right on my ass! I ran as fast as I could and he [Norman] had one of those big heavy half-tons with big tires on it and the bear was chasing me and he was happy to see me run. I think he was having more fun than I was! But he was maybe only 8 feet behind me and I am running as fast as I could. I ran right over the tailgate and right over the cab, and he was right there looking at me and I'm standing on the cab and Norman shot him with the tranquilizing gun.... We skidded him into the bear trap. We put a rope on him and threaded it through and pulled him in there with the truck.... That was as close as I want to get to a bear.... I found it difficult to protect grizzly bears when I had a negligent lawsuit against me for all those years.

He had one more good story while he was working as assistant chief park warden in the town of Jasper, before transferring to Pukaskwa National Park in 1975.

I have another funny one that I always tell...when I was in there [Jasper] in that high use area. I was right across the street from the fire hall [the warden office] and the ambulance and Bev [Hunter] (the warden dispatcher)...she came in and said, "Mac, can you take an ambulance call?" I said, "I guess so, where am I going?" She said, "I don't know. They [the reporting people] are over at the fire hall. They are desperate." So, I went over there, it was about 11:30...anyway there was a guy who had an ambulance parked in front of the door, and I said to him, "Who's going with me?" He said, "Got nobody, got nobody!" I said, "Well, where am I going?" He said, "To the post office." Well, that's just right next building practically [the post office is just across the street from both the warden office and the fire hall]. So, I recruited a guy off the street there and said, "Come on with me...I've got an ambulance call." He was a warden that was in town that day.... He said, "I don't want to do that." I said,

"To hell with you. You are coming!" So, we went over there and I couldn't park. I had to double park in the middle of the street. We got in there and this poor old guy is dead in the middle of the floor. So anyway, we gather him up and we put him in the basket and stuck him in this ambulance and I go to the hospital [emergency] and they are pouring cement. I couldn't get in.... I had to go around to the front door. So, we packed this guy in through the front door.... The doctor said to me, "Mac, why did you bring this guy in here for? He's already dead!" I said, "What do you want to do, Doc? Take him to the landfill?" He said, "No, no take him to the morgue!"...That's what kind of, keeps you going, those things!

During Christine's interview with Mac, Mac's wife Cathy also related some stories about their years at Maligne Lake that give the reader an idea of what it was like for the park warden's wife to live at a warden station and try to raise children. For some while, the road to Jasper from Maligne Lake was only open in the snow-free months – mid-April through mid-November. When Christine asked Cathy, "Did you like the life of a warden's wife?" Cathy answered:

I liked the summertime, [but I] hated the wintertime because you know you are isolated and you are stuck in there. It was fine before we had kids and you could go out and go cross-country skiing, or snowmobiling or whatever, snowshoeing.... But when you have two little ones, then you are kind of housebound. I mean, you take them outside every day to get them out, but still you are housebound. Where do you go? I found it really depressing when the camp, Brewster's [Transport] and Maligne [Tours] would leave in the fall. You could go over and visit them [during the summer season], and then when they were gone, you were there by yourself.

I'd mope around all winter and then in the spring, when those lights came on across the lake again, you knew that you

could go visit somebody if you wanted to. It wasn't so important because it was your choice. Lots of people could handle
that isolation really well. I didn't.... [We moved into Jasper]
when Craig was ready to start school...March of 1972. You kind
of think, "Well, this is the last time I'm going to be driving this
road in the winter and everything and I hope I don't hit a moose
and I hope that we don't get stuck with an avalanche, and we
did." Max Winkler had to come up with the station wagon and
pick us up because we left our vehicles and moving van on one
side of the avalanche along Medicine Lake and got taken into
town. The next day they had to come up with a bulldozer and
clear out the avalanche [debris].

You know when famous people came to Jasper they always
either came to Maligne Lake or they went to Tonquin Valley
or someplace like that. Toni Klettl or Bert Rowe got Princess
Alexandra, but we got Princess Margriet of the Netherlands and
her husband Pieter [at Maligne Lake]. They took them down the
lake [by boat] and when they came back they brought them all
into the house and we served them tea in our house at Maligne!
The next day they came back again, and the tourists had gotten
wind of them, that they were up there. They were going to go
riding that day. Anyway, they were all out in the yard and
Princess Margriet came down and rang our doorbell and invited
herself in! She didn't like all the people bothering her.

ELEVEN

BLUE CREEK

FINALLY, MY OWN PERMANENT BACKCOUNTRY DISTRICT

I was still a young man, in my mid-twenties, when I got the job I had long dreamt of as a backcountry warden in Jasper National Park in 1973. My district was approximately 1000 square kilometres, and to get to the trailhead you had to travel 90 kilometres by truck, mainly on a dirt road. From there it took a further two days on horseback to get to the main cabin.

My uniform started with a light khaki shirt with shoulder flashes, epaulets and two, button-down breast pockets with flaps. My Stetson was baize and had a dark brown band around it with a brass badge mounted on the front. The emblem was of a beaver standing on the wooden thatch of his house with the badge number displayed below and a decorated crown at the top. Green Levi-Strauss jeans that wore like iron and a green jacket with flashes finished everything off. The tie was green, often soiled and usually creased from residing in my saddlebag for long periods of time.

It was busy through the summer; there were hikers, private horse parties and outfitters with their clients passing by. Activity tapered off in the fall, and by late October everyone was gone. No one used this part of the mountains during the winter, and it wasn't until late spring – usually early June – before any activity returned. During the winter months, it was only you and the dog with the odd pack rat or pine marten to share the space with. Once in a while, if the opportunity presented itself, you could team up with the warden in the neighbouring district and do a patrol together.

Travel in the summer was often on horseback, sometimes on foot, and in winter always on snowshoes either Ojibwa style, with a pointed toe and heel, or Iroquois, with a curved front. Sturdy cross-country ski equipment was just around the corner. Besides the main district cabin, I had several smaller patrol cabins. Most of the park cabins were built no more than 13 kilometres apart, but the odd one could be up to 20 kilometres away. My working schedule during the spring, summer and fall revolved around the rhythm of twenty-four days in, four days off, one day getting resupplied in town and then back out again. In the winter that changed, and you could be out for a couple of months at a stretch. Sometimes you were brought to town, maybe to fill in up at the ski hill on avalanche-control work or as a duty warden around town. When the winter snows started to pile up and provide better travelling conditions, we headed back to our districts.

Until you got used to it, you had long lonely stretches you had to adjust to. The longer you're exposed to this type of environment, though, the more precious the solitude becomes. There was a comfort you developed with yourself, as well as your surroundings, a self-reliance you came to depend upon and an attachment to the land that became almost sacred in nature.

What I gained from these solitary experiences bordered on mystical at times. Starlit nights, splashy sunrises, glowing dusks, all rekindled a connection with spirit and wonder and I became immersed in the marvel of it all. A howling wolf or a yapping coyote on a crisp fall night, with a full moon brightening the landscape, added to the magic of the bull elk, bugling his stately presence.

Because of the isolation, communication was important but primitive. A forestry phone system connected the main district cabins along a trunk line to a central communication hub in Jasper, which was located at the town's fire hall. My ring was two long and a short and my ear was tuned to it. Many of the patrol cabins were also connected by forestry line, and those that weren't had at least a single side-band radio. Your lifeline was that phone, and keeping it in good working order was a paramount responsibility motivated by self-preservation.

There was a backcountry district on either side of me: Willow Creek to the east, the Smoky to the west. Al Stendie was at Willow Creek while Marv Millar was on the Smoky. The three of us got along well, and occasionally we would pair up to complete chores that two people were more effective at. During the fall hunting season, which involved patrolling some provincial land, we would occasionally double up. In the evening, if you had someone to play against, cribbage was the card game of choice, otherwise it was solitaire. Hands were dealt and cards counted, usually over a large pot of tea but on special occasions, accompanied by a bottle of whisky or rum. Wooden matchsticks were used as the original pegs had long disappeared and many of the crib boards were homemade from a piece of wood or elk antler.

My western boundary was Snake Indian Pass. The river of the same name ran east through the district and past my headquarters cabin. Blue Creek came in from the north and joined it near this point. The Snake Indian then carried on to Willow Creek, at which point it turned south, eventually reaching the Athabasca River near the site of the old Jasper House and that Native massacre of the fur-trade days.

Each cabin had a small library stacked with westerns and science fiction – rarely did you find anything intellectual. That started to change when university graduates started manning the districts. There was the usual stack of magazines, the most popular being *Playboy* and *Penthouse*, but tamer magazines such as *Argosy* and *Outdoor Living* could also be found. If you were really lucky, you would find a copy of *Western Horseman*.

If you didn't get along with your neighbour it was a different matter. When Toni Klettl was the Blue Creek warden, a decade and a half before me, the Willow Creek warden was Larry Tremblay. Toni was Austrian and Larry was French. They, of course, didn't get along, and the river was often referred to as the Rhine. On the way through to his district, Toni never stopped at Willow Creek and Larry was fine with that. If you listened to one, you wondered how the other could survive back there. If you talked to the other, you wondered how after all those years the first one knew nothing about horses.

GETTING TO SEE THE BLUE CREEK DISTRICT

I had a busy couple of days getting prepared to leave on my first trip. It was going to be a chance to acquaint myself with the land, as I slowly moved upcountry, and it would entail lots of trail clearing and phone-line maintenance. Two of my three ponies knew the district well, which helped immensely, but I needed to know it first-hand. I had spent part of the fall of 1971 in Willow Creek on boundary patrol, and Barb and I had done a side trip to the Blue Creek district cabin, so I was familiar with some of the trails. I would be gone for almost a month, so fresh food had to be purchased. All the cabins were well-stocked with staples, so my ponies weren't going to be packed down too heavy. I also had to stop at the warden equipment store to pick up a few odds and ends that needed to be taken to some of the patrol cabins.

Dennis (Denny) Welsh, the laconic barn boss, was expecting me when I drove up with all my gear into the yard at Maligne Range, where the government horses are kept. He gave me one of those withering, "Where the hell have you been" looks as I walked up to greet him. Gee, I was only five minutes late! He had the horses already in the stock truck with their packsaddles on, and all I had to do was stash gear in the back of the truck behind the horses. Denny had done this often and did not seem too concerned about the horses trampling my saddle, pack boxes or duffel.

The trip up was predominantly uneventful as Dennis was not a big talker and I was soon relegated to looking out the window and watching the countryside pass by. We crossed over the Snake Indian River and gained the east side on a Bailey bridge that dated back to the 1940s. It was suspended high up on the canyon walls, and the approach from the west was down a sharp, curvy road that squared up with the bridge at the last minute. The exit to the east was just as exciting, and both sides could be challenging in the late fall when you had snow and ice to deal with. The road was closed in the winter, as it was never ploughed.

After climbing out of the canyon, we gradually ascended through an extensive set of aspen groves on southwesterly facing grass slopes, until after a few kilometres, the road levelled off in a canopy of mixed spruce, aspen and pine near the trailhead to Celestine Lakes.

The road ran on relatively flat for 16 kilometres beyond this point, until it dropped down onto a comparatively open flood plain nestled in an old oxbow of the river. It consisted of small meadows, aspen stands and mixed coniferous trees. Across the river and next to it was a large, black, shale cliff, and on this side, under the shadow of the face was the aptly named, Shale Banks Warden Cabin.

After climbing up along the side of the valley, the road continued for another 24 kilometres through heavy forest cover and hilly terrain until we reached the end of the road at Seldom Inn. In this last stretch, if you're paying attention, you can hear the roar of Snake Indian Falls, a couple hundred metres off to the west. It a spectacular sight and one of the great points of interest in Jasper that very few visitors get to see. Back then, there was no sign nailed to the tree that announced its presence, just a skimpy trail. Only the odd passing hiker, mountain biker or horseback rider ever heard it through the trees and stopped to investigate.

The other landmark before the falls was the Clay Hill, and it lived up to its reputation on this day. We had just been hit by a heavy rain shower when we arrived at the top of the hill and on the way down we almost went over the side on a tight bend because the road was so slippery. Fortunately, Dennis knew the hill well and had geared down as we headed towards the next bend, but even then, he had to gently apply the brakes and we again started to slide. He stepped off the brakes and let the truck run on the slimy surface of clay, while it was being held back by the transmission. From my vantage point, things were not looking good. He sensed that as he gave me a quick glance.

Looking at the road ahead, he knew that at the start of the next corner, the road surface was reinforced with gravel, which gave better traction. He passed on this important information to me via his eyes and lack of concern. It gave me one opportunity that morning to see some emotion spread across his face. He looked over and gave me an amusing look, and then it was back to stoically driving the truck while I relaxed my grip on the door handle.

Dennis is a salt of the earth type of guy, as capable and trustworthy as you can get, the kind the world needs more of. In any setting with a whisky bottle and a few glasses, say around a kitchen table, a metamorphosis would occur. Dennis became animated and extroverted as he engaged in lively conversations about horses and mountains. This was his unguarded time, something he balanced well in his life. I was experiencing his guarded side that day.

Seldom Inn was aptly named for it rarely saw anyone staying overnight. It was usually used as a staging point for the two backcountry districts. It was an older log structure that was longer and narrower than most, and it had a large fenced pasture, a sturdy set of corrals and some hitching rails standing nearby. It was a place where the horses could be left safely, while a warden was out on days off.

Denny offered to help me pack the horses. I thanked him but said I would be fine. Packing horses alone was something I would be doing all summer, and I was happy to be on my own. I had been to Seldom Inn once before, so I was starting out in familiar country.

My routine that summer was to stop at Willow Creek overnight, on the way to Blue Creek. It was only 13 kilometres from Seldom Inn and a doable distance as a one-day trip from town. If I carried on, it would be another 13 kilometres before I reached my first patrol cabin at Welbourne.

At Willow Creek, from the woodshed looking toward the barn.
DALE PORTMAN COLLECTION

About 11 kilometres up the trail, I entered a large meadow where a trail led west at the north end, passing by two backcountry camp-grounds; one for horses and one for hikers. The trail then carried on as a shortcut to Blue Creek and the north boundary trail. After skirting the meadow, the trail climbed up into the trees for the last kilometre and a half to the cabin. Finally, at the end of the trail stood a familiar large gate made of lodgepole pine and a sign announcing Willow Creek.

As I swung the gate open and led my horses through, I saw to my right a corral and a surprisingly decent barn with a couple of sets of hitching rails out front, while on the far side, another set. To my left, a wooden locker or shed, and just past it and set back a bit, was a tack shed. More to the front of everything, overlooking Willow Creek, facing west, stood the cabin. In front of it was a tall white flag pole that couldn't be missed. An equally tall weather tower, much like the mast of a ship with telemetry and probes on it, was located on the far side of the cabin. A white screen box at its base housed a couple of thermometers and a hydro-thermograph.

There were probably 200 metres between the barn and the cabin but what grabbed my attention was the huge meadow spreading out in front of me, with Daybreak Peak off in the distance. It's a view that stays with you, and when a new cabin was built facing north a few years later, it had one of the most impressive porch views in all of Jasper's backcountry. What drew my attention away from this pastoral setting was the smoke coming out of the chimney and someone standing on the porch.

Al Stendie was the district warden and someone I had chummed around with and known for a few years. There was no need for me to try to impress him, or visa-versa; we knew each other well. He was a steady, easy-going guy who loved a good joke – someone you could trust. With a guitar in his hand, he could channel Roger Millar, and when he had the time, he played in a local band, The Road Kill. His biggest failing was he was the worst Ukrainian whist player north of the Panama Canal.

From the porch, Al was telling me to leave my saddle horse at the barn and just bring the two packhorses over. With Al's help, both horses were unpacked in short order, and then I led them back over to the barn where Fife, my saddle horse, was standing, nervously waiting for some company. I loosened off all their cinches, letting them stand while I filled their feedbags with oats and then placed them over their heads. While they munched away, I unsaddled and placed the riggings on the racks in the barn. Once they had finished their oats, I pulled the bags off, hobbled and belled them and kicked them loose in the big meadow for the night.

After a hearty supper, we sat down and caught up. Afterwards, I conned him into playing a few hands of whist. We were waiting for the usual 8:00 PM radio call on the single side-band radio. Once we had checked in and let the dispatcher know our plans for the next day, we signed off and went back to the card game.

I had my horses in early, before breakfast, and was packed up and gone by 9:00 AM. It was going to be a 26-kilometre ride. Halfway to Blue Creek was Welbourne Cabin, where I planned to stop for an early lunch. While sitting on its low porch overlooking a willow-strewn meadow, a small herd of elk appeared. Behind them, off in the distance, was a palisade of peaks, and nestled below them somewhere around a shoulder was my district cabin. I had come this way once before on boundary patrol, so it wasn't a new view but it was a fresh and exciting one, with all the expectations and anticipation holding my attention longer than expected. I was entering a new chapter in my life.

At mile twelve, after the sulphur springs and Mud Creek, I passed by Kelly's Pond, the only significant landmark of note. From this point, the next 5 kilometres were as straight as an arrow until I reached the drift fence with its closed gate. From here it was 1.5 kilometres to my destination. The trail quickly climbed onto a tree-covered esker and followed its spine until I saw a meadow to my left, down through the trees. On closer inspection, I could see the back of a cabin. Centred on its outside wall, a galvanized washtub was hanging from a peg. A hundred metres later I was at the main gate.

The enclosed meadow was only a few acres in size, and at the far end was a tack shed with two hitching rails standing out front. Behind was the water supply, a spring-fed creek that ran all year. Off to the left was a large but frail corral. The main cabin had been recently built, (eight years earlier) and was one of two designed and constructed this large; the other was the Brazeau district cabin in the southern part of the park. Both cabins had a cement foundation and a porch that was quite large, as well as, two bedrooms and a main living area. Between the main gate and the cabin was the toolshed with a set of hitching rails on the far side towards the cabin.

I spent a good part of the week here, getting familiar with how everything operated, making sure the wood supply was adequate and that there was lots of kindling. There was a hand pump nearby and the well provided the best drinking water imaginable. There was a clothesline set up near the well, strung between two tall poles with a stand at one end. The cabin was well-stocked with provisions and it had a trapdoor and a ladder that accessed a small cold room or cellar.

I settled in quite nicely and spent the evenings planning my summer.

My first patrol from here was going to be up the Snake Indian River to Hoodoo, 26 kilometres away. Most of the work would be cutting trail, fixing the phone line and splitting firewood. I left Blue Creek excited about seeing new country but concerned about how things would go in a strange setting.

Blue Creek enters the much bigger Snake Indian River at a point where it storms out of a canyon and scuffles its way downstream for a short distance. Depending on the time of year, it can be tricky crossing it on horseback. Upstream a short distance, just before the canyon, was a narrow hiker bridge that was not an option. The horse crossing was cobbled together with large stones and it could be tricky footing. It was located at the mouth of Blue Creek, right at a bend where it enters the larger river. Exiting on the far side was also a challenge as there was only one spot where the bank sloped gently to the water. It provided no room for a mistake. When the river was high, if you missed the exit point, there was a good chance you could be carried out into the main current, downstream, and you didn't want that to happen. You would be carried into a stretch of the river that is extremely difficult to get out of. Cut banks and heavy timber block you in on either side.

Our crossing was uneventful as Spider did a good job leading us across. One of the reasons I was riding him and not Fife was that he was quite familiar with the crossing, and it helped that Rusty, the packhorse, was his usual cool and focused self. Fife brought up the rear, following attentively.

Just past the cut off to the upper Blue Creek valley, following the north boundary trail, I had my first glimpse of the Snake Indian Lakes, a number of large but shallow backwaters extending out on both sides of the river.

Thirteen kilometres up the valley was a log shack referred to as Three Slides. It was named as such because of the three avalanche paths nearby that provided graze for the horses. The cabin was in a small opening at the edge of a heavily timbered slope, overlooking a scrubby clearing. It was a dark place with huge Engelmann spruce towering over the cabin, providing scant opportunities for daylight to reach it. The steady rain did not improve the gloom but somehow it made the cabin seem more inviting than usual.

I stayed and did a quick inventory of what was there. The rain quit overnight but moisture continued dripping down off the trees onto its tin roof. Out in the meadow, morning broke bright and sunny, leaving the cabin in dark contrast. I moved on to Hoodoo.

Hoodoo is in a manmade clearing surrounded by coniferous trees in a setting that is a step up from Three Slides. Up the trail a ways was a willow-choked meadow that had just enough feed to keep the horses around for a couple of days, if they didn't poke their eyes out trying to get at the grass. Once they got bored, though, I was hopeful they would pull out, up the valley, to a horse camp at Oatmeal where the grass was better, instead of down towards Blue Creek. There was a rickety drift fence in place to discourage them. The Oatmeal campsite was conveniently located about halfway to Snake Indian Pass.

I spent several days at Hoodoo, and the next morning I found the horses in the nearby meadow. After that, though, over subsequent mornings, I found them farther and farther up the valley towards Oatmeal and on the last morning they were right at the campsite. On that morning, it turned out to be a 10-kilometre jingle as I was heading for Blue Creek, so it made for a long day.

During my stay, I took an inventory of what needed to be done in that stretch of the district and dug a new hole for the outhouse. I scratched my head as to how to move the structure over to the new hole and decided to leave it for another day. The cabin's interior certainly needed a new coat of paint, and the exterior of the tack shed and the cabin's porch was due for another coat of grey paint. I would pack in the necessary paint on the next shift. Later, I added some reinforcement to some of the weaker spans on the drift fence, which was there to stop the horses from moving down the valley towards Blue Creek, and replaced some decking planks on an older bridge.

On a day ride a few days later, I rode up to Snake Indian Pass. The approach to the pass was long and the alpine was extensive and it was a beautiful ride on a sunlit day. On the other side of the pass, just as you reach the subalpine, was Byng Warden Cabin in the Smoky District. It was a beautifully located cabin in a high meadow, providing views in all directions. I had lunch there on the porch looking out at the country that spread to the north and the Smoky River valley, far off in the distance.

There was another pass, Byng, to the northeast that is separated from Snake Indian Pass by a wide, gentle ridge. It was an alternate route back to Hoodoo. I followed up a clear creek to Byng Pass and there stopped to take in the view. High up in the green tundra I took out my binoculars and glassed the nearby slopes.

I had time to investigate the alpine bench that extended across from me to the east, with its deep-seated basins that looked so inviting from above. I discovered a myriad of small lakes, snuggled down in exquisite pockets, and several alpine tarns in full display, spread out like little mirrors across a malachite setting, giving the terrain a velvet-like texture. All of it stretched out high above the valley like a lost and hidden paradise. It was with reluctance that I finally left and headed back to Hoodoo.

FINALLY, THE UPPER BLUE CREEK VALLEY

It felt like home as I rode back into the yard at Blue Creek after my stint at the head of the Snake Indian, and the horses seemed to be excited about getting back. I found over the years that they never seemed relaxed or ready to embrace the area around Hoodoo. They always seemed apprehensive, restless and quick to spook. Al Stendie spent time as the Blue Creek warden a few years before and had the same feeling about the place.

I spent a couple of days at Blue Creek, getting some paperwork done and doing an inventory of the buildings. I was really getting excited about going up the Blue Creek valley and spending time at the Topaz Cabin. So, a few days later, with the chores completed, Spider, Fife, Rusty and I headed up the valley to the cabin 18 kilometres away.

Blue Creek District Warden Cabin from a distance, midwinter in the mid-1980s.
DALE PORTMAN COLLECTION

I took along a little Baker tent that I could set up as a base, up the valley past the cabin. These were good tents for fly camping, structured like lean-tos. They provided protection from the elements but at the same time you could see unobstructed out the front, and although they were made of canvas, they were reasonably light for the time. The cooking area was under an awning connected to the tent and held up by local poles and secured by guy lines.

The first 8 kilometres was up the west side of the valley, well above the canyon, where the trail gained over 200 metres. The best description of the area is: a rocky, undulating, timber-choked, piece of boredom that didn't end until I saw Blue Creek below as it exited a vast meadow, just before taking a rocky trip down an ugly stretch of canyon.

Once I reached this point on the creek and crossed to the other side, the trip became a much more interesting experience. From here it was 9 kilometres to Topaz and the rocky trail magically turned to sand, as it meandered through an open pine forest. The trail remained

One of my favourite places to stay: Topaz Cabin up the Blue Creek valley.
DALE PORTMAN COLLECTION

on the east side of the valley and was often broken up by dry meadows. These clearings provided great platforms for viewing wildlife and the surrounding countryside. These scenic oases were separated by open stands of snarly pine, growing up through a carpet of caribou moss and lichen. Scattered amongst the forest floor were old charred stumps, which lingered from the last forest fire, decades ago.

I arrived at Topaz in the early afternoon with plenty of time to check out the provisions in the cabin, split some firewood and add to the kindling box. In the creek near the cabin was an inviting pool of water that begged for a fishing lure to break its calm surface. I managed to drop a red, panther martin into the transition point between the pool and the faster water above. Immediately I had a strike. A nice rainbow was on the line. He fought vigorously, launching himself out of the water, dancing on the surface one minute then diving and darting around the bottom the next. When I landed him, he was a nice two pounder that barely fit the frying pan and became the main course for dinner with enough left over for breakfast.

After supper, I went for a walk up the trail to the first meadow and spotted a cow moose and her calf standing by the creek edge, looking my way. She gazed at me for a while then nonchalantly turned and crossed the creek with her young one in tow. It wasn't until she entered the timber and broke into a trot that she showed any concern. I walked into the middle of the meadow to get a better view of the eastern side of the valley. It was dominated by an uninterrupted wall of limestone known as the Ancient Wall that ran for miles in either direction. I glassed its lower slopes looking for game with no luck.

The following day, I went back up to the first meadow and took an obscure trail that led across the creek and up the hillside. I was amongst scattered pine with caribou moss and lichen abounding on the forest floor. From the height of the ridge, I could see a side valley below and a large lake that filled it. I had a filtered but decent view of Topaz Lake through the trees. I dropped down to the lake and rode at the edge of its shoreline, following along as it slowly curved to the west.

Finally, I urged Spider back up towards the summit of the ridge, to gain some elevation and possibly find a viewing spot. On the crest was an opening where I could see past the lake to the upper reaches of the valley. I sat there taking it all in and had my lunch. As I sat, a tragic play unfolded before me; a least weasel was chasing a ground squirrel, almost in circles, and then they disappeared for a short while. It didn't bode well for the squirrel. Shortly thereafter, maybe 15 metres away, the slight weasel could be seen dragging the chubby ground squirrel off to its lair.

I was eager to get going the next morning, and after a quick breakfast of cereal and toast, I was saddling the ponies. Again, the trail travelled through stands of white bark pine, carpeted with bearberry and the ever-present caribou moss. Once I broke out of the trees, which was often, I was exposed to long continuous meadows. I encountered purple monkshood sprinkled about on the small dry hillsides next to the trail. Later in a rare stand of spruce, which showed signs of moisture, I was presented with a lovely display of bog orchids.

The western side was endowed with countless side valleys, all, I imagined, hiding secret lakes. The eastern side showed the unbroken terrain of the Ancient Wall. Eventually, though, the wall gave way to open green hillsides, above a band of older spruce. On a few occasions, the trail passed close to the creek. I was happy to find more stretches of the trout-filled stream, meandering about with its azure pools.

While riding up the middle of the valley, I happened to look up and see a band of sheep bedded down on a grassy hillside. There was between fifteen and twenty of them, all lying peacefully in the sun, taking in the view, no doubt watching me and the horses coming up the valley. I was about to reach for my binoculars when suddenly, higher up, I caught something dark and dangerous running pell-mell down towards the resting sheep. It was a grizzly bear coming quickly, and he was almost in their midst before there was any apparent notice from the lounging group. Suddenly there was an explosion of activity. The bighorn were scattering in all directions. The grizzly never hesitated, continuing through the dispersing sheep with now one obvious intention, the valley bottom. Were we now his quarry?

I could hear him crashing down through the timber, heading in our direction. All the horses were now attentive to the ruckus but showed no panic as they followed the sound ploughing downward off the hillside. With my heart in my mouth, I expected at any moment to see him burst into the meadow. My eyes darted about looking for any sign of him. Where was he coming out? Then there was only silence. The sheep had settled down and the spell was broken.

I nudged Fife on while the others eagerly followed. The bear never appeared and I've always wondered what his intent was; it was such a strange and puzzling event. Maybe he just wanted to put on a show. I can picture him now, running through the sheep, chuckling to himself, looking down at us frozen in place in the middle of the valley. It must have made his day.

Keith Foster sitting in front of a Baker tent a few years earlier on boundary patrol, near Vega Basin.
DALE PORTMAN COLLECTION

Not far from where this happened, there was a break in the Ancient Wall and you could see a high col off in the distance, which later I found out was 44/40 Col. The trail across the col is well-defined, which shows evidence of substantial game use. Rather unusual for such a high pass; at 2500 metres, it is only 300 metres below the surrounding summits. Years later, I hiked up there and found a pronounced game trail leading over its summit. There was sign of elk, sheep, goat, wolf, coyote and grizzly bear.

I was now in sheep country, highlighted by the natural arch I had heard about, farther along. To the west, the mountains had turned red and contrasted surreally with the rest of the landscape. A couple of kilometres beyond, after stepping across a creek that came in from the east, we came to the end of the meadow. It was a perfect spot to set up camp. With the timber at my back, I could look south down the meadow with an unobstructed view. There was running water nearby and an abundance of firewood that only needed to be gathered off the ground. I had been stopping to cut deadfall off the trail, which had accumulated over the winter, but for the last 8 kilometres, there had been very few fallen trees blocking the way.

Once the packs were off and the tent was up, I got busy building a saddle rack. I unsaddled the horses, belled and hobbled them and turned them loose. When the sun finally set they were still only a hundred metres away on the other side of the creek. The weather looked good for at least a few days, so I set my small kitchen up in front of the awning. Two pack boxes were put together to act as a table, while one of the remaining two became a bench. The remaining one held all the plates, cooking pots, utensils, easy-to-reach condiments and food. That night I sat under a canopy of stars. When the moon appeared as a full globe and the stars faded, I could still see the horses not far off in the distance, a comforting tinkle crossing the creek becoming music to my ears.

The stream that passed in front of my camp was upper Blue Creek. It came in from the north, its source being Azure Lake situated on the northern boundary of the park. Its final kilometre before reaching us travelled down through more than 250 metres of jumbled rock and cliff, in a sequence of waterfalls and canyons. This oxygenated water was the clearest and as thirst quenching as you could imagine.

After bringing the horses in the next morning, I went to work gathering and cutting firewood. Once I had enough to keep me going for several days, I headed off on foot with a chainsaw in hand, to cut out the 5-kilometre trail to the first Caribou Lake. The two lakes are located off to the northwest and sit in a U-shaped valley. They are full of trout and provide good habitat, ensuring plenty of future trout populations, both in the lakes and the streams below.

After cutting my way to the first lake, I stopped for a bite to eat, and then I pulled a collapsible rod and reel out of my pack. I had one on in my second cast, and within a few minutes I had two that were about a pound each. I continued up the north side of the lake until I came across an unusual formation protruding out of the ground. Standing a metre and a half high, it was shaped like a cone surrounded by a multicoloured bed of wet moss and water. The major tones were of red and ochre, the colour of the surrounding peaks.

The next day I saddled Spider and headed up the right side of Blue Creek where I picked up a decent trail. It was easy going as we climbed the steep terrain through the trees, with only a couple of deadfall encountered that I could easily skirt around or ride over. I would come back the next day and removed them. After a couple of kilometres, I rode out of the trees into a wide-open valley. There were probably 8 kilometres of open terrain ahead, with scattered stands of timber on the periphery and steeper side slopes. Off to the right was the col Jim and Leonard must have come down from on their trip into the valley in 1967. You could see the heavy talus below, and it was not something you would want to bring a horse down.

Though the valley ahead looked enticing, it was difficult terrain for the horse, as the low willows hid miles of boggy ground. This persisted all the way up to a startlingly blue lake at its upper reach. Every side creek coming off the Ancient Wall had a boggy area around it, which required examination and navigation. Some crossings were much easier than others, while others proved too be deep and formidable. Spider spent much of his time, head down, sniffing the ground. His nose and eyes inspected every wet section. He was being cautious but surprisingly quick when he needed to be. It was tricky travelling, and even though the trail was spotty, it was important to follow it if you could. When we lost the trail, I took the time to reconnect with it. With all this wet and boggy ground, it was important to re-establish contact with it. It made for slow going as we picked our way up the valley.

Finally, we reached a point just below the lake. Off to the right was a huge, open, grassy slope covered in wildflowers, mainly deep-blue lupines, rising above the scattered remnants of yellow arnica, red paintbrush and purple fleabane. It was a sunny day, and the hilly terrain was awash in brilliant sunlight. The sloping terrain stretched off into the distance for a couple of kilometres until it reached a jumble of rocks and shallow, layered cliffs. Farther back and hidden from view was Hardscrabble Pass, one of the most remote but spectacular and unusual passes in the Alberta Rockies.

Azure Lake and Blue Creek valley from near Hardscrabble Pass.
JILL DAFFERN COLLECTION

We crossed over the small creek to gain the west side of the valley, which would give us a dry route to the lake. Azure Lake was aptly named, its waters as clear and as deeply blue as you could imagine. It had that clear yet impenetrable translucency of a precious stone. Running midway through the lake west–east was the imaginary park boundary. On the other side of the shallow pass were provincial lands, the Wilmore Wilderness and the upper reach of Rockslide Creek, whose course eventually drops down through a tangle of timber and rock to the Smoky River off to the northwest.

I hiked up the steep terrain on the west side, above the lake, looking for a lunch spot and a good view of the surrounding country. It looked like something you might see in a rural Irish postcard, the subalpine meadows and the undulating alpine spreading out in all directions. It was an emerald wonder. Scattered around the lake were krumm-holz – clumps of alpine fir, gathered together in communal protection from the lash of harsh winds often present at that elevation. Again, with some reluctance that summer, I headed back down to the lake and retrieved Spider.

I might have been loath to leave the place but Spider couldn't vacate soon enough. He was eager to get back to his pals and the rich grass in the meadow next to the campsite. I gave him his head as we wound our way back through the open valley. He had some urgency in his step but still checked each suspicious spot carefully with his nose. He was guided along by the scent trail he had left on the way up. He solved things quickly and didn't waste time connecting the dots. Soon we were standing at the edge of the meadow and our little campsite.

Next morning, I hiked back up the trail with the chainsaw and removed the deadfall. That done, I headed down the valley a kilometre or so to check the outfitter camp and look for the trapper cabin Jim had told me about. I had a pretty good idea where to search, and in a half-hour, I found it. It was just like Jim had described. Inside on a dusty shelf I found a large baking powder can amongst a clutter of other things, and I unscrewed the lid. Inside, rolled up were several pamphlets. I pulled them out and unrolled them. Each had a pale cover and there was about ten of them. They had the same cover design and inside were a half-dozen typed white sheets. The front covers were bordered on each side by tall, slim pillars, which supported an elaborate roof and a base, decorated with a long row of fancy crosses. In the centre of the cover was an elaborate cross with a rose at its centre and in Latin at its base was scribed, *Rosae Crucis*. Near the top, just below the roof border was, in less-than-bold lettering: Rosicrucian Order.

I had this strange feeling that I was inside an Egyptian sarcophagus, as if I were some tomb raider, deep within the bowels of an ancient pyramid. I only scanned a page or two of one pamphlet as I was in such a rush to put them back in their resting place, feeling like an intruder. I screwed the lid on and put it back on the shelf. The next day I packed up my little camp and grudgingly headed back to Topaz for a few more days, before heading off to Blue Creek Cabin.

HOODOO CABIN, DEEP INTO THE FALL SEASON

My last shift extended into early November. I left Blue Creek for Hoodoo on a cold and crisp day in the latter part of October. I spent

Marv Millar packing up at Hoodoo.
DALE PORTMAN COLLECTION

several days doing chores around the cabin: cutting and putting up firewood, splitting kindling and putting a new coat of white paint on the cabin's interior. At Oatmeal campground, I replaced the old and broken top rail extending between the hitching posts. I also put up some firewood and tidied up the camping site. There were several fire rings that I removed, hoping people would be encouraged to build their fires in the big central one.

Another cold night gripped the land, leaving a skiff of snow on the ground. I lay in bed engrossed by a novel as a Coleman lantern purred over my head. The book had just come out and a lot of psychologists and psychiatrists were concerned that it would lead to an increase in people thinking they had multiple personalities or were possessed. The book was *The Exorcist*.

Once in a while, I would have to get up and throw some wood in the stove and then hunker down with it again. It was about one in the morning when I heard something outside on the wooden porch.

Suddenly there was a thump at the door. My heart was in my mouth, pounding away, when there was a second thump. I was a long way from nowhere, in the middle of the night and there was this thumping at the door.

Can this really be happening to me? I thought. I cautiously lifted myself up out of bed, crept towards the stove and then slunk over to the front window. All the while my asshole was clamped so tight, you couldn't have driven a knitting needle up it with a sledgehammer. There on the porch, caught in the slanting light from the window were two porcupines. What a relief! I chased them off the porch with the mop. I closed the book, turned off the lantern and tried to get some sleep. Hoodoo was always a weird place, not just for the horses but for me, as well.

I was expecting Marv Millar to ride over Snake Indian Pass from his district. He was closing down his cabins for the winter and intended to join me at Hoodoo and help me move the outhouse over the new hole I had dug earlier that summer. He normally accessed his district from the west through Robson Provincial Park in British Columbia, but as this was the end of the season, he decided to help me and end his trip at Seldom Inn.

He showed up early the next afternoon from Byng with a bottle of whisky he had squirrelled away for just this occasion. We spent the rest of the afternoon working the outhouse onto the new hole I had dug, and we levelled and secured it on a new foundation. Over a game of crib, I told him about the fright I had the night before and he laughed heartily, fuelled by the whisky.

The grass was poor this late in the season, and there was a good chance the horses would pull out if we turned them out to graze. With the prospect of a long ride the next day, we decided to keep two of them in for the night. This made it more likely that the rest would stick around, but if they did move out, we could round them up much quicker with two saddle horses. There were two old bales of hay in the tack shed – who knows how long they had been there – and we fed them one in the corral.

We found the rest of the horses close by in the small meadow the next morning and headed for Blue Creek with our personal effects. I had already winterized Blue Creek, so after just one night we were off to Willow Creek where we were hospitably met by Al Stendie. "How are you two clowns doing?" What made the evening even more memorable was the arrival of Brian Wallace who had come to spend time in the district on boundary patrol. He had brought enough alcohol to put all of us under the table for a good part of the night, paralyzing us to the furniture.

We were pretty hungover the next morning when we went looking for our horses. After a greasy breakfast, we packed up. We left Brian standing on the porch holding his head low while the three of us headed out for Seldom Inn, each leading two packhorses. When we got there, we left our horses in the pasture and closed the gate. We piled up all the saddles, blankets, tack and duffel into a huge pile in the back of my truck, an old Dodge Power Wagon. On top of this mess we placed our three dogs, which somehow found small cavities to tightly curl up in and safely secure themselves.

The first part of the drive was uneventful. We stopped a couple of times to check on the dogs and the load. We descended a final hairpin turn to the Snake Indian River, crossed the bridge, then the old truck churned up the road to where it levels off. At this point we were fortunate the truck was old and underpowered and we weren't doing much more than 30 or 40 kilometres per hour, because I realized I had no steering. Al and Marv looked on with horror as I spun the steering wheel a couple of full revolutions with nothing happening. "I don't have any steering," I yelled, as the truck left the road. Fortunately, we didn't hit anything and came to a stop after I applied the brakes. That was close! There was no damage, but we had to call for assistance on the truck radio. When help arrived, the mechanic discovered that a pin had sheared off in the steering column. We were lucky it hadn't happened when we were coming down to the bridge; we could have quite easily gone over the edge into the canyon.

Truck loaded with tack and dogs at Seldom Inn.
DALE PORTMAN COLLECTION

The truck in the ditch after losing its steering.
DALE PORTMAN COLLECTION

Freighting at Willow Creek in the spring. The cowling has been removed to help cool the engine.
DALE PORTMAN COLLECTION

SNOWSHOEING, SKIING AND SNOWMOBILES

In early December, Marv and I conducted a snowshoe trip through his district. We started at Mount Robson Provincial Park on the BC side and went up to Berg Lake, which is located under the towering face of Mount Robson. From here we reached the height of land between British Columbia and Alberta and we headed down the Smoky River as far as Lower Smoky Cabin, a distance of 54 kilometres.

This was the last extended trip I ever made on snowshoes. I often used them to build trails to outhouses, woodsheds and tack sheds but never from cabin to cabin. They were also handy for laying a trail that a snow machine could follow, hours or days later, after the snow had set up. Strong fibreglass, cross-country skis with metal edges were now appearing in some sporting goods stores in western Canada, and they were much lighter than the traditionally heavy alpine touring skis with their heavier boots and bindings. Several us younger wardens adopted them.

Al and I spent January and February in our districts freighting supplies in from town by snowmobile. In the fall, we had trucked a variety of things in to Seldom Inn: bales of hay, bags of oats, building supplies, food staples and upgraded dining chairs for the cabins. In December, we had broken a trail up the road. In January, we headed back in by snowmobile, each dragging a sled. After putting in a snowshoe trail from Seldom Inn to Willow Creek, we started freighting our cached supplies up the trail where the hay and oats were stored in the barn.

February was a cold month with the temperatures dipping down to −40°C. We stored the machines in the barn to keep the frost off them and brought the carburetors in to keep warm. This gave us a much better chance of getting them started in the morning. We broke a trail to Blue Creek using Welbourne as a staging point. Hauling large grain shovels, we levelled out the side hills, and after a week of work we started freighting again.

The snowmobiles were Alpine Ski-Doos that had a double track and a reverse, which were handy features to have when freighting supplies. We spent the remainder of the month freighting all that was destined for Blue Creek. By the end of February, we had completed our task and headed back to town for some much-needed time off.

The month of March was spent at Marmot Basin, conducting avalanche-control work. My days included taking weather readings, digging snow pits and throwing hand charges into the trigger zones of the numerous avalanche paths. We also did a lot of ski stabilization when conditions warranted. During that time, Al was working in town as a duty warden, involved with everything that came up daily, which included law enforcement, wildlife management and daily highway patrols.

In April Al and I headed back in after getting some food supplies, and by mid-April we were back at Willow Creek. We had come in to split firewood and restock the woodsheds at Blue Creek and Willow Creek. This time we had our own personal machines: single track, 320-cc Ski-Doos. They were much lighter than the double-track machines we had been using for freighting, but they lacked a reverse. The 320s were also easy to manhandle when they got stuck, and they were great in deep snow. Often in open spaces, one of us would go ahead until we started to bog down and our momentum slowed, then the other would pass, coming in front and continue the trail breaking. In this fashion, we leap-frogged along, making good progress.

One day we were heading to Blue Creek, pulling empty sleds, and we broke out into a large meadow. Suddenly a crazy notion popped

A time for some fun. Al driving his machine through the powder.
DALE PORTMAN COLLECTION

into my head that I still chuckle over to this day. We had perfect travelling conditions: a hard crust with 10 centimetres of fresh snow on top. I
was following Al's sled when I got this wacky idea to pull up next to his
sled, step off my machine onto his sled and then, with stealth, creep
up on him without him noticing. It worked perfectly. He never noticed
the weight transfer from my machine to his sled and my machine just
slowed down and came to a stop. He was totally focused on driving
and any lack of noise from my machine or my presence on the sled was
masked by the noise of his engine. I managed to creep up to the front
of the sled, stretch out my arm and tap him on the shoulder. I swear at
that moment he almost had a heart attack as he swung his head back
in my direction with absolute horror on his face. When he realized it
was me and not some drooling troll, he stopped the machine and, with
puzzlement, was trying to sort out how it was all possible. I was in
absolute stitches, and he was so pissed off, he wouldn't take me back
to my machine, which was a couple hundred metres back. How could
you blame him? Then he got the idea of driving off with me on board
and creating a bigger distance from my objective. I had to bale off the
sled into the snow and post-hole back to get my machine. It is still one
of my most cherished memories of Al on the north boundary of Jasper.

TWELVE

YOHO

MEETING THE MERCURIAL HAL SHEPHERD

I first met my future boss, Hal Shepherd, when I went to Yoho in the spring of 1974, looking at a possible transfer there. When I arrived in Field, BC, I went to the small park administration building to meet him. I walked into his office and introduced myself. He stood up from his desk and, with his one good eye – his other one was covered with a black patch – looked directly at me then he firmly shook my hand. He was wearing a peaked field or forage cap that almost covered a big hooked nose that hovered above thin, determined lips. He was a robust man, wearing an immaculate warden tunic that looked almost military. He was close to what I could imagine General McArthur looked like. He stood there eyeing me up and down, not saying a word, and then he reached into his desk drawer and pulled out some photographs and handed them to me.

I was shocked more by his gesture than the carnage depicted in the pictures. It was the mauled body of biologist Wilfred Etherington of the Canadian Wildlife Service, lying on the ground. Nearby was the helicopter that had just chased the bear off the fatally mauled man.

I don't know who took the photos, either the wildlife photographer or the helicopter pilot, Jim Davis. Hal never said anything as he returned them to his drawer and again stood in front of me. "Does it look like I'm wearing a handgun?" he asked.

"No!" I said, wondering what was going to happen next.

With dramatic flair, he took off his tunic and revealed a shoulder holster that secured a firmly placed revolver. "I've been wearing this around the office for the last week and the Sup [superintendent] hasn't noticed. He doesn't want me packing a handgun." I didn't know what to say.

Finally, I managed, "Is that a .38?"

"No, a .32," he replied, as he put his jacket back on. "Let's go for a patrol!"

We got into his park station wagon with a red light on its roof, and no sooner did he have the engine started than he spotted a guy walking his dog. Suddenly the red light was on, the siren was going and in a cloud of gravel and dust, we headed off chasing the two. We quickly caught up to them, and Hal came to an abrupt stop, rolled down his window and in a deep controlled voice said, "Don't you know, dogs have to be on a leash in my town?" The guy turned out to be Steve Thomas who I knew from working at Rogers Pass, and I was shocked and embarrassed.

Steve said, "Oh, man, it's not that bad. Ginger's a really cool dog. He just needs some free time. How would you like to be tied up all the time?"

Shepherd gave him one of his classic, wild looks and said, "You get that dog on a leash and take this encounter as a warning."

"Yes, Sir," Steve said. Then, after putting the dog on a leash, he saluted Hal. By now I was slunk down in the seat hoping Steve hadn't recognized me.

As we drove away from the crime scene, he called the duty warden, Bill Walburger, on the radio and ordered him to drop by his house for coffee. There was no, "If you're not busy drop by." It was an order. We got there about the same time. I was introduced to Bill as we sat down around the kitchen table. Hal was making coffee and as it percolated, he walked into another room. He yelled back, "How would you like some Napoleon Brandy. It's a very expensive bottle. An airline pilot friend brought it back from Paris for me."

I gave Bill an inquisitive look. Bill yelled back, "Yah, draw two."

Hal walked in with two brandy snifters with at least a couple of ounces of brandy in each. He put them down in front of Bill and me and explained he couldn't drink. He'd had anti-abuse pills placed in the lining of his stomach that made him violently ill if he drank any alcohol. He might not have been drinking at the time, but he sure seemed to like handling it. I was soon to learn a lot more about the drama that surrounded Hal's life. He would often reach the edge of his own dark abyss, only to come back bigger and bolder.

Bill took his brandy and quaffed it down in one gulp much to Hal's disgust. I made sure I sipped mine, savouring the taste and expressing how superb it was. I saw that I'd made a hit with him. "Wow!" I thought. Did coming to Yoho mean that brandy at 10:00 AM was a normal thing around here? Bill later informed me that it was the exception, and he was just trying to impress me. I wasn't sure how to take the compliment. I was now single again. And though I enjoyed a good party and had been known to frequent the occasional bar, I never thought of myself as an excessive drinker. I went back to Jasper wondering who the hell this man was who I'd just met. Our meeting only reinforced every outlandish thing I had already heard about him.

I had been looking forward to another year in Blue Creek, but circumstance played out a little differently than I imagined. Barb and I divorced in 1973, a mutual decision, and in early 1974, I got my promotion to full-time warden. With the permanent job and the divorce, a new address and surroundings started to make a bit of sense. If I transferred, I was going to miss Jasper where I had made several good friends. The scope of Yoho would be nothing like the much larger wilderness boundaries of Jasper. Still, the new park was very beautiful and one never loses sight of friends when working for the warden service. My job requirements would be broader, encompassing most of the general duties that wardens are responsible for.

I was conflicted about my possible move to Yoho, though. I had found Jasper to be a rewarding place to work, and I really liked the town. The people were friendly and the business operators seemed less aggressive than their counterparts in Banff. It was a railroad town more than a park town, and it had a great sense of community spirit. I also had history there. I finally decided I needed to move on and get a fresh start in Yoho.

I MOVED TO YOHO AND WAS VISITED BY TURMOIL FROM JASPER

I moved into a bungalow at the west gate of the park in June of 1974, and for the next couple of years I took over backcountry and law enforcement responsibilities. The bungalow was fairly isolated from town, near the west gate of the park, and it wasn't long before I was encouraging people to drop by. In fact, I had barely moved in before the worst offenders – Bob Sandford, Gord Irwin and Jim Renney – showed up on my doorstep. Jim worked for the CNR in Jasper, and Gord was an interpreter in Jasper, working for Parks Canada. Gord would eventually become a park warden, get certified as a mountain guide and head the public safety program in Banff. Bob and Gord were travelling together during the summer of 1974, getting into trouble, and Jim was tagging along. Twice that summer they ended up on my doorstep, creating a bit of chaos in my life.

The first time they showed up it was with good intentions (hiking up the Ice River for a few days), and they needed a place to stay for the night. They brought along a supply of alcohol, specifically beer and Scotch, and we passed an enjoyable night reminiscing. The next morning found them too hungover to seriously think about an overnight hike, and so they went to town to pick up more booze, giving them an opportunity to graciously invite half the town to a party at my place. Everyone showed up, and it wasn't until Sunday that I managed to get rid of the hungover crowd and lock the door. Just as I was saying goodbye to the Jasper crowd, who should walk up to the door but a couple of people who turned out to be Jehovah's Witnesses. On seeing them, Bob and Gord really picked up their step getting to their vehicle, leaving me with the unwanted arrivals. Their timing couldn't have been better.

A few weeks later the party-happy twosome showed up again on a weekend. They were still planning on hiking up the Ice River but this time with a couple of other well-intentioned hikers. I knew they were coming, so I threw a party to get even and again invited the town. When they saw the crowd, their willpower failed them and again they were thrown into the midst of a truly great Field hoedown. The party carried on throughout Saturday and into Sunday. It was a wild and woolly affair, and again the Ice River became an afterthought. I think at some point Gord and Bob did get up the Ice River that summer, but they sure as hell didn't invite me along or drop by to scrounge a bed.

Yoho is a much smaller park than Jasper, 1800 square kilometres compared to Jasper's nearly 11,000. The backcountry consists of small watersheds and valleys draining into the Kicking Horse River, which runs the length of the park. The two most popular areas for hiking are Lake O'Hara, which has bus and trail access only, and the Yoho Valley, which has a public road leading to it. Another popular area was Emerald Lake, with connecting trails to the Yoho Valley. The lake was very popular, and Emerald Lake Lodge, on the shores of this beautiful, deep, green-blue lake, was first class. The Ottertail and Porcupine tributaries, which entered the Kicking Horse, were the only two valleys with no road access or trails, making them the true wilderness of the park. The park itself is bisected by the Trans-Canada Highway, which often clings to the banks of the Kicking Horse River as it carves its way across gravel flats, over waterfalls and through canyons.

With Hal as our boss there was never a point when we felt we were out of his reach. On rare occasions, he would stroll into the warden office at Boulder Creek, not far from the Emerald Lake turnoff, and after a while you knew he had been drinking. It didn't take long for the anti-abuse pills to wear off. He was in uniform, and we had our suspicions. He was never intoxicated – he was always steady on his feet – but you could see it in his mannerisms. That's when you knew that Norma must be out of town. It was at these times that he would get philosophical and chummy and wanted to talk to his boys. This is when he would drop his guard and wanted to engage with us on a personal level.

BEING A WAR HERO IS NO EASY MATTER

Hal Shepherd understood the misadventure of war, but he also embraced the warrior spirit even as he became a victim of this destructive conflict. He was a damaged man because of his war experience, and he had put his life on the line several times for his men and his country. As he put it, it was an honourable war to fight, even though he knew the Allied armies were guilty of some war atrocities at times.

If Hal had not survived the war, he and Norma would not have gotten married and had four wonderful boys who grew to be as accomplished and successful as they did. Norma's life might have been more peaceful and less challenging with another man, but she had grit and when Hal returned from the war, damaged as he was, she married him. All of us who worked for Hal found her to be one of the most loyal and classy women we had the good fortune to meet. There was a great deal of lore that swirled around Hal. At times, he was bigger than life, but if you worked for him, you were loyal, even if on occasion he was a pain in the ass.

Winston Smith knew Hal when he worked in Prince Albert National Park, and he was captivated by his life story. He did a lot of research on Hal's war years and his early childhood. I helped him with some later stories and what it was like working for him in Yoho. I was able to use Winston's research paper, "A Conflicted Veteran or an Original Man?" to fill in a lot of the blanks in his life here, and I thank him greatly for it. Don Mickle also worked with Hal in Yoho and provided a lot of insight to both my story and Winston's.

Hal Shepherd was born in Lancashire, England, in 1919, but his family immigrated to Canada when he was four years old and settled in the community of Riverbend, Quebec. The area was predominantly

French-speaking so he was brought up exposed to both official languages and could speak French fluently. Most of us thought he had lost his eye during the war, but it wasn't so glamorous. When he was five, a piece of glass from a broken bottle flew up into his eye, and he lost permanent sight in it.

He always dreamt of being a pilot, so when the Second World War erupted in Europe, he thought he had a chance to enlist as a pilot and fight for his country. It was an audacious attempt on his part, but he was rejected because of his eyesight. That didn't stop him, though, and when he heard that the Finnish Embassy in Ottawa was looking for Canadian pilots to defend Finland from an impending Russian invasion, he signed up. The country was desperate for pilots and not concerned about his visual impairment. Before he could get over to Finland, however, the Russians invaded and wiped out the Finnish Air Force. He had a boat ticket already supplied by the Finnish Embassy but had no one to report to.

Russia had three times as many men in uniform, thirty times as many aircraft and one hundred times as many tanks but it failed to achieve any measurable gains as the Finns were as famously tenacious as Hal was. They fought the Russians in the forests, in the open meadows and on the frozen lakes, getting around on skis like ghosts, while cloaked in white anoraks. It became known as the Winter War. The League of Nations declared the invasion illegal, and a peace treaty was signed in March 1940.

Now that there was no reason to fight for Finland, Hal turned his attention to the Canadian Army. He tried to enlist five times but was turned down each time by the same doctor. The Quebec Royal Rifles Regiment was being funded by Price Brothers, a big employer near where he lived, and he begged to be considered. Finally, after getting a different doctor and memorizing the three eye charts they used, he was enlisted. They soon became aware of his eye, and he voluntarily signed a waiver, absolving the regiment and Price Brothers of any wrongdoing should he be injured or killed.

He rose to the rank of Company Sergeant Major and he was

Hal in trench coat, fearless, looking tough as hell.
DON MICKLE COLLECTION

eventually shipped off in the fall of 1941 to help reinforce the British defense garrison in Hong Kong. Two battalions, the Quebec and Winnipeg Rifles, were part of a larger regiment, the Royal Rifles of Canada. Just under two thousand men arrived in mid-November to augment the British and Indian troops already there. The Japanese invaded on the morning of December 9, 1941, the same morning (technically a day earlier because of the International Date Line) they invaded Pearl Harbor and brought America into the war.

The Japanese met stiff opposition, but in less than a week, after relentless attacks, the British and Commonwealth forces abandoned the mainland and took up position on the island of Hong Kong. Less than two weeks later, their position on the island also became untenable, and they surrendered on Christmas Day. The survivors became prisoners of war and the attrition in the camps was as bad as the battle itself.

Hal and his men were shipped to Kyushu Island in Japan where they worked the coal mines for Furukawa Industries. Keith, one of Hal's four sons, who was on the Canadian Olympic downhill team in the late 1960s and early 70s, and later head of financing for Parks Canada in Jasper, remembers his father's war experiences well. He put it best in this description in an interview with Winston Smith:

I doubt that anyone really knew his Hong Kong career beyond the surface information. That in his mid-twenties he became the senior NCO [Non-Commissioned Officer] at a Japanese Prisoner of War camp where he went in at a healthy 175 lbs. and came out a yellow-skinned 136 lbs. At the same time, he managed to be successful enough in looking after his men that he earned an MBE (Member of the Order of the British Empire) for the survival ratio of the men under his command, a survival ratio that far exceeded any other Japanese POW camp, whether commanded by senior or junior officers or other NCOs. Traits of protectiveness for his men and sheer bloody-minded stubbornness that caused him to be bayoneted in the shoulder for refusing to send his sick men into the coal mines and for striking the Japanese NCO who attempted to compel the sick men into the mine. And which allowed him to withstand the psyops of being stood up to be shot for that offense daily and having the "Ready, Aim, Fire" commuted to "Ready, Aim.... No. We do it tomorrow, while the wound heals." I'm sure such a personality made a number of chief park wardens and later superintendents feel [challenged as] they attempted to manage the tension that was Hal Shepherd. From a son's point of view, he was great in a crisis but not very stable in the calm golden times where he often seemed to do his best to create that familiar tension.

We all knew he survived the war physically but he was amongst many that had to just suck it up when he got home. And when the memories and nightmares were too much for him, he would go off and get drunk for a week or so, followed by a long period of sobriety and stability, when he devoted his attention to Norma, his sons and his wardens.

When he returned to Canada, he was only home for a short time before he was sent back as an interpreter for General MacArthur's group at the Tokyo War Crimes Tribunal. He was there for ten months. He had been the only one in his POW camp who could speak French, outside of a senior Japanese non-commissioned officer, who he conversed with, but by the time the war was over, you could add Japanese to his language repertoire. He also told me at one point that he picked up Czech and German and that he knew six languages altogether. Everyone knew he was brilliant, and someone told me that when he was in school he was given an IQ test and considered a "genius."

He met several influential military personal at the war crimes tribunal, and I'm sure he met some of Canada's highest ranking military officers. He returned to Canada and married Norma, who he met when he was stationed in Newfoundland before being shipped out. In Newfoundland, he was assigned to teaching dispatch drivers how to drive the old Harley and Indian Motorcycles they had been issued. One assignment he relished while in Newfoundland was teaching the first Red Cross unit, preparing to go overseas to England, how to march the army way. One of the young women in the unit was Norma, who agreed to marry him when they both returned from the war.

Immediately after the war they started raising a family, and Ian was the first born in 1946. He was followed by Keith a year later. About that time, Hal had been notified that he was to receive a Distinguished Conduct Medal in a ceremony held at St. James Palace and overseen by the Central Chancery of the Orders of Knighthood. But that was upgraded to the MBE, July 25, 1946.

In 1953 Norma and their three sons (Mike was born in 1949) followed Hal's dream to move west and become a cowboy. They settled on some land near Cold Lake, Alberta, where he got a job building the new air force base there. They had six horses and two were registered thoroughbreds. It was here that a fourth son, Don, was born in 1956. I remember after finding this out that I thought, "Finally, after all these years, I understand where Hal got his horsemanship skills," outside of those he gained from the warden service.

THE DARK AND LIGHT SIDES OF SURVIVAL

In 1972 the superintendent of Yoho National Park, Don Macmillan, held a competition for the vacant chief park warden position. They knew what they were getting when they interviewed Hal. He aced the competition and did so well they had to give him the job. With his new role and its subsequent responsibilities, his bouts with the bottle diminished significantly but never really ended. Donny Mickle and I were on hand a few times when he fell off the wagon while Norma was away, but he didn't need alcohol to add to his expanding reputation of being the intrepid warrior he personified.

When the coalition of Arab nations led by Egypt and Syria attacked Israel on its holiest day of the year, Yom Kippur on October 6, 1973, Hal Shepherd, ever the combatant, took notice. The Syrian Army with its tanks had recaptured the Golan Heights while the Egyptians had successfully crossed the Suez Canal with their tanks and were racing across the Sinai Peninsula. Israel was frantically trying to mobilize.

Hal's old friend, Moshe Dayan, now the Israeli minister of defense, someone Hal understood well, was in a jam and he thought he could come to Dayan's aid. Both had been interpreters together at the war crimes trials in Japan. They were both missing an eye and both sported a black patch as a badge of honour. Now that he had a pilot's licence, Hal envisioned serving his old friend who was at war with formidable foes this time. So, with a couple of his buddies as witness, he managed to get through on the phone to Dayan and offered his service to the beleaguered nation, possibly as a transport pilot. They chatted for a while, but Dayan turned down his offer, thanking Hal but telling him that he was probably too old to pass the physical.

After Hal's offer, the Israeli Army, although outnumbered, pushed the Syrians off the Golan Heights with their superior tanks and well-trained tank crews, back towards Damascus, while in the Sinai the two armies fought to a standstill. A ceasefire was put together after nearly three weeks of fighting, and a peace treaty was signed with Egypt's Anwar Sadat. It didn't take long for that news to make the rounds in the beer parlours and coffee rooms of the four mountain parks.

On one occasion, early on in my career in Yoho, there were a few bikers, part of a gang, who had been raising hell with the campground staff up at Takkakaw Falls. As the park's duty officer, Hal called Bill Walburger and I to his house before we could head up there. We walked in the door and there he was, dressed like Mussolini, wearing black leather gloves and slapping a black, shot-loaded, leather quirt into one hand. The thwacking of leather against leather echoed throughout the house. He looked at us with that "We're not going to take any prisoners" look and said, "I'll wade into the middle of them and you two look after my back." He was wired and ready for action. His thin lips spread around the circumference of his open mouth, as his nostrils flared like a winded horse, giving him a very scary look.

Bill and I looked at each other in disbelief, and then Bill said in a moment of sanity, "Hal, you can't go up there. You're the duty officer and you have to stay here near a phone." That set Hal back, and he immediately grabbed the phone and dialled the superintendent. Once he got connected, he wanted permission to leave his post but was turned down. Thank god. Bill and I went up there and diffused the biker situation after leaving Hal, who was almost in tears, standing there in resigned silence.

Donny Mickle and I remember another occasion when Hal displayed his unique way of handling things when the RCMP decided to escort a gang of Hells Angels down to our overflow campground area at the Ottertail Flats. They were headed home from a rendezvous at Coronation, Alberta, and this was the best place to put them. Later, someone sent a young female campground attendant down there to collect the fees. Hal was shocked at the position this woman was being put in, so he called her on the radio and said he would escort her there, much to her relief. They drove down together in his park station wagon.

He drove into the site and stepped out of the vehicle, as she described it later, dressed in his George Patton / Douglas MacArthur attire. He escorted her around to all the sites and collected the fees, and then they climbed back into the vehicle and started to leave. As they were driving away, one of the bikers flashed a limp right hand in the air in a Nazi salute and uttered a sarcastic, "Seig Heil." Any thought of her getting away safely was now thwarted by this challenging gesture. Hal slammed on the brakes, jammed the car in reverse and came to a cloudy halt in front of the offending biker. Hal jumped out as the park attendant looked on in total disbelief. Hal approached the guy with this startling response: "If you're going to do that at least do it properly." Then Hal sprung into attention, looking as tall and strong as he could manage, then thrust his arm in a straight, rigid, Nazi salute, clicking his heals together and in a booming voice announced, "Seig Heil." They probably thought they were watching an authentic SS officer. He then calmly got back into the car and returned to town. He certainly had a risky sense of humour.

Winston Smith recorded Keith Shepherd's stories of Hal as he talked about his dad's time in Yoho and the effectiveness of his tenure there, and what it was like living in Field. Keith recalled Jean Pilon, the superintendent who Hal had great respect for, as well as his wife Lisa. Keith felt these were Hal's most productive years when he enjoyed training many wardens of considerable talent. Among them were Peter Whyte, Darryl Stinson, Dale Portman, Don Mickle and Canada's first female warden, Kathy Calvert. Keith emphasized that Hal believed that women could be as competent as the men working in the field. He was respected by his peers for his forward thinking and generosity. He also pioneered the hiring of Aboriginal trainees for the warden service and hired Tim Laboucane, who had passed the qualifications for seasonal warden. Yoho National Park was one of the first to have a First Nations man employed in this capacity. Hal was progressive and liberal in his outlook on life. He was well ahead of his time in that fashion.

Though getting on, Hal had never abandoned his first passion for flying planes. In the mid-1970s, at a gathering of chief park wardens from across Canada who were meeting at the Palisades Training Facility in Jasper, two of the chiefs from the Maritimes (Ben Roper was one) happened to mention that neither of them had ever been up in a propped aircraft. On the following weekend, with two days off, the chief wardens were taken in a hired bus from Jasper to the industrial airport in Edmonton to go on a turbo-propped flight in a DC-3, in honour of the two who hadn't had the opportunity. This was organized and paid for by Hal. Along with the pilot was a co-pilot and two stewardesses who handed out drinks to the flabbergasted men. Financially he had no concerns, for his chief park warden salary was supplemented with a substantial military pension.

We can't cover Hal's time in Yoho without a flying incident. Warden Eric Langshaw in Banff got a report on his radio that an aircraft had landed on the highway near Saskatchewan River Crossing. As he approached the plane, whom did he see standing beside it but Hal Shepherd in a forage cap and a fleece-lined leather bomber jacket, sporting aviator sunglasses. "What the hell are you doing landing here?" Eric asked.

"I was forced down by low clouds," Hal replied, as a mischievous smile crossed his face. Langshaw looked up in the sky and saw one or two small puffy clouds.

"Now I have to set up road blocks to clear the traffic so I can get you out of here," Eric replied. He told us later, "Hal was on his way back from Jasper to Golden, BC, where he kept his plane. He just stopped by for coffee and to show off his airplane."

Two other well-documented episodes occurred while he was the chief park warden in Yoho. Both incidents involved the local RCMP, who thought Hal was someone out of the Wild West and was only here because of some weird time warp. A prison break that had occurred near Vancouver, BC, and a hardened criminal had managed to escape with a stolen car. He was last spotted east of Golden on the Trans-Canada Highway, heading towards Yoho. The RCMP had a description of the car and its licence plate. The RCMP officer set up a roadblock nearby with red and blue lights flashing, flanked by park warden trucks. Suddenly there was Hal, standing like Wyatt Earp in the middle of the Trans-Canada Highway, a shotgun across his chest, when the convict appeared in the stolen car. As the vehicle approached, Hal raised the shotgun to his shoulder and aimed at the windshield. The vehicle came to a halt in front of Hal and quickly an RCMP officer approached the car, gun drawn. The convict gave up immediately. He later told the RCMP that he had been in prison with a lot of hard men but the look that guy gave him scared him rigid. The seasoned criminal said he knew Hal would not have hesitated to shoot him.

The other incident occurred when Vi Sandford, Bob's future wife, was robbed at the West Gate Visitor Centre in Yoho. A lone guy came in wielding a knife and stole the cash out of the cash register and then cut the phone line and ran outside. Vi didn't hesitate to follow him out, managing to get the licence plate number of the vehicle. The bandit didn't realize she had a park radio and was able to notify both the RCMP and the duty officer, who was Hal that day. The RCMP closed the Trans-Canada Highway to Golden and set up a barrier near Boulder Creek, a few kilometres west of town. Again, Hal had it all figured out. He would stand in the middle of the road with the shotgun, and we would cover him with our rifles from our trucks. He was disappointed when the RCMP caught the guy on a logging road just west of the park gates. He'd been robbed of saving a damsel in distress, but he complimented us on being professionals. We felt like wooden characters in a puppet show.

HE KNEW WHEN TO HANG UP HIS SPURS

Hal never had the same rapport with the superintendent that replaced Jean Pilon, who was transferred back to Ottawa in 1976, and was sorely missed by many of us. Donny and I had vivid memories of Jean and Lisa at their official residence in Field on Saturday nights, when some of us would get together with the couple, joined by Hal and Norma. Randy Robertson, another long-time warden in Yoho, was also often there. We would trade stories that would captivate them, especially tales about being on the trail with the Mickles. They thoroughly enjoyed our re-enactment of the chicken dance and were quick to participate. This contrasted greatly with the dour and humourless superintendent who replaced this engaging and committed man.

The new superintendent immediately disliked the warden service, and Hal had difficulty with how he ran the park. Three of his park wardens (Don Mickle, Randy Robertson and me), along with the head of interpretation in the park, were continually warning Parks Canada in Calgary's regional office about the verbal abuses this man directed at his female staff in the park administration office. This led to a serious confrontation between the two men. When Hal found himself lying across the superintendent's desk with the man's tie in his hand, as both of their faces turned red, he realized it was time to quit. He had managed to have one superintendent removed during his career but he doubted if management would remove another. It was time for Hal to retire.

I organized a big send off for him and Norma at the Lake Louise Inn, and the boys (men now) attended. We had a great turn out, and he retired in good style. He gave a great speech and even got teary-eyed delivering it. He and Norma moved to Sicamous, BC, located on Shuswap Lake. He traded his airplane for a boat, a Great Lake Cruiser "Commander," circa 1947. He loved the boat. The mahogany hull and the teak deck and galley were kept in first-class shape. Early in his retirement he had a couple of part-time jobs to keep him interested in life. He became a horseback-riding instructor, which was a shock to me. I had never seen him on a horse, and suddenly he was teaching horsemanship. He followed that up by becoming a golf instructor at the local golf course. That was even more shocking to me. In all the time I had known him, I had never seen or heard of him golfing, and now he was a golf pro. He was either the biggest con artist imaginable or he really could turn his hand to anything. I found out later he was a pretty good golfer.

In 1983 they moved to Westbank, BC, near Kelowna and joined the Kelowna Yacht Club. He soon became a member of the Yacht Club Board and then quickly moved on to become the Power Squadron Commander. His life seemed to even out after retirement, and it was probably the most happy and tranquil period of Norma and Hal's life together. He had had a successful, though tempestuous and sketchy, career as a park warden during which he produced four sons of whom he was very proud. What I thought was his greatest achievement was keeping Norma, as classy a lady as you could find, by his side all those years.

By 1990 the maintenance and upkeep of the boat was becoming too much for the two of them. He sold the boat and bought a motorcycle. In the early 1990s, at the bi-annual Warden Days, held at Maligne Range near Jasper where the wardens kept the horses, who should show up driving a Harley Davidson Roadster but Hal, decked out completely in black leather. Every person there who had never met or heard of him all said in varying tones, "Who is that?" He came up again two years later with a couple of his buddies, this time driving a Harley Davidson Fat Boy. The three of them were part of the Kelowna bike club called the Blue Knights Club. They were all ex-law-enforcement officers who on weekends would take off with a pup tent and sleeping bags strapped behind the seat and tour about.

He died of lung cancer in 1994 at the age of seventy-five. At his request, Norma and the boys scattered his ashes on Okanagan Lake and several of us from his Yoho days made it to his funeral. It was a celebration of his life and an opportunity to visit with Norma, Ian, Keith, Mike and Donny again. I spoke a bit about Hal as a chief park warden and what he meant to all of us. He was a huge part of our experience working in Yoho National Park and living in the tiny community of Field, BC. He was the most fearless man I had ever met, and as a park warden working in the mountain national parks, I have met a few in my time.

Hal once said to me that death was a mystery to many human beings but not to him. He understood it as a veiled doorway we enter. He said his life was challenging at times, difficult for Norma and the kids growing up, but he had faith in its outcome. His war years must have cemented that belief. This explained to me his unwavering fearlessness in facing life's challenges.

THE WARDEN SERVICE CHANGES

In the spring of 1974, the warden service hired the first two female park wardens in the country, Jan Cadeaux and Kathy Calvert. Jan started out in Pacific Rim National Park but Kathy was asked to run the women's Conservation Corps in Waterton Lakes National Park in southwestern Alberta. The following summer, Hal accepted Kathy as a seasonal park warden. In his usual military fashion, he insisted that all of us slovenly men turn up in our best uniforms and look professional for a change, with pressed shirts, buttons done up and clean ties. The last thing he barked was, "Trim your mustache Portman. How can you eat anything with that in the way?"

She was an hour late because her aged car had broken down in Banff, so Hal held court in the coffee room trying unsuccessfully to calm everyone's tension. The only calm person was our faithful secretary, Pat Rutherford. We settled into a long lecture from him on how important it was to introduce both Aboriginal people and women to the rank and file of the warden service. We were all well turned out, and he eyed all of us critically, while he looked and acted like the field marshal of a dubious troop. When she finally arrived, we all sprang to our feet and almost saluted we were so pumped up by Hal's hype and expectations. She, of course, was shocked at this jack-in-the-box event and looked at us like we were either nuts or robots. After introductions, he tried to address business as usual. Hal was progressive and liberal and when there was controversy and concerns about hiring women and Natives, he was the first to step up. As I mentioned earlier, his next step was to hire Tim Laboucane as one of the first Indigenous wardens in western Canada.

BOB COMES TO MY RESCUE AFTER HE FELL DOWN A MILLWELL

Later that night, Kathy's boss, Warden Dave Reynolds, invited her down to the bar after work for a beer. Some of us joined them. At some point, I was telling her the locally famous story of Bob Sandford falling into a millwell on the Saskatchewan Glacier. At the time of the accident, Bob was a seasonal naturalist working for Parks Canada and stationed at Saskatchewan Crossing. This was before he moved up to Jasper in 1973. Bob wanted to explore the Saskatchewan Glacier and visit the Castleguard Meadows for his interpretive work. He went with a small group but all he had to wear on his feet were cowboy boots with crampons strapped to them. As he had only two days off, he would have to walk up the glacier and into the meadows on the first day and return the second day. The accident happened on the return trip, when exhausted and unroped, he started taking shortcuts across the ice. Crossing one of the many streams on the surface of the glacier he was picked up by the current and carried down a millwell that, much like a sink drain, was spiralling clockwise and vanishing into the depths of the glacier. This fascinated him, but he got too close, lost his footing and slipped in, boots first. He got carried down to the bottom of the glacier and found himself bobbing along in a stream (the source of the Saskatchewan River) much like a cork in the deep bowels of the ice. He eventually saw a light at the end of a long tunnel, surrounded by glowing blue walls. Who knows, maybe his whole life was flashing before his eyes. Low and behold, he popped out at the toe of the glacier, suffering from mild hypothermia but nothing more.

Being a climber, Kathy was listening to my story and thinking it was probably the biggest pile of hooey she had ever heard. "That's impossible," she said. I was set back by her sudden retort and felt any credibility I had built up with her was rapidly vanishing.

I said, "It's true," and she rolled her eyes. At that very moment, someone I hadn't seen for a while walked through the door of the bar. It was none other than Bob Sandford, and I said, "And there he is now! Now you can ask him." It was amazing. Bob had been a student in her lab class at university where she earned a modest income as a teaching

A head shot of Kathy wearing her new, well-kept warden hat.
DALE PORTMAN COLLECTION

assistant while working on a master's degree in insect physiology. With my credibility somewhat restored, I ordered another round of beer.

Here's the six degrees of separation factor. Bob had told me about his epic on the glacier when we first met in Jasper but it was authenticated by one of his companions at the time, Eugene Nowick. Eugene hadn't witnessed the event per se, but he had travelled up the glacier with Bob on his way to meet his friend, Ken Forest, who just happened to be Kathy's twin brother. I later talked to Ken about it, and he said that he had, in fact, met Eugene on a different trip but still, everything else was true about Bob's story.

HOW KATHY MET BERT MICKLE

The town of Field was a CP railroad divisional point, and the park headquarters for Yoho National Park. It was a pleasant mix of CPR workers, retirees and young Parks Canada staff with an assortment of small business people mixed in. In a smaller sense, it had that hippie feel about it that you still get in places like Smithers, Rossland or Nelson, BC. As you entered Field from the highway, the first small white house on the left was referred to as "buckets east," and as you left town on the back road there was another place called "buckets west." If you lingered by either one, you might pick up the pungent odor of marijuana, wafting from an open window, being enjoyed by an eclectic collection of people inside. In the 1980s, I had a working dog trained to detect narcotics, and he never failed to wag his tail when we drove past these houses in my Suburban truck.

By the time Kathy came to work in Yoho, I had moved to a cabin located at the government barn near the Emerald Lake turnoff. The cabin faced a large horse pasture to the south while behind was a slough, more a backwater of the Kicking Horse River. The slough was segregated from the "ranch" by the CPR tracks, whose broad curve defined the enclosure. In the evening, the headlight of the train lit up the bedroom, announcing its eastbound approach. This was followed by the wheels screeching as it made its way around the bend on its approach to Field. It was a beautiful spot, very peaceful in the evenings, unless the train happened to be passing by. Off the highway on the way in was a barn, a tack shed and large, gravel parking area. Some days it was the centre of activity in the park.

It was here that Kathy first met Bert Mickle. It was her second summer working in Yoho, and we had been dating for a while. One morning at the ranch house, on our day off, we woke up to the rustle of grass outside and the sense that people were out there. We were both awake now and heard someone say, "They must be in here somewhere." Then we saw two people slink by the bedroom window. Donny was in uniform while Bert was wearing his fall red-plaid jacket and a black hat, a cigarette hanging from the corner of his mouth. They didn't knock. They came through the front door and, without hesitation, walked into the bedroom. Kathy kept asking me, "Who's that old guy?" She was shocked by the audacity of the two, as she grasped the top of the bed cover. She said later she felt quite vulnerable.

I said to her, "Meet Bert Mickle!"

All that was said as they left the room was, "Get up and make us some coffee."

THE FATHER AND SON ON CATHEDRAL MOUNTAIN

In 1976 I took over the public-safety and avalanche-control responsibilities from Gordon Rutherford who was now going to run the resource-management part of the operation as well as the collection of scientific data for a biophysical of the park. The data was coming in from several different natural science contractors working on the various components of the project. It would eventually turn into a mosaic map, highlighting the park's flora, fauna, hydrology, soils, geology, typography and geomorphology. It was a huge undertaking that was happening in all the national parks across Canada in the mid- to late 1970s. Most of us lent a hand in helping out with the mapping.

Although I was overseeing the public-safety function in Yoho and administrated the budget, Tim Auger was our premier warden in the field. He conducted the training and was the field rescue leader when we responded to accidents. Occasionally, Hal Shepherd would inject himself into this small hierarchy.

I remember one rescue at Lake O'Hara where Tim was stationed. We were both down at the warden office at the Boulder Creek maintenance compound when Hal showed up to tell us there was a missing father and son on Cathedral Mountain. Of course, in his usual authoritative manner, Hal told Tim and me how to go about conducting the search, which Tim took with a grain of salt in his usual laid-back manner.

Hal was old school and had participated in several rescues back in the days of Walter Perren. He was also a colourful product of the Second World War and, as noted before, had a passion for spiffy uniforms, was a disciplinarian and liked things done in a snappy and efficient fashion. We left him standing in the middle of the room as we headed off to the rescue room. Tim muttered something under his breath. He was the most free spirited of all of us, and he chaffed under the tyranny of Hal's sometimes-confrontational style.

A father and his fourteen-year-old son had neglected to register going out for a climb and when they failed to return the following day, Hal got a concerned phone call from his wife. She said they were thinking of climbing Cathedral Mountain. Tim knew the father because he had been involved with him on two other occasions, also when he failed to register with the park. Normally a cheerful and thoughtful fellow, Tim was in a dark mood, following the events of this day. He told me that the father lacked respect for park regulations and the legal process. If this should turn out to be a rescue and they were found alive, Tim was planning on charging the father for "Failing to Register Out" under the National Parks Act. This was unusual for Tim. He usually stayed away from the law-enforcement component of our responsibilities.

We drove up to Lake O'Hara and hiked into the Lynda Lake area and up into Cathedral Basin, where we found an abandoned tent perched below the south face of the mountain. A note was pinned to the flap of the tent saying, "Gone to climb south face of Cathedral Mountain." With some weariness, we looked up at a dreadful snow gully with footprints marching up the middle. Tim considered it to be a dangerous choice for a route at any time of day. To him, climbing that route was no better than rolling the dice to decide your fate.

We climbed up onto a big boulder and with little hope of success, we started yelling at the top of our lungs, "Are you there? Are you all right?" When we got no response, Tim got on the radio and called Hal to explain the situation. The face of the mountain was vast and extended 760 metres to its summit. It would be impossible to search without the aid of a helicopter, and so Tim requested one. It was getting late, and the pair would soon find themselves out for a third night. Tim's decision was the right call. There was a long silence on the radio, and then, with typical clarity and great authority, we received our instructions from our Supreme Leader. In a less than gentle voice, he issued his instructions, "Tim! This is what I want you to do! Proceed to the foot of the gully and climb it until you establish contact with the party. Report back to me!"

Don Mickle, Jean Pilon and his son at the upper end of the Ice River.
DALE PORTMAN COLLECTION

Following this announcement, a steady flow of profanity passed from Tim's lips to my ears. I was dumbfounded by Hal's military response, and neither one of us knew how to answer. I had a sense that Hal's disembodied good eye was looking down on us from the sky, with a stare that could pierce steel. Tim could not fathom how you would not spend money on a helicopter in a situation that might mean the life or death of a young boy. Though, I don't think he had the same concern for the father.

I was concerned about how Tim was going to respond to Hal's instructions on the radio when we heard a faint cry. It was surreal and astonishing all at once. It was a feeble cry for help. We spotted them. They were descending by a completely different route, and we set out like Hal had instructed and climbed up towards them. We assisted them down to the safety of their tent, at which point they got a lengthy tongue lashing from Tim.

After an extended discussion and debriefing with Hal in his office the next day, he reneged on his position about the helicopter. To his credit, he never questioned the use of a helicopter again with us. He knew how valuable Tim was to the public safety program in Yoho. If Tim left for greener pastures (Banff), he and the park would be in a difficult situation. Tim did just that a year later and took a promotion in Banff.

THE LAW OF EBB AND FLOW

As mentioned earlier, about a year or two after I arrived at Yoho, we lost our beloved superintendent, Jean Pilon. The new man who had parachuted in from Ottawa was not nearly as likeable. For one thing, he felt wardens interfered with the way Ottawa wanted things to be conducted in the national parks and that we had too much power. He was also more pro-development than most superintendents were back then. He felt the "conserve and protect" mandate laid out in the National Parks Act interfered too often with business development. As park wardens, we were empowered to enforce the act, so we were an inconvenience to him and how he wanted to run the park.

We were banging heads right from the get-go. He felt we were nothing more than prison guards who oversaw too many environmental issues. He also had little respect for scientific data. To qualify the townspeople of Field for northern allowance, which was a tax break, he had a sundial set up in his backyard. It was a nice gesture on his part, but he was fudging the data. By setting it up under a tree, most of the sunlight was blocked. It was a deliberate attempt to skew the data in favour of getting the tax break for the town. We also had a sundial out at Boulder Creek, which we checked every day.

A sundial operates in this fashion: when the sun is out, the rays pass through the glass globe and burn a line on a cardboard strip that is placed behind it. As the sun moves from east to west along the calibrated slip of cardboard, the burned portions stretch across the paper and you can read how many hours of sunlight there are on any particular day. The strip needs to be changed every day and the date recorded on it.

Because of his flawed data and our accurate readings, we now had data for two microclimates, 8 kilometres apart, one that had far more sunlight than the other. We brought the matter up with him, which only enraged him, and he became more adamant on getting the results he wanted. One day we snuck into his backyard and took the glass globe and replaced it with a grapefruit of similar size. We then put the globe in a large soda cracker box and padded it with newspaper. We wrapped it in brown paper, put the required amount of postage on it and addressed it – Park Superintendent, Yoho National Park, British Columbia, V0A 1G0 – and mailed it. A few days later I got a call from Hal asking me if the globe was missing from our sundial at Boulder Creek. It wasn't but I played my role and told Hal I would go out and check then call him back. On returning to the office, I phoned him and told him it wasn't missing. He said, "That's strange because the superintendent's globe isn't missing either. I wonder who belongs to the one we just received in the mail. I'm going to get to the bottom of this. I'm sending it off to the crime lab in Kamloops and get some fingerprints lifted off it."

That was a bit alarming, even though I had made sure that every-thing had been wiped clean. Things were not going as planned. We had hoped that the missing globe would put a spotlight on the flawed data and the fact it was located under the canopy of the tree. Now we had what seemed like a criminal investigation going on. And it was being conducted by our own chief park warden, who didn't like the man any better than we did, but he didn't know about the inconsistent data.

The big mystery for us was: how could he change the daily card-board chart and not see the grapefruit? One of my accomplices got tired of driving down the back alley, looking into the superinten-dent's backyard and seeing the grapefruit. This park staffer solved it by knocking on the superintendent's house after work and telling him there was a grapefruit in his sundial. It was embarrassing for the superintendent to go back and check, then come back and admit it was missing. Even worse he had to report it to his chief park warden. What really surprised Hal was that when the crime lab report came back, they said there wasn't a fingerprint to be found on either the globe or the box it was packaged in.

The superintendent began to focus on the warden service with an even more baleful eye after that. His humiliation over the grapefruit was a direct result of our tampering, which he could scarcely fail to deduce. We often thought his apparent frustration at work was a product of his domestic woes. It was quite apparent that the woman he'd married wore the pants in the family. She seemed to dominate him at any function he attended. She would get him to bring back all the written reports his staff and secretaries produced and edit them for grammar and spelling mistakes. She used a red pen to highlight everything she deemed wrong and it took all of us back to our school days. As noted, he also was overly abusive to his female staff. My theory was that his wife was bullying him and he was taking out his frustration on these women.

I had heard stories of his temper tantrums, which usually preceded the verbal abuse. One day I was sitting with a couple of other people, eating lunch in the coffee room in the basement of the administration building. We sat facing the small room that held all the personnel files. He came downstairs and went to that door and found it locked. He was livid that the woman who was the personnel officer had locked the room up when she had gone for lunch. I found it amazing that with all that personal data inside, why he would not think it should be locked. He picked up a big metal garbage container with a steel ring around the bottom and started hammering the door with it. It was one of those double doors that split in half and could be opened independently, with a small shelf on the top of the bottom one. We were sitting there with our mouths open, sandwiches to mouths, frozen in disbelief. He flailed away at the door, totally oblivious to our presence for a time until he was exhausted. It was a tough door but well beaten up when he finally gave up and went back upstairs in a huff. We looked at one another and I think in unison said, "What was that all about?" The shelf was hanging down over the lower door and took some of the damage. We didn't hang around to see what was going to happen to the poor woman who worked there after she returned from lunch. Later, I felt like a coward.

The abuse of the women intensified. It became so bad that we helped the head interpreter draft a letter to our regional office in Calgary, complaining about the superintendent's abusive nature, and the three of us signed it. A week later personnel from the regional office sent out a couple of people to interview us over the allegations. They returned to Calgary promising action. Nothing came of this, and the unrelenting verbal abuse went unabated. It continued and we repeated the process, and again we had someone come out and again promise that something would be done. Nothing was done. Three times they came out. It was always a different person; the last one was the head of personnel. The formal approach to getting a resolution was going nowhere. This was when Hal Shepherd wisely decided it was a good time to retire from Parks Canada.

Once Hal was gone, a nice accommodating gentleman from the prairies came in as the chief park warden. Gordon Cullen was an easy-going, very approachable man who brought some normalcy to the job. But he was no match for our demented superintendent. Soon after his arrival, we started hearing a rumour that three of us wardens were having an affair with the woman who owned the corner store. She was a married woman who was annoyed by the rumour but was sensible enough to realize it had no credibility in town. None other than the superintendent had started the rumour. After work, we would often drop by the store, pick up the *Calgary Herald* and chat with her. Often the superintendent would see us there and eventually he came to the wrong conclusion. There was also the possibility he just made it up. The accusations, of course, were false.

IF PARKS CANADA DOESN'T WANT TO DEAL WITH OUR CONCERNS, WE WILL

I happened to be in Lake Louise one day, talking to Claire Israelson, the head of public safety there, who asked me how we were getting along with our superintendent. He had heard all the stories. I told him what he needed was a pie in the face. He said, "Well I know two guys up at the Chateau who would do it for you." The seed had been planted.

I organized fifteen park employees to donate ten dollars each to pay for the hit. I had already negotiated a price with the two gentlemen, both university students from Ontario, studying law. We agree that it should be a cream pie with a cherry filling. On the designated day, it felt like High Noon in Field. I borrowed a Super 8 movie camera to record the event. I was in the living room of a park house, right across from the school and next door to the superintendent's house. It was sunny spring day with not a hint of a cloud in the sky. The rest is history. It wasn't long before we had a new superintendent. Over the years many have criticized the tactics used in replacing the man. They would say, "There are better ways to go about it." Or, "You should have tried a more mature approach." To a certain extent they might be right, but we did try to deal with it through proper channels and it didn't work.

THE "RITE OF SPRING": THE YUCCA FLUTZ

One event of the year gave us relief from the crazy work atmosphere that we seemed to face every day. This was "Yucca Flutz," which we sponsored every spring in Yoho. It was very much a warden event in its creation, but soon it expanded beyond this small branch of the government. The name first appeared when Bob Sandford and I were living in Jasper. He adapted it from a drink that originally came from the American southwest derived from the Yucca plant. Having no Yucca plants in Canada, Bob was forced to alter the formula and embroider the name.

He was visiting Field one day in the spring of 1976, and I asked him for the recipe. I had just come up with the idea of a spring break, hoping to hold it sometime in late May or early June. It would celebrate the arrival of warmer days, which were late in coming to the mountains. We agreed it was a great idea, and soon I was planning the event.

I put together an organizing committee, and Bob provided a sample for us to taste. In a one-gallon glass pickle jar with a wide mouth and lid, he added mixed fruits, a cup or so of sugar, a jar of maraschino cherries and a bottle of vodka. We then crammed it full of ice. He wrapped a wet towel around the outside of the jar and we all took turns shaking the contents. We did this until the towel froze to the outside of jar. Then he twisted the lid off, popped in a half-dozen, long

Jay Morton with jar in hand next to Donny Mickle.
DALE PORTMAN COLLECTION

straws and passed it around. It was delicious, and so the annual rite of spring became known as the Yucca Flutz.

It was just a party that first year, but we had invited the townspeople, and many of them showed up, as well. The following year, a race was added to better justify the party, and we further elevated it with an award ceremony. The relay race had three components: a running section, a canoeing section and a road-biking section. The runners left from the barn at the horse ranch to the Kicking Horse River below the Natural Bridge. The baton was then passed to the canoeists, who paddled down the Kicking Horse River to the Chancellor Peak campground. The last members of the various teams biked back along the Trans-Canada Highway to the party site at the ranch.

Everyone had a good time fuelled by a lot of steaks, baked potatoes and a giant Caesar salad, which were spread over a foil-covered four-by-eight sheet of plywood. One of the things that snuck up on people, especially the women, was the fruit, which was now laced with vodka and deceptively sweet. I always suspected the women

Doug Gibbs arriving from Sun Valley, Idaho, with the gang.
DALE PORTMAN COLLECTION

thought they were not really drinking alcohol if they just ate the fruit.
The following morning could best be described as carnage, with people
lying everywhere both inside and outside the cabin. This rite of our
mountain spring carried on well into the 1980s, long after I left Yoho
for Lake Louise. The race gradually became bigger with more participants coming from farther abroad. Even when I was involved, we had
teams from all over the East Kootenays, as far north as Jasper, as far
south as Waterton Lakes and as far east as Calgary.

Not all our time was taken up by parties or dealing with bad superintendents, of course. There was a very serious side to the job in Yoho,
particularly in mountain rescue and dealing with the numerous motor
vehicle accidents and fatalities that plagued that stretch of the Trans-
Canada Highway.

One of the stranger events we dealt with in Yoho happened in December 1976 on Chancellor Peak, a huge tragedy for the families involved. The peak is located at the south end of the park and can be easily seen from the Trans-Canada Highway, especially if you're travelling eastward. At the time, the avalanche hazard was extreme. The hazard developed from an abnormally cold November with below normal snowfall. This caused a layer of hoar frost to develop at the base of the snow pack. It could be best described as sugar – no adhesive quality to it at all. This was followed by a modest amount of new snow in late November and early December.

We started to notice avalanches set off by mountain goats crossing gullies high up on the mountains. You could see the goats were instinctively crossing slightly above the trigger zones, successfully completing their traverses across the mountains. But just their movement above seemed to release a slide just below, showing how fragile the conditions were. We quickly notified the climbing community of the treacherous conditions and discouraged any enquiries from people wishing to sign out for a climb.

Only one man ignored those warnings, a world-renowned Himalayan climber who had been on the successful 1972 American K-2 expedition. He had a reputation for being independent and seemed particularly resentful of government interference, especially from the warden service. When it came to avalanche conditions, he should have known better. We also had other concerns about him. On a few occasions, he neglected to self-register with us. Registration was put in place for everyone's safety but also to eliminate unnecessary search and rescue operations. So, we were extremely concerned when we got a phone call from his wife saying that he was overdue on a climb of Chancellor Peak with their teenaged son and his friend. They were from Golden, BC. I had checked the registration booth at the west gate that morning and no one had registered out.

His wife was upset with the warden service because we hadn't initiated a rescue sooner, but at the time we had no indication they were even up on the mountain. But no amount of explanation could calm her down. She also said she had expected them home the previous night.

I sent in a request for the helicopter from Banff, and then I drove down to the west gate to check the registration booth again. I looked at the registration form and I flipped through its pages. There in the back part of the unused section of the book, which had about a hundred pages, was his registration, concealed from sight as though it was deliberately hidden there. For some obscure reason, the man decided on this course of action, making his registration difficult to detect by anyone. This was strange. His desire to climb a mountain in those conditions made me wonder if he had a death wish. There was also a cryptic note from the climber saying that if he did not return, the park was to contact Tim Auger who was now stationed in Banff.

We quickly got our gear and rescue equipment together. I had a feeling the guy knew what the outcome was going to be, and it wasn't going to be good. I didn't contact Tim, as it was far too early in the operation to call personnel in from another park. It was incumbent upon us to do what we could before taking that step.

With what daylight remained, Jim Purdy and I flew the upper reaches of the mountain looking for their tracks. We saw numerous goat tracks crossing the treacherous gullies and the slides they had set off, and then we found the party's ascending foot tracks. They led into the upper reaches of a long, wide basin that faced westward towards the highway. You could see where their tracks crossed towards a large, open gully, ending in a small avalanche. The slope was between 20 to 25 degrees in steepness, and the snow was no more than a foot deep. You could also see the skid marks their bodies made over the scree slope as they were carried down by the small slide they had triggered. The avalanche started above them and broke to the ground, carrying them towards the steeper terrain below. It led to an extensive gully that ran down to the foot of the mountain. We flew into the gully and saw that a larger avalanche had been triggered in a second gully that fed into the main avalanche path creating a more significant mass of debris at its base.

We flew down to the avalanche deposit near the terminus of the gully, believing they could be found in the debris. I called in the search and rescue dog team from Lake Louise, and we continued to search the gully from the air but found no evidence of them on the surface. It was now going to be a foot search. We landed at the base of the mountain to rig the sling gear under the helicopter in the Hoodoo Creek Campground.

Jim and I slung in to the deposit site and unhooked from the helicopter. Immediately we found part of a climbing rope on the surface and followed it along until we got to the first body, then we turned around and followed the rope back to the second body and subsequently the third. Light was fading fast, so I asked for a cargo net, to sling the bodies out in one trip. The pilot was Jim Davis from Banff, and he had a net in his cargo bay, which he brought to us. We placed the three bodies into the cargo net, brought the corners together and fastened them. We signalled for the helicopter to fly up to our location. When it arrived, we hooked up to the end of the sling line and watched as the helicopter lifted it off the ground. All three bodies were frozen solid and some of their feet and hands stuck out of the course netting. They hung above each other in awkward positions, bizarrely disconnected from one another. Just as the helicopter flew down with the bodies, the RCMP unfortunately arrived at the site with the distraught spouse. Not knowing we were flying the bodies out at that point, the RCMP gave in to her request to go to the staging area. It was an understatement to say this was bad timing, and totally unintentional. This was the first sight the distraught woman had of the three deceased.

It couldn't have been any more shocking and macabre a scene for her to arrive at. We had instructed the RCMP to keep the woman away from the rescue scene while we conducted the operation. But when the bodies were uncovered, we requested an RCMP member to attend, to act as coroner. Field was a two-man posting with usually only one member on at a time. This was the case so he brought her along with him. It was a failure of communication between the RCMP and us. We should have realized the situation he was in, and he should have told us about his situation with her aboard. Unfortunately, that didn't happen.

THIRTEEN

YOHO AGAIN

A FAMILY RESCUE ON THE PRESIDENT GLACIER

Kathy and I cemented our relationship during her second summer
in Yoho, and then I was introduced to her father, Don Forest, a celebrated climber. I also met other members of this energetic family as
the summer wore on. Over the next few years we did a lot with her
family. With Don, the activities usually involved outdoor pursuits,
and not all of them were scripted or planned.

One of the mountaineering accidents that stands out from my
years in Yoho occurred in the fall 1978, and it involved some of Kathy's
family. We now call it "the family rescue." It started with a group of
Alpine Club of Canada members going on their annual clean-up trip
into one of the ACC huts on the Thanksgiving weekend. That year they
headed for the Stanley Mitchell Hut up in the Yoho Valley. Don Forest
was part of the group, along with Kathy's youngest sister Sylvia.
Many of them planned to climb Mount President, while a few stayed
back to prepare a fine turkey dinner for the evening celebration.

Among the climbers were three young lads from Calgary, hoping
to gain some leadership skills and get some route-finding experience

behind them. It was decided they would take turns breaking trail and selecting the route up the glacier. The three fellows were travelling together on one rope while Sylvia was just behind, leading the second rope of three, which included her father, Don. The first three had come upon a crevasse and decided to skirt around it to the left. But before setting off again, they changed leaders. The new leader ascended above the crevasse, while the remaining two below anchored him. Suddenly a small avalanche broke above them.

The volume of snow the avalanche contained would not have been enough to bury a person on an open slope. But the leader was now above the open crevasse and was dangerously exposed. The debris knocked him off his feet and carried him into the crevasse, which absorbed most of the avalanche deposit. It never reached the climbers below the crevasse. It had been a soft-powder avalanche, and a cloud of snow settled around the group, obscuring the other two rope-mates for a time. Once it cleared, they saw that the remaining two were safe but the young lad leading the group was gone.

Everyone was now galvanized into action. They followed the rope into the crevasse and started digging with their hands, hoping he was just under the surface. What shocked the group almost as much as the accident was that no one had brought a collapsible shovel with them. It was mid-October and no one was anticipating avalanche activity. It was quickly apparent that help was needed as the boy appeared to be deeply buried. It was very difficult digging when all they had were hands and ice axes. One of the surviving boys on the rope, who was in the lead just before the accident happened, was deemed the fastest and fittest, the best candidate to be sent out for help. He was accompanied by a few others, who helped get him safely off the glacier.

He headed for the warden cabin located in the same meadow as the ACC hut, but no one was there. It was only a patrol cabin and infrequently occupied. Unfortunately, the boy did not know this and decided to wait for the warden to return. After some time passed, he realized no one was coming, which left him no choice but to hike out to Takkakaw Falls trailhead and drive to the main office in Field.

Up on the mountain, the rescuers were desperate for some assistance as they made slow progress towards the victim. By now it was early afternoon, and they were wondering why they had not yet heard an approaching helicopter.

I received the report at 1:00 PM and immediately called the rescue helicopter in from Banff. I headed for the rescue room to get geared up with Gordon Rutherford. The boy had told me that they needed shovels, so we grabbed several along with our personal gear, and the avalanche rescue pack. We met the helicopter at the landing pad at 2:00 PM and loaded everything on board, including the slinging gear that would be needed to sling rescuers and supplies in and out.

Ironically, Kathy Calvert and Warden Randy Robertson were doing a horse patrol near Twin Falls when they saw the helicopter headed for Mount President. They suspected something was up and immediately headed back down the valley to the trailhead. Once there they got on the radio and were updated on what was happening. They loaded the horses and headed back to the warden office, to gear up if needed for the rescue. Once they arrived back at the office, things got hectic.

The survivor ran up to Kathy saying, "Don't worry, your dad's all right." But before she could clarify what he was talking about, a call came in to dispatch reporting a two-ton truck had careened off the Trans-Canada Highway on the Field Hill and the ambulance was needed. Just then, Jim Davis, the helicopter pilot, on returning from the first flight, walked into the office, spotted Randy and Kathy and told them to get their gear together to fly in. Randy couldn't go, as he was needed to drive the ambulance to the truck accident, so Warden Eric Langshaw was enlisted in his place.

Prior to this, Jim had managed to land Gordon and me near the crevasse, by landing on one skid. We tossed the rescue gear to the waiting climbers and jumped from the helicopter. Those waiting their turn to dig quickly apprised us of the situation. I knew some of the people there but was surprised when I heard a female voice say, "Hi, Dale," which was followed by a male voice, "Hi, Dale." I was greeted by Sylvia, popping out of the hole followed by her father Don. Don had a laceration between his eyes, which had started to ooze blood. He seemed oblivious to the wound and had a faint smile on his face as he greeted me. (We later found out that Sylvia had walloped Don on the forehead with her ice axe in a spurt of digging frenzy.)

It was apparent to me that the shovels were not going to be enough, and I ordered pails be sent up on the next flight in. I then started shovelling down into the confined space. It was slow going as I followed the rope into the throat of the crevasse. There was room for only one person at a time, and I needed to be roped up and belayed in case the snow below me collapsed in the crevasse.

Kathy was the first to be slung in hanging under the helicopter with pails dangling from her hips. To Kathy, it seemed as though she had just left the valley, but now she was back, dangling in mid-air above a bunch of small figures looking up at her. Suddenly a person popped out of the crowd with blood running down his face. "Dad," she cried. "What are you doing here?" Before he could answer, Sylvia joined him with an ice axe in hand.

Sylvia cried out: "Kathy, what are you doing here?" It was a family reunion on a tragic long weekend.

A large plastic pail attached to a rope was lowered to me. I rapidly filled it and it was pulled to the top, emptied and thrown back down. By now the tunnel was 3 metres long. In quick fashion, we followed the rope down another ten feet to his body. When I reached the victim, he was completely covered by the weight of the snow with a space of a foot or so under him, then more snow. He had been hanging from his harness with the entire weight of the snow on top of him, and I don't think he lasted long.

In Kathy's biography of her father, *Don Forest: Quest for the Summits*, Sylvia talks about the moment when we finally brought the victim to the surface. She remembers how quietly the body was brought up in the darkening afternoon and solemnly slung out to his family waiting far below in the town of Field. She related to her sister later: "I watched in morbid fascination as the wardens wrestled with him, trying to get him packaged into the body bag. He had stiffened in an awkward position and when one leg was being forced into the bag, the other leg shot out and kicked me. I was devastated."

Slowly people became aware of their own safety as night was coming on quickly. About half the group had left for the ACC hut shortly before the body was found. And now the remaining few, including Don and Sylvia, gathered their gear in the encroaching gloom. Sylvia retained an indelible memory of "looking back up the glacier at Kathy and Dale amid all their equipment, standing alone on the glacier waiting for the helicopter to come." Sylvia was only sixteen at the time.

As Kathy put it, "Darkness was coming on fast and so was an impending storm. We anxiously waited for Jim to return as the wind whipped around us and the cold settled in. Suddenly Jim was on the radio. He announced: 'It's getting dark, there's a storm coming in and I'm running out of fuel! I can make only one pass and if you are on the line I'll get you out. Otherwise you're on your own.'" Kathy recalled, "A swirl of wind and snow as a red ring swung towards us, Dale reached up to click on his rescue carabineer, then I clicked on, then both of us were jerked violently forward. The bulky gear attached to the sides of our harnesses prevented us from flying backwards, as is normally the case, so we flew face forward, rushing headlong towards the valley so fast that tears spilled from my eyes."

One minute we were standing there with all this gearing hanging from our harnesses and the next, we found ourselves sailing face first, swooping across the crosshatch of crevasses below. Within minutes the meadow was below us and we touched down. We unclipped, while the helicopter landed 50 metres away. The clouds had closed in, obscuring our view of the President Glacier. We quickly sorted out the equipment, unhooked the slinging gear, attached to the under-carriage of the machine and turned down an offer to stay for supper. In fading light, we made our way in the helicopter, back to Field and the compound.

The Stanley Mitchell Hut.
DALE PORTMAN COLLECTION

Sylvia added a poignant memory: "Thanksgiving dinner that night seemed unnecessarily gleeful to me. People were laughing and smiling and telling stories. How could people be happy when someone had just died? Maybe that was the difference between being an adult and just a teenager. I crawled upstairs to the sleeping area and cried."

When you are a climber, death can sometimes be just around the corner. Maybe they were reacting to the fact that it could have been them. Most were seasoned climbers and later, in a quieter moment, reflected on the mishap and the need for a shovel. But in that situation, even several shovels would not have changed the outcome; he was buried so deep. The next day we drove to Calgary and got on a plane destined for Europe and a much-needed break from work.

A CLIMBING TRIP TO THE LYELL GROUP WITH DON AND KATHY

It was 1977, and Kathy had just returned from the first All Women's Expedition to Mount Logan, and we were now seeing a lot more of each other. I was soon going to get some opportunities to get out on climbs with Don and his mountaineering group. By this point, Don had climbed four peaks of the Lyell Group, but had not yet summitted Peak #4. He wanted to put it behind him. Kathy and I took time off from work to help him in his quest for the peak.

We set out in dubious weather at the Glacier Lake trailhead with big packs, hoping the weather would turn in our favour. We left the trailhead at 8:30 AM and after a few hours we encountered one of the valley's resident black bears on the shores of Glacier Lake. We sat on our packs having a break and he eyed us as a source of easy food, content to keep his distance until nightfall. With a smirk on our faces, we headed for grizzly country and dared him to follow.

With an excess of energy, typical of someone half his age, Don kept busy clearing the trail of deadfall, moving everything that was not anchored down or attached to a root system. Soon Kathy joined him and I followed suit. This was my first trip with Don, and I remember how impressed I was with his strength. He was not a big man, and although he was fifty-seven, he was fitter than anyone I knew at his age. I was nearly half his age and I realized I needed to upgrade my fitness.

Nine and a half hours after starting out, we set up camp in the same meadow in which Don had had a famous encounter with a grizzly. The next morning looked like a day that would break with clear skies, so we quickly ate a small breakfast and were on our way by 5:00 AM. By 10:30 we were at the far end of the glacier, beneath the col between Peak #4 and Peak #5. Suddenly the weather started to turn on us. Dense clouds hidden behind the peaks descended rapidly, and we were engulfed. We groped our way towards the col and reached it at noon.

After a long lunch, waiting and hoping it would clear, we were still in a whiteout. Finally, we decided to abandon the climb and descend back to the glacier. Halfway across it, we passed out of the clouds and the wet snow turned to rain. An hour later we were off the glacier and looking down on our camp. Something wasn't right, and I said to Don and Kathy, "Doesn't the tent look funny to you?" They shrugged their shoulders then started working their way down the slope. We arrived back at the camp and found the tent completely collapsed with everything inside soaking wet. It was in a hollow and was hard to reposition on drier ground.

We wrung our sleeping bags out as best we could and Kathy and I gave Don our dry down jackets while the two of us tried to stay warm that night in the three wet sleeping bags. A small lake slowly grew in the middle of the tent, pushing us in increments to the periphery and contact with the wet walls. The temperature dropped to freezing, while a firm wind drove the rain and snow. It was a cold and miserable night that kept both of us awake and was made worse by Don's ability to sleep through it all.

The next morning broke with clear skies and frost all about, but once the sun came up, steam rose all around. We hung everything out to dry on the numerous bushes and small conifers scattered about. By noon everything was dry, and we packed up and headed out. To reach the trail we had to cross a stream that had swelled considerably after the rain. Don soon found a crossing upstream of a deep pool.

He went first, smoothly jumping across the fast-flowing stream onto a slab of rock. A narrow ledge, a few centimetres deep, provided purchase for your feet, while near the top of the slab were a couple of handholds. Once this dexterous move was accomplished, it was easy to scale the rock and be on your way. Don made it look easy, but for Kathy with her smaller stature and large pack it would be more difficult. She made it and gave me a triumphant look. Now it was my turn. As I leaped towards the slab, I missed the foothold – I missed the handholds. I was suspended momentarily in place like a frazzled coyote in a Road Runner cartoon. There was the sound of scraping on the surface of the rock followed by a frantic struggle to reach the handhold as I slipped into the stream that pushed me into the cold blue pool below.

I bobbed about treading water, my hat floating nearby, while Kathy and Don laughed hysterically. I got my pack off and tried to pitch it on shore, but the banks were too steep and it kept rolling back. I wasn't getting any help from them as they continued to roll on the ground like a pair of hyenas. I was pissed off, so I dragged myself and my pack out of the pool like some drowned rat, threw my pack on my back and hit the trail, never looking back.

They scampered behind trying to catch up, squawking something like, "Maybe you should stop and change into something dry," followed by another burst of laughter. It was their droll, ineffective attempt at concern. In soaked boots, fountains of water spurting out at my ankles, I sloshed along in complete disgust, water streaming off me, leaving them a wet trail to follow. It was now a hot day as we walked along. Everything slowly dried on me, and by Glacier Lake, in outward appearance anyway, it was like nothing ever happened. The only thing that took a long time to dry out was my pride.

THE ELUSIVE MOUNT RECONDITE

Kathy and I moved into a small duplex in Field, located at the west end of town. It was the house that Don and his climbing buddies often arrived at to bum a ride up one of the gated and locked fire roads. This allowed them better access to the unclimbed peaks they sought in Don's quest for the 11,000-foot summits.

One of the last remaining peaks was that of the elusive Mount Recondite, hidden deep in the Siffleur Wilderness, at the head of Martin Creek on the boundary with Banff National Park. It barely qualifies as an 11,000er, touching the sky at 11,010 feet. But that was of little concern for Don. His first attempt on it was made in the summer of 1977, but they were turned back because of inclement weather. Don returned during the summer of 1978 with Kathy, Bill Hurst and Vic Bennett, a local climber from Field. Once again, on reaching the base of the mountain, they were turned back by heavy rain. Getting back to the highway was a challenge.

They had four river crossings to confront, made more dangerous by high water. Crossing the Siffleur River was going to be the most difficult challenge of the trip as it was the largest river and it didn't level out on the stretch of the valley they were in. The bottom was strewn with large, round, rolling boulders. The biggest problem for Kathy was the safety of the dog, a mutt named Morley, who had been abandoned on the side of the Trans-Canada Highway near Rogers Pass. She had been working there the previous winter and had rescued it from the Canadian Army, who were keeping it as a mascot. As Kathy put it, "The dog lacked confidence in everything except chasing bears and wolverines."

To help get Morley across the river, a couple of the climbers were stationed downstream on the far bank of the river. They would try to retrieve the dog if he got that far. To Morley's credit, he had good reason to be terrified. He wasn't going to jump in voluntarily, so tough love was at hand and she threw him in. It didn't look good for the poor mutt. If he got by the spotters, Morley could quite easily be lost in the rapids that broke shortly below them. Once in the water, Morley had no choice but to let instinct kick in, and he started paddling for the far shore in desperation and gained it above the spotters on his own. Kathy and Don made their way across the river, arms linked together, trying to maintain their footing in the glacier-fed water. In order to keep your footwear dry, you have to cross streams in sock feet. In cold stream crossings, your feet get numb quickly and can be battered about by rolling boulders. You don't feel any of this bruising on your feet until they start to warm up on shore. That's when the pain comes.

Don was seriously intent now on finishing off the remaining four 11,000 peaks that he hadn't scratched off his list. He decided to make a third attempt on the stubbornly evasive Recondite. Kathy couldn't go because of work, and I was more than flattered to be asked along instead.

I was thrilled to have the opportunity to join the group, which included Gary Pilkington and Mike Galbraith. We departed from the Helen Lake trailhead on the east side of Icefields Parkway near Bow Lake. We skirted Helen Lake, which is a blue gem set in emerald-green alpine. From there we gained the summit of Dolomite Pass. Our goal that first day was Isabella Lake, located 24 kilometres away, and the cozy patrol cabin sitting on its western shore.

We headed out early the next morning from the cabin and after 6 kilometres, reached the horse crossing on the Dolomite. The cobbled streambed was tricky but not deep, and soon we came to the main crossing point on the Siffleur River, which Kathy and Morley remember so vividly. The crossing was deep but the current was manageable, and soon all four of us were on the far shore. We bushwhacked up a treed ridge, which extends out from Mount Kentigern, gained its crest and dropped down into the side valley below. Don called it "Laughing Bear Creek." It was a small valley that I was familiar with in my guiding days with the Mickle family.

We travelled up the valley and found a nice green patch of moss and grass nestled in and around a jumble of large rocks. The camp had protection from the wind, and easy access to a stream nearby. We were up very early the next morning, gearing for a 5:00 AM start. It was only going to be me, Gary and Don, as Mike had blistered his feet badly on the way in and decided to give them a day off.

We climbed up through a jumble of moraine to a tangled field of talus, which skirted the odd silt-laden tarn to gain the southeast col. From here we followed the ridge up towards the peak at a nice pace, in terrain that required no technical climbing. The weather was mostly cloudy but the sun came out on occasion, lighting the way and highlighting the distant summit. Near the summit there was a cleft in the ridge that forced us to downclimb before we could climb out and gain the last part of the ridge again. This was the crux of the climb. It was a testy downclimb because of the exposure to the steep east face, which towered above the numerous alpine lakes at the head of Martin Creek. We did it without a rope, and I had to be careful about where I placed my feet and hands. Downclimbing is tricky in most situations, and I took my time. Climbing up the other side was easy in comparison.

After a four-hour climb, we were on top of Don's fifty-first 11,000er; he had only three more to go. We sat viewing the jumble of surrounding peaks. One of them looked to be a little higher than us, and an active debate ensued. If it was slightly higher than Recondite it would need to be added to the list as a newly discovered 11,000er. Don was soon rummaging in his pack and came up with a gizmo that he could look through – some kind of levelling device. He was an engineer and was always inventing things and possessed all kinds of weird and wonderful gadgets. By looking through a lens and lining up the distant summit of the other peak and consulting a level he could determine whether it was higher or lower. Luckily, it was lower.

Below the summit, we hunkered down out of the wind for a bite to eat and a drink of water. As we sat there munching on biscuits and GORP, we noticed that Don had fallen asleep. I found out that day from his climbing mates that Don was famous for taking catnaps at the unlikeliest times. After about fifteen minutes, Gary and I woke him up to continue the descent.

He obviously wasn't fully awake. He was working his way down an innocent cliff band shortly after his nap when he pulled out a rock, hitting himself on the head. Blood was spurting out of the puncture wound near his temple, but in true Don fashion he carried on as if nothing had happened. He just shook his head and told us he was all right. I insisted that he hold up so I could tend to him. He stopped and let me apply some first aid. Using a hanky and pressure, I managed to staunch the bleeding, but by now his face was covered in blood. I tried to tell him his appearance wasn't that great, but he waved me off and we continued down the mountain.

When we walked into base camp Mike was there to meet us. When he saw Don come strolling in, a look of horror crossed his face and he said to me, "What happened to him?"

I said, "It's just Don with another head wound." Don was famous for injuring his head.

We packed up the next day, climbed over the ridge and then crossed the Siffleur River and gained the main hiking trail. We split up here. They had an extra day and were going up to the head of the Siffleur to camp next to one of the alpine tarns that are scattered throughout the undulating alpine. The next day they climbed over a high col, which Don named "Quartzite Col." It is a shorter way down into the Mosquito Creek valley, which took them out to the highway. For me, it was a long hike out over Dolomite Pass that day. I needed to be at work the next day. It was getting dark when I got to my vehicle.

DON'S CLIMBING BUDDIES: THE GRIZZLY GROUP

The Grizzly Group, which I briefly introduced to the reader earlier, could best be summed up in an introduction paragraph to an Alpine Club of Canada publication written by Bob Sandford, "Once upon a Mountain." Bob writes:

It doesn't take much time traveling in mountaineering circles in Western Canada to hear about the Grizzly Group. The first I heard of them was a passing reference to a legendary circle of old mountain men who had been climbing together for decades. When I explored the myth, I discovered that some of the members of this elite group were people I knew. I also observed that, though they may be somewhat grizzled, the members of this circle could hardly be said to be old. I soon discovered, as well, that the group's loosely established objectives were based on traditional mountaineering values that focused more on friendship, mutual reliance and fun than on the mere measure of accomplishment.

For me, the group was more like an extended family. In Sylvia's potentially difficult teenage years, Don took her to the mountains with his friends. It helped keep her away from falling in with the wrong crowd, which might lead to the use of drugs and alcohol. I don't think he had to worry, but Don was thorough in everything he did, even if at times his actions seemed unconventional. Kathy and I often had Sylvia along on trips we did together. On Don's invitation, we also went out on several Grizzly Group outings. As far as Kathy and I were concerned, Sylvia was one of the original Grizzly Group members, even if she was only thirteen at the time of its inception. Her climbing abilities were established very early in life.

One of Don's philosophies was that a bad day in the mountains would always trump a good day in the city. That was a pretty common attitude amongst the group. They got their name in July 1973 while laden with heavy packs and trudging up the steep trail

Don Forest reciting Robert Service on the Yukon River.
DON FOREST COLLECTION

that led to the Lyell Meadows, from the lateral moraine below.

When they finally reached the meadow, one of them spotted a big pile of dung, still steaming in the cool air. While the rest of the group took refreshment from a nearby creek, Don went off with his pack, looking for a suitable campsite. Partway along, he dropped his pack and carried on. He and the grizzly saw each other at the same time. Don slowly backed off saying, "Woof, Woof," like a dog. He passed his pack before he realized he was leaving it behind. Continuing his dog impersonation, he started moving slowly forward to retrieve his pack. That's when the bear stood up to survey the group. After getting a good whiff of them, he dropped down on all fours and lumbered away, up a slope and out of sight. After that encounter, they started calling themselves the Grizzly Group. As they put it later, "The name stuck like bear dung to a sleeping bag."

The five original members of the group were Glen Boles, Don Forest, Leon Kubbernus, Gordon Scruggs and Mike Simpson. Lyn Michaud soon joined the group as an active member. Those that followed were

Frank Campbell, Walt Davis, Jim Fosti, Bill Hurst, Bob Jordon, Ron Matthews, Rollie Reader, Peter Roxburgh and Bruno Struck.

Years later, while working on her book about her dad, Kathy asked several members of the group to define themselves and they answered in various ways; it was Mike Simpson who summed it up best.

> The Grizzly Group sort of epitomizes what we would call camaraderie in the mountains. The level of trust between four or five people that existed initially was a total one. I mean, you didn't have to be concerned about your safety or whether somebody would come to the rescue if there were a problem. And all our objectives, our interests were common – the fact that the whole trip was important, not just getting to the summit. Over the years we ended up developing a great interest in other things besides mountaineering, like geology through Gordon Scruggs, our resident geologist.

Don added that one of the group's distinguishing traits was the use of the rope. As the group aged, he claimed their motto became: "If we have to take out the rope we must be on the wrong mountain. Since we took out the rope a lot, we were often on the wrong mountain."

Another one of the other traits they had was breaking into the odd warden cabin when conditions were warranted or dictated by circumstance. Before becoming park wardens, both Kathy and Sylvia admitted to having entered one or two cabins in a surreptitious manner – usually through the window. But Don was probably the worst, and I mean this in a light manner. Maybe he had a premonition that down the road he would have ample opportunities to gain legal access to them with two daughters in the warden service.

Kathy related one story to me about her father and the Grizzly Group, breaking into a cabin in their endeavour to summit Mount Willington in the winter of 1973–74. She said, "March was a fine month for travel as the heavy snow and consistent temperatures made for a stable snow pack. Don had been taking avalanche safety training and

A painting of the Grizzly Group by Glen Boles for an Alpine
Club of Canada publication by Robert Sandford.
ALPINE CLUB OF CANADA

probably felt more confident knowing how to better judge dangerous
conditions. It likely gave him confidence for his second attempt on
Mount Willington on the twenty-third of that month with Walt Davis
and Mike Simpson."

The most direct approach to Mount Willington is from the Icefields
Parkway. It involves travelling up Mosquito Creek and climbing over
a high col north of North Molar Pass. Don named it "Centre Pass." As
it turned out, Centre Pass led them into the Pipestone watershed not
the Siffleur, leaving them a long way from their destination.

Their incredibly steep and daring route could only be done in ideal
conditions and has probably never been done in the winter since.
Reflecting on this, Walt [Davis] told Kathy:

I figured someone was looking after us. We didn't have any Pieps [early avalanche transceivers or beacons] or anything like that. I think I had an avalanche cord and I probably did drag it.... I can remember it was really dangerous because of the avalanche hazard – but Don knew there was a warden cabin [Pipestone Cabin] down there and that's where we headed. Anyway, we got to the warden cabin and it's getting pretty close to pitch black. Of course, no keys – I mean we didn't have any "in" into the warden cabin in those days and we took our ice axes and pried off the window. We had to dig down to it first and we went in and it was spotless. The warden service really looked after them. And we stayed there.... We went in and out the window – because of the big lock [on the door].

Mike Simpson reported the next day, "It was snowing with a low ceiling and the same conditions existed the next day so we gave up and came back." They returned over North Molar Pass, the highest pass in Banff National Park that has an existing trail over it, at 2560 metres. It took them seven hours of hard trail breaking, which is a good time on that trail, even in the summer. They were a fit bunch.

I had the opportunity years later, on a trip to Fraser Pass with Mike Simpson and his family, to chide Mike about their propensity for breaking into warden cabins. Our route was up the Whirlpool River, then up its middle fork to the pass into BC and on to Fraser Pass. It was going to be an epic final day to the pass so we spent the night at Middle Forks Cabin. I said to Mike as I unlocked the door, "It must be unusual for you to enter a warden cabin through a door rather than a window, eh?" He gave me a sheepish look, and we both chuckled about that.

DON FOREST AND THE QUEST FOR THE SUMMITS
As someone once said, Don was one of the more colourful and easy-going characters to fall out of the pages of the Canadian West. He was an electrical engineer who co-owned an engineering company

(Wiebe–Forest) in Calgary and for a long time, much of his energy went towards growing the business. But, later in life, he added another business into which he could pour his boundless energy.

This new career had an inauspicious start when Don was forty-three, at a time in life when many dial back on their outdoor activities. Kathy and her twin brother Ken had joined the Alpine Club of Canada in 1963 at the age of sixteen, and they had roped their father into driving them to club-sponsored climbs in the mountains. After spending occasions sitting in the car waiting for them to return, he finally said the hell with that and joined the club.

Through the ACC, Don met his climbing buddies, which would eventually coalesce as the Grizzly Group. With help from Mike Simpson, Glen Boles and others, Don successfully summitted all fifty-four 11,000-foot peaks in the Canadian Rockies. Shortly after, he climbed all the 11,000ers in BC's Interior Ranges. He was the first person to do so. By this point, he was in his early sixties. At that point, he and his Grizzly buddies started to focus on canoeing. Their attention was now drawn to some of Canada's more challenging and remote rivers, like the South Nahanni and the Yukon. On the Yukon River, in 1984, he was in his glory with his friends. Every night around the campfire he would recite one of Robert Service's poems, helped along by some of Don's potent "Take Off" (overproof rum and Triple Sec).

In 1986 Don and three others, John Northwood, Dick Howe and Mike Galbraith, went on an expedition to Nepal. Their objective was to climb Island Peak and get some trekking in. The people and the culture, though, became the highlight. In 1991 at the age of seventy-one, Don became the oldest person to climb Mount Logan, Canada's highest peak. It was a big moment for him to be standing on the summit, guided there by Chic Scott. In November of that year he was presented with the prestigious Summit of Excellence Award at the Banff Mountain Film Festival.

Don had been a past president of the Alpine Club of Canada, and it was no surprise to many of us when he was chosen as the patron of the Alpine Club of Canada's 2000 Guides' Ball at the Chateau Lake Louise.

The cover of Kathy's biography of her father, Don Forest.
ROCKY MOUNTAIN BOOKS

In the spring of 1994, I took Don with me on a business/pleasure trip to China. We started our adventure in Hong Kong but soon found ourselves in Guangzhou (Canton). Then we headed up the Pearl River in a rickety, old overnight ferry to Wuzhou where we caught an all-day bus to the spectacularly scenic town of Yangshuo. After spending a few days biking and boating through the gorgeous karst landscape the area is famous for, we boarded a bus for the city of Guilin, an hour north. Here we were introduced to a Chinese tour guide, Sun Lu, who agreed to set up future tours to China for me. Then it was on to Kunming in China's southwest province of Yunnan and the limestone labyrinth of the area's famous formation, the Stone Forest. At Chongqing, in the west central part of China, we visited the famous Chaotianmen Dock, which is the start of the Five Gorge Yangtse River trip and the shorter and more popular three-gorge section. Chongqing was followed by a stop in central China at Xian to visit the archaeological wonder that is the terracotta warriors. Then we travelled to the coast, finally arriving in Shanghai to take in its famous riverfront view of the Bund. We found ourselves back in Hong Kong after a tumultuous and challenging thirty-six-hour train ride to Canton followed by a four-hour trip on a much more modern train. We had a wonderful time together; he was the most adaptable, inquisitive and pleasant person to be on a trip with.

MORLEY AND HIS TORN RECTUM

Morley was the first of four dogs Kathy would take in. Because he was abandoned at such a young age and did not spend the necessary eight weeks with his littermates, he became difficult and aggressive around other dogs. He bonded better with people, especially when he was young. He was a yellow dog with a black nose, which made him look like he had had been dipped nose-first in a pail of black paint. He was brought up at the government ranch, in a rural setting, and he soon uncharacteristically bonded with a young coyote about his age. When we went riding and had the dog along, he and his pal often joined us, trotting along behind. He had quite a personality and eventually we simply were not surprised by anything he did.

One day in October we were returning from the Ya Ha Tinda Ranch after trailing the government horses back from Lake Louise for the winter. It was a week before we planned to fly to Europe for a holiday. We had arranged for a truck to be dropped off at the ranch so that we could drive back to Banff over the gravel Cascade fire road. It was a crew cab maintenance truck, which had a tool box in the back situated under the rear window. On the way out we passed two mountain bikers peddling up the road. They gave us the strangest look but we were too tired from trailing horses all day to worry about what had startled them. I was driving, and as we approached a small bridge, I had to brake. Suddenly, out of nowhere, Morley came flying past the windshield, landed on the hood of the truck, bum first, with enough momentum to send him off the hood and onto the road. We were all shocked at what had just happened as I furiously tried to stop before running over him. We found him sitting on the road, but he quickly got up and bent around to examine his ass. It was bleeding and it looked like he had a laceration between his tail and his rectum, caused by the sudden contact with the gravel road.

Morley with Kathy on mountaineering trip with the Grizzly Group to Mount Recondite in 1978.
DALE PORTMAN COLLECTION

While we had been driving down the road he must have managed to climb up onto the toolbox in the back of the truck where he gained access to the top of the cab. There he lay, or more likely, sat, taking in the scenery. No wonder the two bikers had given us such a strange look, seeing a truck approach with a dog sitting on its roof. When we got to Banff, I took him to the vet. He had torn his tail away from his rectum so the vet stitched him up and then handed me some ointment I was to put on the wound, three times a day.

Bob and Vi Sandford were to look after him while we were in Europe. They were now living east of Edmonton just outside Vermilion, where Bob was teaching at the local college. He was going to visit Banff, so I had the opportunity to drop Morley off with them there. I brought Morley to the door and handed him over to Bob. As I was leaving, I remembered the ointment I had in my pocket. I turned, approached Bob again, standing in the doorway and said, "Oh, I forgot. This ointment needs to be smeared on his torn ass three times a day." I handed it to my friend who stared at me in total disbelief, but I left before a look of revulsion overtook his features.

As I walked back to my vehicle I heard, "I'll get even with you someday, Darter." That was his nickname for me. I chuckled all the way back to Yoho.

AN UNCHARACTERISTICALLY DISOBEDIENT LUCKY

When we returned from our trip and picked up Morley from the Sandfords, we heard all about Morley's many escapades while in their care. Years later, we can all chuckle over the many Morley stories we witnessed but none was better than the ointment caper. While on the subject of Morley, I cannot help sharing a couple more stories that come to mind, for dogs were a big part of most wardens' lives.

Joe Halstensen was a park warden in Banff when I first started with the warden service. Of Norwegian extraction, he came from a skiing background. He was assigned to town in those days, which offered little activity in the fall after the tourists were gone. One of his duties was to pick up stray dogs. He was in the centre of town at the corner of Banff Avenue and Wolf Street when he saw a dog cross the road in front of him. It looked like his dog, Lucky. He stopped the truck, puzzled how the dog had gotten out of the fenced yard. Maybe one of the kids had left the gate open.

He parked the truck in the middle of the road put his red light on and called Lucky to come. The dog ignored him and carried on. Over the years, Joe's dogs were always obedient so he was surprised when the dog was unresponsive to his command. He called him again. Lucky continued on. Joe was now furious. He caught up to the dog, grabbed him by the scruff of the neck and hauled him back to the warden truck. By now he was gathering a crowd. He had left the driver's side door open, so he hurled the dog into the cab and climbed in beside him. The dog growled at him and Joe cuffed him. The two just glared at each other as Joe put the truck in gear and drove off down Banff Avenue.

As he drove home, he was perturbed about Lucky's unusual behaviour. The dog gave him one last low growl as he settled into the passenger side of the truck. During the ride, the dog kept a wary and intense eye on Joe from the far side of the seat. When he drove up to the front of the house, who was there to meet him but good old Lucky, quivering with excitement and wagging his tail. Joe said later that the last thing he wanted to do was to make eye contact with his passenger. With a fearful lump growing in his throat, he opened the door and stepped out of the truck, leaving the door open when he walked into the yard. He petted Lucky as he passed and walked into the house, feeling foolish about not recognizing his own dog. When he returned to the truck, the dog was gone.

LIKE OWNER, LIKE DOG

I have so many good dog stories, but the funniest one involves an old friend. Al Stendie was a good travelling companion during my time in Jasper, especially when we had backcountry districts next to each other. He had a dog named Kelly who was part German shepherd. Kelly had selective hearing, and it would seem at times that he was almost deaf, especially when Al asked him to do something. This story takes place in the early 1970s, before I had taken over the Blue Creek District. Al and his new seasonal warden, Sid Marty, were hiking down the trail towards Snake Indian Pass. Kelly was along, running here, there and everywhere. Not far from Oatmeal campground, Kelly could be seen happily scurrying about, chasing ground squirrels, and Al seemed oblivious, but not Sid. Al's a great guy but like some of us, he could be stubborn. Sid was much more idealistic in how he thought the job should be done, possibly because he was still new working for Al. They were opposites and they often talked past each other, not really connecting. It was like they were on different frequencies.

Over the years, Kelly sometimes got lucky and caught a ground squirrel. Like most dogs though, he never caught a red squirrel. It was the red squirrels that always won, tormenting him by chattering continuously from the tops of the trees. Kelly was more motivated chasing ground squirrels, anyway, and soon returned with one in his mouth. Sid was alarmed that maybe a hiker had seen the event. Al being a farm kid saw nothing wrong with Kelly's action and could not understand why catching ground squirrels would bother Sid. Sid's discomfort finally came through to Al when he announced, "Dogs should be on a leash, not running around and certainly not killing wildlife, especially in clear view of the park visitor."

Sid did not want to be disrespectful of his boss, but he could not help pointing out that what the dog did was terrible. He basically said to Al, "You can't allow your dog to run around like that in a national park, killing animals, especially when you're wearing a park warden uniform."

Al stopped and considered what Sid had said. He replied, "You're right, Sid. I never thought of it that way. He could get one of those little bones stuck in his throat and choke to death." All Sid could do, as he shook his head, was file it away in his mind for another day.

FOLLOWING IN THE TRAIL BLAZED BY HUNTER S. THOMPSON

It was 1980 and Gord Irwin and I dreamed up an idea for Bob's stag. At first, we struggled to find a suitable location to hold it. Gord came up

Bob Sandford years later, being distinguished.
DON FOREST COLLECTION

with the notion that only a place as big and bold as Las Vegas would do. I thought it was a great idea, for it was as "over the top" as Bob Sandford could be. The two of us immediately started organizing. We convinced a group of fourteen others from various locations throughout the mountain national parks to be part of it.

For some it was hard to determine when the stag ended and the wedding began. But many of us had to sober up quickly and go to work. There are those who would say we were excessive and irresponsible;

they are probably right. But the episode epitomized the spirited free-dom of the late 1970s and early 80s.

Years later, one park superintendent was so enamored of the stories of Bob's stag that he tried to duplicate it. He, along with his managerial staff, headed for Las Vegas for a few days of rest and relaxation, all on the taxpayer's dime. When the regional director found out, all hell broke loose. The superintendent lost his job, but the incident was hushed up so well by the office in Calgary that the press was com-pletely unaware. Even park employees didn't hear about it. I wouldn't have known, either, but someone in the know leaked it to me.

My days working in Field, BC, came to an end in 1980 when I took a promotion to Lake Louise as a law enforcement coordinator and dog handler. And with that an important episode of my life came to an end. We continued to live in a house we built in Field for a few more years. Kathy continued to work as a park warden in Yoho. Then in 1982 we moved to Lake Louise and rented out our home to the federal youth group, Katimavik.

EPILOGUE

CONSIDER THE 1980S MY GOLDEN years. The decade began with me becoming a dog handler. I had the necessary qualifications. I could relate to dogs, having owned several over my lifetime. I had a wild and almost feral nature about me. I was hard to manage like so many head-strong dogs I've trained over the years. And those were my good qualities. I was considered notorious by most of the wardens' wives in the period between marriages – 1973–83 – and their husbands soon picked up on this. When they came home much too late at night or in the early morning, I was often the excuse, even if I was nowhere in the country. I was a handy alibi, but I would be remiss if I didn't admit some complicity. It was almost like some wives took out a notice on the local radio station, warning of my pending arrival: "Hog tie your husbands and throw them in the basement. Portman's coming to town."

After Kathy and I were married, a collective sigh of relief emanated from the many wives in the numerous warden homes of the mountain parks. It has been a challenge for her to be married to someone like me, and she deserves a meritorious award of some fashion after all these years. Maybe the Victoria Cross, for spousal duties conducted in a dangerous landscape.

I started as a dog handler in Lake Louise in 1981, and in 1986 we moved to Jasper where I filled the dog handling vacancy on Alfie Burstrom's retirement. Many stories spring from this fertile period in my life, and I was blessed with good health and great opportunities to travel, especially to the more remote areas of the four mountain parks and wilderness areas in BC and Alberta. After visiting Europe in 1978, Kathy and I continued to seek foreign lands and arrived in China in the mid-80s. We were reaching the end of the decade when we visited East Africa, where we attempted Mount Kenya. We ended up rescuing a Yugoslavian who had fallen while trying to climb the same route we were on. The weather rolled in afterward and the window of opportunity to summit closed. In 1989 we went back to Europe for a month, renting a car and touring the Mosel and Rhine Valleys and the mountains of Austria, Switzerland and Italy.

The 1990s arrived, and my health was now being challenged. I was diagnosed with malignant melanoma, and the doctors gave me a 50/50 chance. This was a midlife crisis, and I had to adjust. I embraced my doctor's strategy for my survival and recovery, but I also became much more holistic in my attitude towards life. I joined the Rosicrucian Order and sought alternative healing methods through visualization and meditation. I continue down this path today and firmly believe it is the most effective tool in any person's toolbox. That said, you must have faith in the process, and that does not come easily for most.

This decade was a challenge for both Kathy and me, and I must say, on reflection, that I had doubts on occasion that either of us would survive. In 1993, after taking a year off for my health issues, I started an adventure travel company. The Green Horse Adventures conducted multi-day horse-supported hiking treks in the Canadian Rockies. We also conducted three tours to China and organized a fourth trip for an adventurous group from Calgary.

I wrote my first letter of protest in 1995, when I foresaw the demise of the warden service, but I was a lost voice in a workforce that was being carried along with a new mission statement and a utopian vision. This was a challenging period for me, as well as my supervisors, whose responsibility was to keep me reined in. I retired as a park warden in 1998.

We continued to travel extensively. Kathy was seasonally employed and had most winters off, while I collected my overtime and put it towards journeys abroad. In late 1990, we headed for Chile and Argentina, and two years later we were back in South America visiting Ecuador and Peru. In between I went back to Europe, accompanied by an RCMP dog handler. We were there to observe the German Bergwacht's program of avalanche search and rescue, pertaining to dogs. There were participants from across Europe.

We spent some time with friends in the Cayman Islands who worked there. We relaxed and SCUBA dove, and I got my PADI (open water) certificate. Kathy went back to university and got her master's in waste stream management, and we celebrated by going on a second conventional holiday to Hawaii. We finished things off by travelling to Central America in 1998, and I returned on my own to Mexico in 1999.

The turn of the century was a challenge for us on a personal level, and after retiring we moved to Calgary. It was a difficult and challenging period for me; during that time, Kathy wrote a wonderful biography of her dad that was published in 2003. I published two books on either side of it, one on rescue dogs and the other on chasing wild horses in the foothills of Alberta. The warden service continued to do poorly as it was evident that Parks Canada wanted to see the last of the outfit as an organization. It was a very vindictive and tumultuous period. A group of us retired wardens formed the Park Warden Service Alumni Society as we saw what was unfolding before us. It was established to protect and preserve the warden service's culture and heritage for some form of posterity. Parks Canada certainly wasn't.

In 2006 we moved to Cochrane, Alberta, to be closer to the mountains, and under Kathy's determination and direction, we jointly wrote a book about mountain rescue in the Canadian Rockies and Columbia Mountains, *Guardians of the Peaks*. In 2006 Kathy came down with an aggressive and particularly nasty form of breast cancer, and she went on a regimen of hard-hitting chemotherapy. I trained her in meditation and creative visualization, helping her battle the disease.

Our travelling didn't slow down as we kept to an active schedule as backpackers, seeking and experiencing as much of the globe as possible. Often, we were gone for up to six weeks at a time. We visited Cuba in 2007. We returned to Mexico in 2008, touring Baja and part of the mainland in a rented car. We headed for Southeast Asia at the end of 2008, when the Canadian loonie was on par with the US dollar, and it seemed that by the time we landed in Singapore it was trading at 80 cents. This was a two-month venture, and we knew it was going to be our last overseas trip for a while. Along the way, we visited Malaysia, Thailand, Laos, Cambodia and Vietnam and left Ho Chi Minh City for home during the chaotic throes of Chinese New Year celebrations.

We continued to get out to the mountains as much as possible, both in the winter and summer. Every year throughout the 2000s we volunteered to work in Jasper (two weeks at a time) using the park's horses and cabins as we painted buildings, cleared trail and did repairs to corrals and other infrastructure. In 2008 we were told by Parks Canada our services were no longer needed as volunteers. No reason was given outside of the fact we were taking jobs away from unionized staff. What unionized staff? There was no one else out there when we were there. It was the start of a steady corrosion of trails and infrastructure in our four mountain national parks. In the spring of that same year, with mean-spirited intent, Parks Canada broke up the warden service.

In 2009 the warden alumni decided to celebrate the once-proud organization and its historic accomplishments. It had been one hundred years since the first park warden was hired in Banff. Parks Canada was not happy with this development, as they had already dismantled the organization and the last thing they wanted was public attention being directed towards their nefarious act. They put a lot of effort into trying to sidetrack our centennial endeavour, but we prevailed in the end. Over six hundred people attended the gala event, which was held over three days in Banff.

The warden alumni have remained feisty throughout the years and continues to advance the warden cause. A quote from a Banff superintendent in the 1990s shows the mindset at the time: "Why should you, as a group, be respected for your integrity, when it should be shared by all of us?" In 2008 Parks Canada handled the termination badly and today its own structure and delivery could be classified as a mess. It will eventually bounce back – everything does that doesn't succumb to extinction – and hopefully it will again be a proud organization that provides quality service not only to those who frequent the high-use areas but also the backcountry visitors.

We were now focused on road trips in Canada and the Pacific Southwest. We've completed several tours to the north, taking in the Yukon and Nunavik. One of the highlights was canoeing the Wind River with family and a friend. We culminated our Canadian experience with a trip to Atlantic Canada and Newfoundland in 2015, discovering again what a great and diversified country we live in.

In the fall of 2015, Kathy's book *June Mickle: One Women's Life in the Foothills and Mountains of Western Canada* came out. Finally, after so many years of research and personal interviews, helped along by Don Mickle's dedication to the project, Kathy brought forward an impressive window on June's life, and the life she represented, being raised in the shadow of the mountains we've all come to love.

Today you would be hard-pressed to find six people within Parks Canada who can ski to a warden cabin. That's out of a staff of half-a-hundred. When we were out there, all we had was our wits and common sense. Mac Elder once said that "common sense is illegal in Ottawa," and I think that quote certainly applies to the mandarin there now. Even if you had the skills to get back there, it takes a week to complete the paperwork the bureaucrats require. You must prove that you: have a valid first-aid certificate, know how to light a wood stove, have an approved avalanche certificate, taken a chainsaw course and completed a cabin-maintenance course (how to fill up a wood box and mop the floor). Most superintendents and resource managers now have little connection with the backcountry of our mountain national parks.

That aside, as I write this, Kathy has just finished the editing on a new book. She was contracted by the warden alumni to write the compelling story of the Ya Ha Tinda Government Ranch, which the alumni plan to celebrate in 2017. The ranch will mark one hundred years of being a working government horse ranch.

Hopefully, the day will come later, rather than sooner, when the old lamplighter returns to extinguish our flame and optimistically carry what remains off to a distant place. I have a lot more to say. Both of us do. But if we can't, we both know we've experienced a rich and challenging life, full of hills and valleys with not too many plains to rest our heads upon.